The Maya and Catholicism

UNIVERSITY PRESS OF FLORIDA

Florida A&M University, Tallahassee
Florida Atlantic University, Boca Raton
Florida Gulf Coast University, Ft. Myers
Florida International University, Miami
Florida State University, Tallahassee
University of Central Florida, Orlando
University of Florida, Gainesville
University of North Florida, Jacksonville
University of South Florida, Tampa
University of West Florida, Pensacola

The Maya have invited a priest, Bishop Ruiz of San Cristobal, to celebrate a mass for their village patron and founder, St. Lawrence, to whom their own prayer officials (lower right) also plea for village prosperity while village shamans and officials (upper right), who having previously sought the help of St. Lawrence, pray to their ancestral gods residing in the sacred mountains for the same purpose.

The Maya and Catholicism

AN ENCOUNTER OF WORLDVIEWS

John D. Early

University Press of Florida
Gainesville/Tallahassee/Tampa/Boca Raton
Pensacola/Orlando/Miami/Jacksonville/Ft. Myers

11 10 09 08 07 06   6 5 4 3 2 1

Early, John D.
The Maya and Catholicism : an encounter of worldviews / John D. Early.
p. cm.
Includes bibliographical references and index.
ISBN 0-8130-3025-0 (alk. paper)
1. Mayas—Religion. 2. Mayas—Rites and ceremonies. 3. Maya cosmology.
4. Indian Catholics—Latin America—History. 5. Catholic Church—
Missions—Latin America—History. 6. Christianity and culture—Latin
America. 7. Christianity and other religions—Latin America. I. Title.
F1435.3.R3.E37 2006
261.2'97842—dc22   2006023026

The University Press of Florida is the scholarly publishing agency for the State
University System of Florida, comprising Florida A&M University, Florida
Atlantic University, Florida Gulf Coast University, Florida International
University, Florida State University, University of Central Florida, University
of Florida, University of North Florida, University of South Florida, and
University of West Florida.

University Press of Florida
15 Northwest 15th Street
Gainesville, FL 32611-2079
http://www.upf.com

To Jacky
Thanks for . . .

Contents

Tables

Illustrations

Preface

This research is the long-delayed outgrowth of the author's dissertation, "The Sons of San Lorenzo in Zinacantán," written as one of the early members of the Harvard-Chiapas Project under the direction of Evon Vogt (Early 1963–64, 1965). At that time I was a Catholic priest, a Jesuit, finishing my doctorate in the former Social Relations Department at Harvard University. After Frank Cancian had limited his interest in the *cargo* system to its economic and prestige structure, Vogt thought that I was a natural for research on its rituals.

Leaving Boston in a second-hand Volkswagen "Bug," I arrived in San Cristóbal seven days and almost four thousand miles later, in late December 1962. A few days later I had an automobile accident with the despised son of the state governor who was entering town with his hated entourage to collect tax money, was jailed briefly when I refused to talk to the police until I had an interpreter, had an open-air trial for the accident on the town square that drew a large, supportive crowd for this unusual event, and was judged guilty and relieved of a hundred dollars for damages to a fender. Several days later I was introduced to the residents of Zinacantán by Bishop Samuel Ruiz and the local circuit-riding priest and asked to lend assistance by celebrating the midnight Christmas mass. In a church dimly lit only by shimmering candlelight and guided by the Zinacanteco *fiscal* in a completely unfamiliar ritual preceding the mass, I sat in a chair before the altar holding the "infant saint" while Zinacantecos came forward to kiss it. I was not sure if I was functioning as a Catholic or Mayan priest.

The experience was not completely unexpected. In my intellectual wanderings I had obtained MA degrees in social philosophy (St. Louis University), theology (Woodstock College), and sociology (Fordham University). I had read in comparative religion, especially Mircea Eliade; had delved into Max Weber, Paul Tillich, and the wonderful phenomenology of Reinhold Niebuhr; at Harvard I had taken a course with Talcott Parsons and a seminar with Timothy Leary, a portion of which introduced me to psychedelics. But perhaps the best preparation was the stimulation of excellent courses in biblical studies by professors trained under the incomparable William Albright of Johns Hopkins University. The Albright students treated the sections of the Bible as religious literature that needed to be understood against the background of the languages, archaeology, history, literary forms, and cultures that produced them—anthropology at its best from a source not usually associated with professional anthropology.

In Zinacantán I did not function as the town priest, although I would sometimes help the nonresident priest with mass and baptisms. Most of the time I was just another Harvard graduate student spending time with the fiscales and members of the cargo system, learning what they did. I was well received and I think they liked having a priest who was interested in their activities.

My dissertation—highly descriptive as I never mastered Tzotzil—was the result of that experience. One particular question stood out in my mind and stayed with me during and after the writing of it. It was obvious that the Zinacantecos were not orthodox Catholics, that they had their own religious system with rituals conducted by their own specialists, the shamans, the fiscales, and the occupants of the cargo positions. Why, then, did they go to all the trouble and expense to bring in a non-Mayan Catholic priest for masses and baptisms when it would have very easy for one of their own specialists to perform these rituals? They had seen the rituals many times and were quite capable of doing them themselves. Why didn't the residents just do away with the Catholic priest, especially since he was a *ladino* (usually a person of Spanish descent or a mestizo) a member of a group they did not trust? I pushed this thought further by wondering why they were so insistent on incorporating the mass and baptism, rituals of obvious Spanish origin, into their own system.

I returned from Zinacantán and spent several years trying to define my role as a priest-anthropologist within the Catholic bureaucracy while bouncing around in it like a pinball in a game machine. I became a marginal man. Many priests thought I was crazy because I was an anthropologist. Many anthropologists thought I was crazy because I was a priest. Part of this time I spent working with the Oklahoma Diocese that was sponsoring a program (Micatokla) in Santiago Atitlán in Guatemala inspired by liberation theology, although the term was not yet in use at that time. The staff was composed of priests, nuns, and laity who administered various development efforts that included agricultural, credit, and weaving cooperatives; a medical program with a large clinic and later a small hospital; a literacy program that included a small radio station (Early 1973); a Montessori school; and a pastoral program that attempted to develop a liturgy that would convey the basic concepts of Christianity in a meaningful way. I was involved as a consultant to these programs and also assisted with the first Peace Corps efforts in Guatemala.

I was overwhelmed by the malnutrition in the community and the resulting child mortality. The situation was much worse than what I had seen in Zinacantán, although this may have been due to the funnel effect of the clinic in Santiago, where many seriously ill patients were brought. To understand the problem and help the medical program in its allocation of generous support from the Oklahoma medical profession, I sought information about the mortality levels and their causes. After consulting experts in Guatemala and the United States, I found that few really knew about this kind of situation except the late John Gordon of the Harvard and MIT public health departments who encouraged me. So I started my own research, which was my initiation into population dynamics, a combination of ethnography, demography, and clinical studies (Early 1970a, 1970b).

During this period I found no support in the Catholic bureaucracy for the contributions that the social sciences, especially anthropology, could make to population problems, social justice (human rights), or ecumenical religion. This was not only a policy failure, but also a failure to draw on their spirituality to face the contemporary problems of the world community. The decision makers of the bureaucracy were locked into the worst aspects of their own system while adopting the worst aspects of secular systems. In frustration, I resigned from the priesthood. (While I married two years later, Vogt 1994: 378 is incorrect in implying that I resigned in order to marry.)

I took a position at Florida Atlantic University and continued building on the population work I had started in Santiago Atitlán, expanding it to all of Guatemala (Early 1982, 2000). Unable to return to Guatemala due to the political situation and the work I had done there, I helped further collect and analyze data originally compiled by those with long-term residence among the Yanomami of Brazil (Early and Peters 1990, 2000) and the Agta of the Philippines (Early and Headland 1998). But all during this time that question of why the Maya kept insisting on the Catholic elements in their religion remained with me. I published an article that reflected an early attempt to find some threads of the complex historical weaving behind this question (Early 1983). Finally in these years of my retirement I have had time to return to it, and this book is the result. An earlier attempt would have lacked the necessary foundation of the scholarship produced by the explosion in Mayan studies in the last three or more decades.

I realized the problem that I was attempting to analyze required looking back over many centuries and covering many topics, each of which was a specialty in itself. To put some boundaries on the inquiry, I have had to treat much of this material in a very general manner. Although I include some of my original research, in some respects the book is a synthesis of primary and secondary sources. The critical issue is, Does the synthesis hang together so that it throws some light on the questions asked? I have tried to limit the inquiry to answering these questions without attempting a complete explanation (something never attained in any field). In so doing, I bring up topics that are either not researched or barely so. I hope this book may help focus some of these questions for future research by others.

In the text I have mentioned the works that I have particularly relied on for various topics. I have used many quotations for several reasons. I see no use in attempting what might be a clumsy paraphrase of what has already been well expressed. These passages give direct credit to the quoted authors for their insights and provide a basis for assessing the validity of my interpretations. I have read works by many other authors that have entered my subconscious, although I don't quote them directly here. To all who have preceded and helped this work, thanks and I hope I have done you justice. To the Maya of Zinacantán, Santiago Atitlán, and many other Mayan towns, many thanks for all you have taught me.

For sacrificing time in their busy schedules in order to read an earlier version of the manuscript and make many helpful suggestions, my gratitude goes to Jacinto Arias of San Pedro Chenalhó, Chiapas; Clifford Brown of Florida Atlantic University; Allen Christenson of Brigham Young University; Edward Fischer of Vanderbilt University; Robert Laughlin of the Smithsonian Institution; Christopher Lutz of Plumsock Mesoamerican Studies and the Mayan Educational Foundation; and James Mondloch of Albuquerque, New Mexico. The final text is solely my responsibility. I would like to express my gratitude to the staff of the Interlibrary Loan Department of the Florida Atlantic University Library for their unfailing assistance in obtaining research materials, and to Christopher Lutz for providing the unpublished Oss materials.

Some editorial notes: I have used *contemporary* or some equivalent term a number of times in the text. It roughly designates the years 1970 to 2004. I have used the term *Christianity* throughout the text. If the text concerns the centuries after the unity of Christianity began to break down, the term refers to Roman Catholicism. For the most part, the other Christian denominations were not involved in the questions investigated here. All the translations from Spanish into English are my own unless noted otherwise. The Tzotzil prayers were translated into Spanish by Domingo de la Torre Pérez, and my translations into English were polished by Mrs. Janet Collin-Smith many years ago. Many of the introductory photographs to the chapters depict various saint images in Zinacantán and Santiago Atitlán. I took all of the photographs in the book except figure 15.3, taken by and a gift from a missionary, now deceased, and figure 14.1, provided courtesy of Allen Christenson. At some future date Allen and I are hoping to produce a teaching CD that employs our photographic collections of Mayan life, especially its rituals.

PART 1

Introduction

The Research

The Maya and Catholicism examines the relationship between many Mayan communities and Catholicism—the priest, the mass, baptism, and the saints—that began in the sixteenth century. The core of this relationship is the insistence by the Maya on retaining the services of non-Mayan Catholic priests to celebrate the Catholic rituals in their churches during Mayan festivals in honor of the saints. What is the reason for this insistence? The relationship continues into the twenty-first century, although around the middle of the twentieth century important changes began to take place within both Mayan communities and the Catholic Church that have radically altered the situation in many communities.

Mayan Rituals and Their Specialists

The Maya have a strong sense of service to their community that includes the performance of rituals deemed necessary for the community's welfare. The rituals and their explanations within the Mayan worldview form a ritual matrix. The Catholic priest is only one of several ritual specialists functioning within this matrix. To put his services and rituals in context, it is helpful to briefly survey Mayan ritual personnel and the purposes of their ceremonies.

Shamans

Shamans perform their rituals to petition the gods for various favors: to make the earth fertile and provide them with crops, wood, et cetera; to cure or protect from sickness; to protect the community from some perceived danger, especially weather damaging to crops; to divine the future; or to bring misfortune upon a perceived enemy (witchcraft). Seldom does a single shaman perform rituals for all these purposes. Some shamans do not divine the future. Other shamans refuse to perform witchcraft ceremonies, considering them a perversion of the shamanic power. Shamans are called to their vocation through dream visions or some type of extraordinary psychic experience in which the ancestral gods appear to them and impart the shamanic knowledge and power. Death is seen as the consequence for refusing this call to community

Figure 1.1. Amid the smoke of incense, a shaman looks on as her assistant places a sacrificial chicken in a small cave, the entrance to the interior of a sacred mountain home of the Zinacanteco ancestral gods.

service. Many shamanic rituals are performed on behalf of individuals or family groups, only occasionally for the entire community. The latter usually take place at important points in the agricultural cycle and in times of crises such as prolonged drought, volcanic activity, or major epidemics. In most Mayan communities there is no formal organization or hierarchy of shamans, although there may be an informal ranking system based on the number of years of shamanic practice.

The Cargo/Cofradía System

Members of these groups are appointed or voluntary roles that are performed on behalf of the entire community in rituals during festivals honoring the saints. The Catholic calendar specifies for each day of the year a saint to which the day is dedicated. From this calendar each community or the local Catholic priest selects certain saints as patrons. The community festivals are celebrated on the feast days of the patron saints. The cargo officials are entrusted with the organization, financing, and performance of these rituals. To provide an understanding of the Catholic elements within the Mayan ritual matrix, the next two chapters will describe the extensive rituals of the festivals.

Figure 1.2. After redecorating a home altar, two mayordomos and their incense bearers pray before the saint images shown in the introductory photograph of part 1.

Figure 1.3. The author with the mayordomos eating a ceremonial meal on the occasion of moving the saint images when there was a change of mayordomos. Notice in the background the saint's freshly washed clothes hanging to dry.

The Catholic Priest

The scope of the priest's role in a community is partially dependent on whether he is a resident of the community or a circuit-riding visitor invited to officiate during the festivals of the saints. Except for some of the larger and more important towns, most Mayan communities do not have a resident priest. Historically, the Catholic priest has been a Spaniard or creole, or after national independence, a Mexican or other North American, Guatemalan, or European. For more than four hundred years, Mayan communities have on their own initiative sought and demanded the services of these non-Mayan priests and their rituals as an essential part of Mayan festivals.

Figure 1.4. A Catholic priest celebrating mass.

The Anomaly

The Maya retain their own pre-Columbian gods as protectors as well as their own priests, the shamans, who in the Mayan view perform rituals for the same purposes as the Catholic priests. Furthermore, during their rituals the Mayan shamans also call upon Catholic saints. In any traditional Mayan community, shamans with lighted candles and burning incense can be seen in the churches offering prayers before the images of the saints. Since cultures tend to be ethnocentric and defensive, the presence of a non-Mayan Catholic priest and the Spanish-derived mass, baptism, and saints is anomalous. Why do the Maya demand that non-Mayan Catholic priests perform Catholic rituals that fulfill the same purposes as the shamans' activities?

A frequent answer in the literature is that the rituals of the Catholic priest are considered necessary for the well-being of the community. This answer is incomplete as it fails to explain the anomaly in the situation. To explain it, some scholars point to the violence of the Spanish conquest and the consequent imposition of Catholic rituals. Although the Catholic priest and his rituals arrived as a consequence of the conquest, the Maya quickly accepted these foreign elements. If external constraint alone was the operative force, the Maya long ago would have dispensed with the Catholic priest.

Others explain the anomaly as a syncretic process whereby the traditional Mayan and Catholic religions have been fused to form a hybrid religion. If so, what are the guiding principles of this hybrid? Does it mean that individuals think of themselves as Catholic one minute and traditional Maya the next by compartmentalizing the religions? Or does it mean they have created something new? Wagley saw the fusion as creating a distinct, new religion, and many have accepted this formulation:

> Ostensibly Chimaltecos [residents of the town of Santiago Chimaltenango, Guatemala] are Catholic and they are recognized as such by the Roman Catholic Church. Obviously, their religion is not Catholicism as we think of it. Their entire culture is a fusion of Maya and European cultures and this fusion is perhaps most striking in their religion. In prayers, for example, Christ, a Catholic saint, an aboriginal day deity, and a Guardian of the Mountain may be appealed to in that order. Their concept of any one of these deities, whether it be of Catholic or aboriginal origin, is a blend of European and Maya beliefs. One cannot say that the Chimalteco concept of Christ is Catholic, nor that the Guardian of the Mountain is a Mayan deity, for the fusion of aboriginal and foreign elements is complete in each detail. The result is not an American Indian religion with a veneer of Catholicism nor is it Catholicism with many aboriginal appendages.

Chimalteco religion is a new form—a new religion—arising out of a historical merging of two religions. Their religion is different from each original ingredient and particular to Chimaltenango. (1949: 50)

This version of the syncretism thesis is purely descriptive and does not analytically explain it. What is the structure of this new religion? What are the new perceptions and the new logics behind the usage of symbols from both traditions?

Another position denies any anomaly. Its answer is simply that the Maya were converted to Catholicism and only a very small number continue to practice the indigenous religions. Robert Ricard's book, *The Spiritual Conquest of Mexico*, is the classic statement of this position: "one of the most noteworthy phenomena of the Portuguese-Hispano colonization is the Christianization, profound or superficial, but indisputable, of the immense territories, or, more exactly, the numerous native groups that were subjugated by the two Peninsular powers" (Ricard 1966: 306).

Regions Investigated

The research will examine the Maya in western Guatemala and two regions of Mexico, the Yucatán Peninsula and the state of Chiapas (see map). These three areas were inhabited by the Maya at the arrival of the Spaniards and remain the areas with the highest concentrations of Mayan populations. These populations have many customs in common, use the Mayan languages, and have similar historical backgrounds. During the colonial period they were considered rustic or backwater districts in comparison with the more developed region of central Mexico centered on Mexico City. They looked to Mexico City for help in governance. The conquest of the Mayan areas used the tactics Cortés developed during his conquest of the Nahua. For most of the colonial period, the dioceses of the Mayan areas were suffragan dioceses subject to Mexico City. The Franciscans and Dominicans who evangelized the three areas followed the patterns originally used by the friars in central Mexico. After independence from Spain, these regions were relatively neglected by their national governments, and the Mayan worldview continued much as it had been prior to independence.

The Chapters

The first step in fully comprehending the anomaly is to understand the structure of Mayan festivals and the place of the Catholic elements within them. This is done in part 2, where chapters 2 and 3 are ethnographic accounts of the Mayan festivals for the saints. These descriptions illustrate the problem to

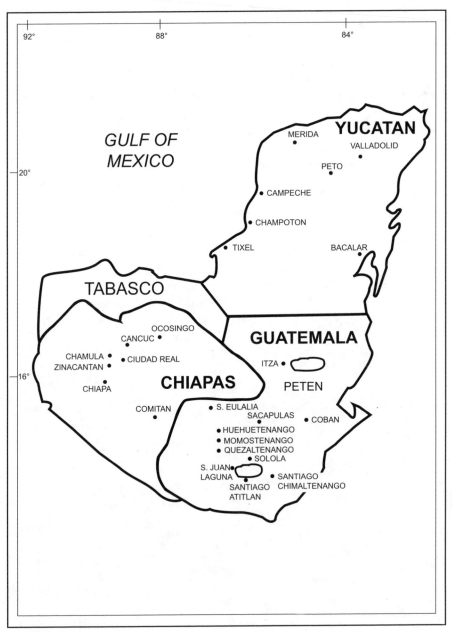

The Mayan Region

be investigated by the remainder of the research. Chapter 4 explores the importance of the priest's role and his rituals. Using historical and ethnographic materials, the chapter shows the enduring persistence of the Mayan demand for the Catholic elements and that they cannot be considered as merely external trappings.

Part 3 begins the search to explain the anomaly. Chapters 5 and 6 investigate those aspects of the Mayan and Spanish worldviews in the early sixteenth century that are pertinent to the research topic. Chapter 7 analyzes what happened to the Mayan worldview at the time of their first encounters with the Spaniards.

Moving into the colonial and national periods, part 4 examines the Spanish worldview of the friars and their efforts to convert the Maya to Catholicism. Chapters 8 and 9 describe the intended theological goals, content, and strategy of the friars' conversion program, while chapter 10 investigates the problems they encountered. Chapter 11 looks at the situation of the secular priests who succeeded the friars in the late eighteenth century. These chapters describe what was actually presented to the Maya in the evangelization effort, thereby helping to explain the direction of their reaction.

Part 5 examines the Mayan reaction. Chapters 12 and 13 describe how the Mayan applied the worldview described in chapter 5 to interpret what both the friars and the Spanish laity presented to them. This part explains the anomaly. Chapter 14 analyzes the role of the fiscal as a ritual specialist and periodic Mayan attempts to install the fiscal in the role of priest. Chapter 15 examines a relationship between the saints and shamans.

Part 6, the last chapter, examines the implications of the findings for some questions frequently raised about the relationship between the Maya and Christianity. Finally, it indicates some topics for future investigation suggested by the research.

PART 2

The Anomaly

Catholic Elements in Mayan Festivals

The following three chapters describe the efforts that Mayan communities put forth for the care of the saints. These efforts involve large numbers of people, a sizable amount of time, and an expenditure of considerable resources. They show the importance that Mayan communities attach to the Catholic saints, rituals, and priests.

The Saints, Their Homes, and Their Servants

The center of ritual activity during most Mayan festivals is the colonial church, usually a large, imposing structure facing the town square.

The Churches

Usually the church is the largest edifice in town, towering over the small, single-room homes with their adobe walls and thatched roofs (see figure 2.1). The thick exterior walls of the church are constructed of adobe brick, wattle and daub, or stone. Typically, there are few windows. Roofs can be vaulted or flat. The interior usually has a single nave, with or without a transept, and an altar at one end of the nave. Some have a side chapel or baptistery. Sometimes there are few pews, the central part of the church being relatively empty. There is little congregational worship among the Maya so there is little need for pews. Also, traditional Mayan women prefer to sit on the floor. They are so accustomed to squatting around the house fire while cooking that they find this a more comfortable position.

The church may look like a colonial Catholic church, but Catholic churches are owned by a Catholic diocese, a legal corporation under the jurisdiction of a bishop. Due to long periods of absence of Catholic priests from Mayan communities and to anticlerical legislation enacted by national governments, many of the churches have come under the jurisdiction of local Mayan authorities for the use of all community members. They are Mayan churches to which Catholic priests are invited guests for reasons to be seen.

The Maya are divided into various groups. The national governments of Mexico and Guatemala in their attempts to integrate the Maya into the nation created administrative units called *municipios* that have some similarity to U.S. counties. The boundaries of these units usually recognize preexisting colonial groupings. Each municipio has a town center and outlying villages administratively dependent on it. In some cases these outlying units can be as large or larger than the town center itself. The colonial church is usually located in the town center, and there may be additional churches in the outlying dependencies if the size of the population warrants it.

Figure 2.1. A view of Zinacantán town center in 1963. The church is in the middle of the picture and some of the sacred mountains are in the background.

Images of the Saints

Upon entering the cavelike church, the most noticeable element is the large number of statues of the saints. Toward the front is the altar with a crucifix and tabernacle. A large statue of the town's patron saint may stand above it, or there may be a painting of the patron saint on a large screen behind the altar or a large retable with niches containing numerous statues. Along the side walls of the church are additional altars or pedestals with statues of more saints. Table 2.1 shows the position of the approximately forty saint statues, crosses, and images in the two churches and a chapel in Zinacantán, Chiapas, during the 1960s (some are shown in fig. 2.2). For Guatemala, Christenson (2001: 52) has made a similar listing of the approximately fifty-eight statues or pictures of saints in the church at Santiago Atitlán, and Cook (2000: 66) has done the same for the more than thirty images in Momostenango. A Maryknoll priest remarked about the church in Jacaltenango, "In this church there are more saints than in heaven" (Montejo 1991: 3). For the Maya, the church is the home of these saints and a visual statement of their importance in the life of the community.

In the Zinacantán churches are eleven statues or pictures of Jesus, eight of the Virgin Mary, and multiple images of other individual saints. Each image or picture may be considered a different saint regardless of like names or Catholic theological interpretations. The people know the names of the more important

Table 2.1. Saint Images in the Churches of Zinacantán, 1960s

I. Church of St. Lawrence

MAIN ALTAR

		Virgin of Purification		
St. Hyacinth	Virgin of the Rosary	St. Lawrence	St. Dominic	St. Peter Martyr

Virgin of Guadalupe (picture)[a]	Sacred Heart (picture)

SIDE WALL LEFT	SIDE WALL-RIGHT
St. Anthony	St. Peter
(pulpit)	Evangelical Cross
Christ	Virgin of Sorrows
St. Sacrament	Jesus in his tomb
St. Teresa	St. Magdalen
	St. John
	Large cross

SIDE CHAPEL OF THE CHURCH OF ST. LAWRENCE

St. Joseph	Virgin of Nativity	Virgin of Easter	St. Resurrection	St. Pilar	St. Lawrence Lesser	St. Rose	Sacred Heart Greater	St. Lawrence Lesser	Sacred Heart Lesser	St. Dominic Lesser

SIDE WALL LEFT	SIDE WALL RIGHT
Jesus Nazareth	
Holy Trinity	Virgin of Immaculate Conception
Virgin of Carmen	

II. St. Sebastian Church

MAIN ALTAR

Lord in tomb	St. Fabian	St. Sebastian Greater	St. Catherine	St. Sebastian Lesser
	Jesus Nazareth			

Chapel of Lord Esquipulas

MAIN ALTAR

Lord Esquipulas (crucifix)	St. Lawrence (picture)

Source: Early 1965:17–18.
[a]All images are statues unless identified as pictures.

Figure 2.2. The interior of the main part of the church, showing some of its saint images, Zinacantán 1963.

saints but are doubtful about the identities of many others. To compile a list of the saints' names requires a long discussion with those in charge of them and other members of the community. Sometimes it is impossible to get a consensus, only a majority opinion. In nonliterate Mayan society the visual communication of the church architecture and the number and aesthetics of the many statues take on great importance.

Each municipio has a saint as its patron. The official name of the town center is usually a combination of the name of the patron saint and the traditional Indian place-name, although in practice often only one of the names is used. San Lorenzo (Saint Lawrence) is the patron of Zinacantán. His life-sized image stands above the main altar of the church in Zinacantán center (see introductory photograph in part 2). At the lower part of the image is a gridiron. In European mythology, Saint Lawrence was one of the early Christian martyrs burned on a gridiron in Rome. This history and the symbolism of the gridiron are unknown to the Zinacantecos. For them he is their patron who arrived in town in the distant past, wanted a place to live, and told the Zinacantecos that if they would build him a home, the church, he would take up residence there and watch over the town as its protector. A similar story is told about San Sebastián (Saint Sebastian), who is the principal image in the other Zinacanteco church (see introductory photo to chap. 13).

In some municipios the saints have additional homes in private houses. In many instances individuals have purchased images and set them up in saint houses as personal deities. In some cases, when the colonial churches were tumbled by earthquakes, the Maya entered the ruins, rescued the images, took them to their homes, and subsequently built typical dwellings as homes for them. When the churches were restored, the priests were unable to persuade the people to return the images.

In this investigation the word *saint* is restricted to the Catholic saints (including Jesus and the Virgin Mary) represented by the polychrome statues in the churches and saint houses or by their images in pictures or on banners. This is a narrower sense than in frequent Mayan usage. Indigenous groups, when speaking Spanish, have a tendency to use the terms *san, santo,* or *santa* for many sacred objects that have no historical connection with Catholicism.

The Caretakers of the Saints

In each municipio a group of men is responsible for the upkeep of the saints. This group is organized as a small bureaucracy with a hierarchy distinctly marked by levels associated with age, prestige, wealth, and function. The names of these organizations vary according to their structures and their relationships to civil authorities depending on the Mayan region and historical period.[1] Two common names are *cofradías* for the structure and *cofrades* for the members; or *cargos* for the structure and *mayordomos* or *cargadores* for the members.

The system in Zinacantán can serve as an example. Zinacantán is the name of both a municipio in the highlands of Chiapas and the town that serves as its religious and civil center. As shown in figure 2.3, the religious organization consists of approximately forty ritual positions assisted by many helpers. The organization is divided into four hierarchical levels: two *alcaldes,* four *regidores,* fourteen *alfereces,* and twenty *mayordomos.* At each level, an individual usually occupies an office for one year in the ceremonial center, then returns to his cornfield or other occupation and may assume a higher office in a future year. Climbing this bureaucratic ladder is the way many Maya perform their community service.[2]

The two highest levels of the system are the two alcaldes and four regidores, divided into pairs by the designation of older and younger brother. These two groups together are known as the *moletik,* the acting elders of the community. They are in charge of community ritual and the cargo system. They are assisted by two scribes who know how to read and write in Spanish. The latter take care of the books of applications for cargo positions and of any paperwork required of the moletik.

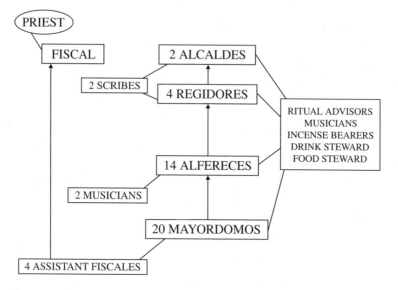

Figure 2.3. The personnel of the Zinacanteco cargo system.

Before government regulations split civil and religious functions in Indian communities, the alfereces were judges in disputes brought before the village authorities. They also performed rituals for the saints as a necessity for properly carrying out their civic duties. Now only their ritual duties remain.

The twenty mayordomos are directly responsible for taking care of the saints. They also work in pairs designated as elder and younger brother. Six pairs are responsible for the saints in the two churches, and another pair, known as the *mayordomo rey* and *mesonero*, for the saint in the chapel of Esquipulas, which also serves as the meeting place of the moletik. There are additional mayordomos who serve only during the festival of the patron saint or during Holy Week, or who take care of the saints in the chapels in outlying communities.

Because the officeholders change every year, each level has a permanent specialist attached to it who functions as an advisor or performs the rituals when needed. The *fiscal* is in charge of the church and all rituals performed there. He is usually appointed by mutual consent of the priest and the alcaldes. Because he must be familiar with all church ritual and be able to read Spanish, the position is permanent. He is especially associated with the mayordomos, as they maintain the church and perform many of their rituals there. He has four assistant fiscales, frequently called sacristans, who act as the civil servants of the mayordomo group. The advisors to the alfereces are two permanent musicians, a violinist and guitarist, who guide them in the performance of their ritual duties.

Many items are used or consumed during the performance of the rituals. For this purpose each cargo member needs the help of various assistants, shown in figure 2.3. Each has one or two elderly advisors who teach the cargo member various aspects of his role. Musicians and incense bearers are needed for most rituals. Care of the saints involves "feeding" them so that large amounts of food and drink are used in the ceremonies requiring considerable logistical support, especially from female relatives.

The Festival Calendar

The festivals of the saints involve a considerable expenditure of time. To use Zinacantán as an example, the forty saints in the two churches and the chapel have twenty-eight festivals dedicated to them, as shown in table 2.2. These involve approximately 166 days of ritual performance for the community saints, or more than 40 percent of the days in a calendar year. On all these days various cargo members perform rituals for the welfare of the entire community. The next chapter will describe this ritual activity.

Expenditures for the Festivals

To finance the rituals performed during the schedule of festivals shown in table 2.2 requires a heavy expenditure by the Mayan community. It would be revealing to know what percentage of the total municipio income is dedicated to providing for all the goods and services connected with the rituals. Such a figure is impossible to obtain in a mostly illiterate society whose economy is only partially monetized. Anthropologists have attempted to find some quantitative indicators:

> Tax (1953) shows that the most expensive cargo costs considerably more than a man could earn in a full year of wage work. . . . In Zinacantan (Cancian 1965), the most expensive cargo costs the equivalent of ten years wage work. Guiteras Holmes (1961: 58) records . . . : One of the lesser religious offices . . . implies an expenditure which is the equivalent of . . . between three and four years of a man's daily wages. Higher positions demand that the Pedrano expend four or five times the above amount. (Cancian 1967: 288)

Table 2.2. Calendar of Saint Festivals in Zinacantán

Date	Saint	Type	Ms	As	Als and Rs	Priest	Change	Days
All Sundays	Esquipulas	Esquipulas			P[a]			52
Dec. 16–25	Two Infants	Mj[b]-D[c]	P	P	P	P		10
Jan. 1	All	D	P	P	P	P	Moletik	1
Jan. 6	Kings	Mj-D	P	P	P	P	As[d]	4
Jan. 15	Esquipulas	Mn[e]			P		Ms[f]	4
Jan. 22	Sebastian	Mj-D	P	P	P	P	Ms	4
Feb. 2	Purification	Mn	P					4
M[g]	Carnival	Mj-D	P	P	P	P		5
Fridays in Lent	Buyer	D	P					4
4th Fri in Lent	Buyer	Mj	P	P	P	P		4
Holy Week	Buyer	Mj-D	P	P	P	P		6
April 29	Peter	Mj	P	P	P	P	Ms, As	4
M	Ascension	Mn-D	P					4
M	Pentecost	Mn-D	P	P				4
M	Trinity	Mj	P	P	P	P	As	4
June	Corpus Christi	Mn-D	P			P?		4
June	Sacred Heart	Mn-D	P					4
June 13	Anthony	Mn	P					4
June 24	John	Mn	P					4
June 29	Peter	Mn	P					4
Aug. 4	Dominic	Mj	P	P	P	P	Ms	4
Aug. 11	Lawrence	Mj-D	P	P	P	P	As	4
Aug. 31	Rose	Mn	P				Ms	4
Sept. 8	Mary's nativity	Mj	P	P	P	P	As	4
Sept. 21	Matthew	Mn	P					4
1st Sun. after Oct. 7	Rosario	Mj	P	P	P	P	As	4
Nov. 1	All Souls	Mn-D	P			P		4
Nov. 25	Catherine	Mn	P					4
Total	28		26	14	15	14		166

Source: Early 1965:221.

Notes: Date: festival date, determined by the Catholic calendar kept by the fiscal.

Saint: the primary saint for whom the festival is celebrated.

Type: the ritual pattern, as described in chapter 3 and summarized in table 3.1.

Ms: the twelve mayordomos; the fiscal, his four assistants, and the two musicians are always present with this group.

As: the fourteen alfereces, usually accompanied by their ritual advisors and musicians.

Als and Rs: the two alcaldes and four regidores (i.e., the moletik), usually accompanied by the scribe (escribano) and the mayordomos of Esquipulas.

Priest: the Catholic priest.

Change: the officeholders who leave and enter their cargo roles on the last day of a particular festival.

Days: the number of days during a festival when rituals are performed.

a. P: perform(s) ritual.

b. Mj: major festival ritual pattern (cf. table 3.1).

c. D: a distinctive ritual occurs during this feast, either by itself or in addition to the major pattern type.

d. As: two alfereces leave and two enter their positions on the final day of the festival.

e. Mn: minor festival ritual pattern (cf. table 3.1).

f. Ms: two mayordomos leave and two enter their cargo offices.

g. M: date of festival moves, depending on the date of Easter.

Summary

Mayan churches are filled with images of Catholic saints, thirty to fifty of them in some cases. A small bureaucracy is established to take care of them and to offer prayers and gifts to them during rituals that fill more than 40 percent of the days in a year. The expenditure for the ritual activity can range from the equivalent of one to ten years' wages of a single individual depending on the rank in the bureaucracy. The willingness of Mayan communities to continually undertake such a burden indicates their firm belief in the saints and the necessity of the rituals that invoke their favor.

Mayan Festivals for the Saints

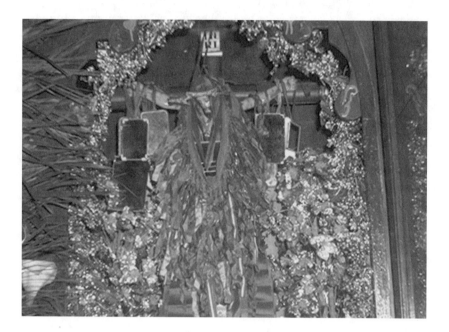

The role of the Catholic priest and his rituals should be seen within the context of all the ritual activity during the festival.

Patterns of Festival Rituals

The rituals of the festivals follow one of several patterns depending on the importance of the saint being honored and the segment of the cargo system involved. Using Zinacantán in the early 1960s as a model, table 3.1 outlines three patterns. The Major pattern provides the structure for the more important festivals (identified as "Mj" in table 2.2), while the other two patterns, Minor and Esquipulas, are shortened versions used for less important saints or occasions. Some festivals have their own distinctive rituals that are added to the basic pattern.

A fourth ritual pattern, the Church-Mountain, is not a festival pattern but refers to predominantly shamanic rituals with processions to the sacred moun-

Table 3.1. Types of Festival Ritual Patterns

Major	Minor	Esquipulas[a]
A. Night before the First Day		
1. Flowers changed in houses of Ms[c]	Same	Same
2. Oath of incoming As[d]	—[b]	—
B. First Day		
3. Flowers changed in churches by Ms	Same	Same (chapel)
4. Atole at homes of outgoing As	—	—
5. As spend night visiting	—	—
C. Second Day		
6. As pray, sing, and dance at church	—	—
7. Ms pray, sing, and dance at church	—	—
8. Atole at homes of outgoing As	—	—
9. As spend night visiting	—	—
10. Ms prepare and place necklaces on saints	—	Same
D. Calendar Feast Day		
11. Mass, baptisms, marriages in church	—	—
12. As pray and dance at church	—	—
13. Ms pray and dance at church	Same	Same (chapel)
14. Moletik presides in chapel	—	Same (chapel)
15. Ms return necklaces	—	Same
16. Exchange of flags between old and new As	—	—
17. All visit incoming As	—	—

Source: Early 1965:283 with revisions.

a. Pattern for feast of Esquipulas: Whenever the moletik meet in the chapel, usually every Sunday and on major festivals, the same pattern is followed except that items 1, 3, and 10 take place on Saturday night or the evening before the first day of the festival if the oath for the incoming alfereces is to be administered.

b. Dashes in second and third columns mean that the ritual in the first column is omitted for that festival pattern.

c. Ms: mayordomos.

d. As: alfereces

tains and churches. Cargo members join the shamans in this pattern when a ceremony is performed for the whole community.

Pattern of Major Festivals

Most festivals last for three or four days, depending on how days are counted. By Zinacanteco calculation the time from immediately after one sunset until the next sunset constitutes a single day, although this covers a two-day span by western reckoning. The Zinacantecos call the first day *chuck-nichim*, flower tying; the second day *ixperex*, vespers; and the third day *k'el-k'in*, the principal day. The community is made aware of the progress of all the ceremonies by a series of loud explosions from skyrockets and handheld mortar-type devices that are ignited at selected intervals during the rituals.

Night before the First Day

This evening the mayordomos refresh the images and altars in their homes while the mayordomos of Esquipulas chapel do the same there (see table 3.1, section A). This prepares the chapel for a ceremony in which the moletik will administer a preparatory oath to the two alfereces who will begin their year of service on the final day of the festival.

Flower Changing Ceremony in the Houses of Mayordomos

After sunset each pair of mayordomos meets at the home of the older brother (senior mayordomo) with their drink pourers, musicians, and two older women carrying bowls of burning incense. These homes have two table altars. One has small saint images clothed in traditional Zinacanteco garments (see introductory photo in part 1). The other altar has coffers containing clothes for these images and for those images in the church that this pair of mayordomos cares for. The practical task for this evening consists of redecorating the altars with fresh flowers and changing the clothes of the images in preparation for the festival. These tasks are incorporated in a ritual ceremony that includes offerings of candles, cane liquor, and incense; the recitation of prayers; and music, singing, and dancing for the saints accompanied by violin, harp, and guitar.

To start, the mayordomos put on their ceremonial blankets, pass in front of the seated musicians, and ask their help during the ceremony:

> See then, my elder brother,
> See then, my younger brother,
> In your presence,
> Before your eyes,
> We will change the flowers,
> We will change the leaves of the tree,
> Of father Saint (saint's name),
> Of father Saint (saint's name),
> Lend me your instruments,
> Lend me your songs,
> Elder brother,
> Younger brother,
> For before your eyes,
> For before your face,
> I will change the flowers,
> I will change the leaves of the tree,

Now we have arrived at his great feast day,
Now that we have arrived at his great festival.[1]

Before every segment of this ritual the mayordomos similarly state its purpose and ask the assistance of their musicians in a formalized speech.

Next the mayordomos place a straw mat on the floor before the altars. Two older women with bowls of incense sit at the foot of the mat. The mayordomos strip the altars of their previous decorations: the green leaves and red geraniums from the two arches over the front of the altars, the cut flowers from the vases, and the pine branches covering the altar supports. A round of cane liquor is passed and the redecoration begins. Fresh leaves and geraniums are piled on the straw mat before the incense bearers, who fashion small bouquets from them. These are passed to assistants and then to the mayordomos, who tie them to the arches. Fresh flowers are placed in the vases and new pine boughs tied to the altar supports. At the beginning, middle, and end of this segment of the ritual, as well as at the same points in all segments of every cargo ritual, a shot glass of cane liquor is passed to all present.

After a short interlude the mayordomos commence changing the many layers of clothing enveloping the images. Once again they pass before the musicians reciting an invocation:

See then, my elder brother,
See then, my younger brother,
I am going to dress,
I am going to clothe,
Father Saint (saint's name)
Father Saint (saint's name)
He will be happy,
He will open his eyes,
At that which is in his sight,
At that which is before his face,
O elder brother,
O younger brother.

After the images are swaddled in layers of newly washed clothing, there is a brief interlude. Then the mayordomos again recite a greeting as they pass before their musicians:

See then elder brother,
See then younger brother,
Let us speak,
Let us move our lips,
We beg for the divine pardon,

We beg for the divine forgiveness,
Before the divine presence,
Before the flowering face
Father Saint (saint's name)
Father Saint (saint's name)

This is the introduction to an extended prayer to the saint recited by the mayordomos and the incense bearers. After placing lit candles on the altars, they kneel and in the customary high-pitched prayer tone, implore the saints. This extended prayer illustrates the typical thoughts and feelings of the Zinacantecos toward the saints. (This particular prayer is directed at Hmanvaneh, the Christ image used on Good Friday. The saint invoked changes, depending on the festival.)

In the name of God Jesus Christ, my Lord,
Divine purchaser of glory,
At dusk,
At dawn,
Day and night may I be in your sight,
Day and night may I be before your flower face.
Receive it then, my father,
Receive it then, my lord.
Not for the smallness of my offering, abandon my back,
Not for this, abandon my side.
Grant me,
Reserve for me,
Thy three graces,
Thy three blessings,
On my back,
On my side.
That there may not overtake me,
That there may not come before me,
A demon,
A demon,
At my back
At my side.
You keep me,
You protect me,
Wherever I go,
Wherever I walk,
At dusk,
At dawn.

You know,
You have seen,
Where I found the small offerings,
Which I lay beneath your feet,
And before your hands,
In fear of you
And shame before you,
On each of your great feast days,
On each of your festivals.
Direct me,
Guide me,
Open my eyes,
Open my sight,
To know how I found,
To know how I received,
The little gift,
The small offering,
Divine and glorious man,
Divine and glorious ladino,
Do not yet put me to shame,
Do not yet abandon me.
May I be a good servant beneath your feet,
May I be faithful to my task beneath your hands,
Divine and glorious man,
Divine and glorious ladino
We have just changed your flowers,
We have just changed the leaves of your tree
Now we have arrived at your great feast day,
Now we have arrived at your great festival,
You will be entertained
You will be happy
On your great feast day,
On your great festival,
Father Saint (name of saint)
Father Saint (name of saint)

This prayer is recited with great emotion, which is evident in the facial expressions, head movements, and body language of the mayordomos and incense bearers (see figure 1.2). At various points in the prayer, there is a forced shedding of tears to express emotion. This crying is so realistic that at first the writer thought it was a spontaneous outburst. Inquiry revealed otherwise, eliciting the comment that it is done "to show our hearts to the saint."

The last part of the ceremony is dancing and singing for the entertainment of the saint. Once again the mayordomos pass before the musicians:

See then, my elder brother,
See then, my younger brother,
Lend me the ten toes of your feet,
Lend me the ten fingers of your hands,
Let us make merry for a while,
Let us amuse him for a while
In the resplendent sight,
Before the flower-like face,
Of father Saint (saint's name)
Of father Saint (saint's name)
He will be happy,
He will be entertained,
On the great feast day,
On the great festival,
Of father Saint (saint's name)
Of father Saint (saint's name)
Although it be for a short time,
Although it be only for two moments,
This has always been the custom,
It has always been performed like this,
Elder brother,
Younger brother.

The musicians begin playing. The mayordomos open the glass door of the image case, face the musicians, and begin to dance. They remain in one place, lifting their feet up and down, bending their knees, and swaying their bodies in time with the music. The incense bearers fall in behind them and pick up the rhythm in the same fashion. Five songs comprise the saint's entertainment.

The first segment varies for each pair of mayordomos and their respective saints. The following example is the song of the mayordomos reyes and mesoneros for the Virgin Mary, who is associated with the moon:

The woman of the sky,
The ladina of the sky,
Now Mary, she is pretty,
Now Rosary, she is lovely
She is present, Mary of the Rosary,
She is here, Mary the ladina.

The second selection is sung by every pair of mayordomos, as are all the following songs:

> We are here together,
> We are united here.
> We are laughing,
> We are joking,
> To celebrate his great feast day,
> To celebrate his great festival,
> Our radiant lord,
> Our resplendent father.

The third song is,

> Our fathers are gathered together,
> Our mothers are gathered together,
> His servants are gathered together,
> His boys are gathered together,
> My elder brothers are gathered together,
> My younger brothers are gathered together,
> La la la la a laaaaaaaa.
> Let his servants dance,
> Let his boys dance,
> Let our fathers dance,
> Let our mothers dance,
> Let our fathers enjoy themselves,
> Let our mothers enjoy themselves,
> Let my elder brothers enjoy themselves,
> Let my younger brothers enjoy themselves.

The fourth song is,

> Let us dance to the songs that reach heaven,
> Let us dance to the songs on the earth,
> Let us dance to the songs beneath the feet,
> Let us dance to the songs beneath the hands
> (Name of saint), our divine lord,
> (Name of saint), our divine father.
> la la la la la la la laaaaaaaa.

The last song is,

> Here we are together,
> Here we are united.

> How good it is beneath the feet,
> How good it is beneath the hands,
> Of (name of saint), our divine lord,
> Of (name of saint), our divine father,
> He is like a flower, our divine lord,
> He is like a flower, our divine father.

During this part of the ritual a party atmosphere takes over. While singing and dancing, the mayordomos smoke, drink cane liquor, tell jokes that often are off-color, laugh, and have a good time.

The Oath of the Incoming Alférez

The chapel of Señor Esquipulas, the patron of authorities, functions as the "office" of the moletik. At one end of the small rectangular chapel is the altar of Señor Esquipulas (a Christ crucifix, see the introductory photo to this chapter). A rectangular table seating about fourteen people occupies the remainder of the chapel. The moletik gathers here every Sunday and during the major festivals to conduct the business of the cargo system and to talk with any member of the community who wishes to see them. Any time the moletik will be using the chapel, the mayordomos reyes and mesoneros must prepare it in advance by changing the flowers and decorating the Esquipulas image (see fig. 3.1).

Seven of the major festivals are the occasions for changing the occupants of two of the fourteen alférez positions. Several rituals comprise the change ceremony, the main one occurring in the chapel of Señor Esquipulas on the evening that begins the first day of the festival. This ritual begins about nine o'clock at night when the members of the moletik take their seats in the chapel along with several civil officials. All lay their batons of office on the table with the silver tips facing the foot of the table. The regidores escort to the chapel the two new alfereces together with their musicians and ritual advisors. The senior incoming alférez enters first and stands at the foot of the chapel table. In order of seniority each alcalde, regidor, scribe, and civil official rises, faces the incoming alférez, and delivers this exhortation.

> My venerable father,
> Now your person has arrived,
> Now your person has arrived,
> Here before the feet,
> Here before the hands,
> Of the Lord Esquipulas
> O, my venerable father.
> You have come to receive,
> You have come to take,

The holy divine oath,
Here before the feet,
Here before the hands,
Of the Lord Esquipulas
O, my venerable father.
You must be a good servant,
You must be faithful to your trust,
During the twelve months,
During the twelve days.
Therefore, you must leave your sins,
Therefore, you must leave your wickedness,
Under the feet,
Under the hands,
Of the Lord Saint Lawrence
O, my venerable father.
For this you are swearing an oath of your person,
For this you are swearing an oath of your being,
For this you will come to the feast,
For this you will come to the festival.
You must be a good servant,
You must be faithful to your trust,
You must leave the cargo in order,
You must leave the cargo prepared.
For the two who will succeed you,
For your two successors,
For a year in the divine world
During a year on the holy earth,
O, my venerable father.
Sufficient is our word,
Sufficient are our two words.

At the end of this exhortation, the incoming alférez kneels, places the tips of his fingers on the table, and bows his head forward between his two hands. The senior alcalde rises, comes to the side of the kneeling alférez, and prays to Lord Esquipulas:

In the divine name of God Jesus Christ, my lord,
Divine Lord Esquipulas, my father,
Divine Lord Esquipulas, my lord,
May everything be done that is commanded, my lord,
May everything be done that is commanded, my father.
He came to receive

He came to take
The holy divine oath,
Here under your feet,
Here under your hands,
Your servant,
Your boy.
He must be a good servant,
He must be faithful to his trust,
For the twelve months,
For the twelve days
Here under your feet,
Here under your hands.
May he see it,
May he watch over it,
As they saw it,
As they watched over it,
His two predecessors,
His two antecedents.
May he leave it in order,
May he leave it prepared,
For the two who replace him,
For his two successors
A year in the holy world
A year on the holy earth
The worker,
The servant,
Of the divine Lord Esquipulas, my father,
Of the divine Lord Esquipulas, my lord.
May he walk in your radiant sight,
May he walk before your flower-like face,
By the blessing of the Father, true God,
By the blessing of the Son, true God,
By the blessing of the Holy Spirit, true God.

During the last three lines of this prayer the senior alcalde makes a motion over the head of the alférez that resembles a threefold sign of the cross. The words resemble the ancient Christian doxology. Aubry (1988: 23) thinks it is a holdover from the blessing used by Dominican priors at *cabildo* (town council) meetings.

Next the incoming alférez proceeds to the altar of Señor Esquipulas where he places a candle, kneels, and prays before the image; then he stands and again faces the seated authorities. The senior alcalde turns the heads of the silver-tipped batons toward the new alférez. Then each official again rises and delivers the same exhortation as previously. After his exhortation the senior alcalde steps forward and presents a hat with a peacock feather to the incoming alférez, a symbol of his new position, which he will wear during the next year when dancing for the saints. The alcalde tightens the novice's red turban around his head and arranges its ends so that they hang straight down the back, the usual ritual manner of dress for an alférez. The same ceremony is then repeated for the junior incoming alférez.

The First Day

Most of the activities today are still preparatory (see table 3.1, section B). They involve the cargo officeholders with few members of the community present.

Mayordomos Prepare the Saints in the Churches

The mayordomos clean the images, pictures, and crosses in the churches, and then decorate them with fresh flowers and dress the images in clean sets of clothes. The statues follow European models, with sculpted clothing typical of the saint's historical period or from traditional Christian iconography. When clothing the saints, the mayordomos put Zinacanteco-style clothing or elaborate cloth coverings over the sculpted clothing. The mayordomos also clean and decorate the church. They change the altar cloths and flowers, and put pine arches over the doors of the church. The ritual associated with these practical tasks involves the same offerings and prayers made the previous night in their houses.

At the beginning of some major festivals saint images are carried from the chapels in the outlying villages to Zinacantán center. All cargo members process out to meet them at the entrances to the center. Then, led by flute and drum, and with the mayordomos and alfereces carrying their flags of office, they process back to the town church where the visiting images are placed until the final day of the festival.

Alfereces Entertain the Saints and Each Other

In the late afternoon the mayordomos, alfereces, and moletik with their assistants and three civil officials gather in front of the church and process to the homes of the two alfereces who are leaving office during this festival. There, each leaving alférez serves coffee, bread, *atole* (gruel made from corn flour), and cane liquor as a gesture of departure at the end of his year of service. In front of the house his two elderly ritual advisors stand at the head of two parallel rows of benches where all the members of the cargo system are seated.

A server carrying containers of atole, bread, and coffee kneels in front of the advisors who recite this invocation.

In the name of God Jesus Christ, my lord,
Father Saint Lawrence   (Here they face the church
Father Saint Dominic,   and address the saints.)
With this, my father,
With this, my lord,
They will receive,
They will possess,
Your ray (the food),
Your shadow,
Your sons,
Your servants,
Your creatures,
Your workers,
Your hirelings.
May there be granted us,
May there be reserved for us,
Your three graces,
Your three benedictions,
Lord Saint Savior,   (They look up at the sun
Lord Saint Manuel,   here addressed.)
Your sons will receive,
Your sons will possess,
Your ray,
Your shadow,
My father,
My lord.
Receive my words, O Calvary,   (Here they turn to the sacred
That there may be granted us   mountain, Kalvario, the meeting
That there may be reserved for us,   place of all the protecting gods.)
Your three graces,
Your three benedictions
My father,
My lord.
The blessing of the Father, true God,   (Here three hand signs of blessing
The blessing of the Son, true God,   are made over the food.)
The blessing of the Holy Spirit, true God,

This prayer invokes the saints as well as the ancestral gods who live in certain mountains surrounding the valley of Zinacantán town center. Food and drink are then distributed to the seated cargo members, who consume some but pass most of it back to waiting kin, who will take it home for later consumption.

Following these visits to the homes of the departing alfereces, the other alfereces with their musicians begin a series of visits to one another's houses. During the visits the alfereces eat, pray, sing, dance, and drink in a manner similar to the ritual of the mayordomos the previous night. These visits last the entire night, with the last one taking place in the early morning of the following day.

The Second Day

Much of the activity on this day takes place in front of the church, where various cargo officeholders sing, dance, and drink for the saints (see table 3.1, section C).

The Alfereces Entertain the Saints

Following the visit to the last house in the early morning, the alfereces process to the church for a day of entertaining the saints. They enter the church and briefly pray. Then they proceed to benches that have been placed in front of the church to the right of the doorway. Here they remain all day, singing, dancing, and drinking to the accompaniment of their musicians. Since the alfereces have been drinking all night, they are quite mellow at this point and still have another day and night of drinking ahead of them. During the day the two alfereces leaving office and the two taking their place perform the "dance of the drunks," a comedic parody of their situation. The dancers gyrate wildly, yell loudly, and take long leaps, their movements becoming more and more erratic and clumsy. They collapse at the end of the dance, then rise and enter the church to pray.

> God Jesus Christ, my lord,
> Lord Saint Lawrence,
> Lord Saint Dominic,
> May all be done that is commanded,
> May all be done that is commanded.
> I am confused,
> I have lost my way,
> So forgive me, my father,
> Forgive me, my lord,

Your flower [i.e., the cane liquor] has knocked me down,
The leaf of the tree has taken me off my feet,
I have lost my reason,
I have lost my way.
Do not completely abandon me,
Do not cease to protect me,
My back,
My side.
I have lost my few belongings,
I have lost my few belongings,
Through the fault of your flower,
Through the fault of the leaf of your tree.
So I am made poor,
So I have become poor,
But receive my word, father,
But receive my word, lord,
Grant me,
Reserve for me,
Your three graces,
Your three benedictions,
On my back,
On my side,
Divine Lord Saint Lawrence,
Divine Saint Dominic
My resplendent father,
My resplendent lord,
Mary of the Rosary,
Mary, ladina,
Woman of the sky,
Ladina of heaven.

The Mayordomos Entertain the Saints

About midmorning the mayordomos and their musicians arrive at the church, enter, and pray before the images. The mayordomos then dance to the accompaniment of the violin, harp, and guitar. After an hour or so they leave the church and sit on benches in front of the church to the left of the doorway across from the alfereces on the right. A drink pourer offers a shot glass of cane liquor to each mayordomo as he passes along the bench. This is repeated a number of times until the bottles, one contributed by each mayordomo, are empty. In this manner the mayordomos pass the afternoon drinking and chatting, watching the alfereces dance and the people who have begun to congregate for the festival.

The Alfereces Continue Visiting

In the late afternoon the alfereces again process to the homes of the two departing alfereces. The ceremony described for the first day is repeated. Then they begin a second round of visiting each other's houses during the night, eating, drinking, dancing, and singing for the saints as previously described.

The Mayordomos Count and Place Necklaces on the Saints

After sunset each pair of mayordomos gathers in the home of the older brother to prepare the necklaces of the saints. These will be taken to the church to decorate the saints for the climax of the festival on the third day. The mayordomos spread a straw mat on the floor in front of the altars. The incense bearers take their places at the foot of the mat. The mayordomos open the coffers containing the necklaces, decorated cloth strips to which silver coins have been attached by brightly colored threads. These necklaces are entombed in a series of from ten to twenty cloth wrappings embellished with the finest Zinacanteco weaving. After unwrapping the necklaces, the mayordomos count the value of the coins attached to each one. The meaning of this count is not clear, but it may be a form of self-evaluation for the mayordomo. The correct count for each necklace is known from previous ceremonies. The mayordomo may count correctly if he feels he has properly performed his service to the saint, or may deliberately miscount and ask forgiveness as an acknowledgment of improper service. The necklaces are then rewrapped in their layers of cloth. In the early hours of the morning they are carried to the church, where they are again opened and placed around the necks of the saint images (see fig. 3.1). On finishing this task, the mayordomos sing and dance for the saints, especially the one whose feast day is being celebrated.

The Third Day

This is the last and most important day of the festival (see table 3.1, section D). During the first two days of the major festivals some people gather in the churchyard and visit the saints in the church, but the numbers relative to the population are small. On the third day many of those who live in Zinacantán center and neighboring villages will visit the church and then spend time in the churchyard talking with friends, drinking, and occasionally watching the mayordomos and alfereces. Residents in the other villages in the municipio of Zinacantán usually attend only on the most important festivals: the feasts of Saint Lawrence and Saint Sebastian, Holy Week, and Epiphany.

Figure 3.1. A mayordomo rey dresses the image of Señor Esquipulas (for the final result, see the introductory photograph to this chapter).

The Catholic Priest

Two days of the festival have already passed with praying, dancing, singing, drinking, and offering food for the saints. At this point the Catholic priest is inserted into the festival matrix. In the morning he arrives in his truck from San Cristóbal to perform the most important ritual of the saint's festival, the mass. His arrival is announced by the ringing of the church bells. People gather around him to make arrangements for baptisms and to have him bless pictures of the saints. He then celebrates the mass with the mayordomos, moletik, and fiscales in attendance. There is little participation by the people who have come for the fiesta. During the mass people may wander into the church, kneel and pray before a saint image, sometimes very loudly, and then leave paying no attention to the mass itself. After the mass, the priest performs baptisms. When these are finished, the tower bells are rung again to signal his departure.

The lack of congregational worship does not mean that the people consider the mass an unimportant ritual. None of the Zinacanteco rituals are congregational. The moletik have collected money from the people to pay for the festival, gone to San Cristóbal to invite the priest to Zinacantán for the mass, and paid the customary stipend for his services. For the Maya the important features of the mass are the priest wearing the colorful vestments, using lit candles, and offering bread and wine while reciting the necessary prayers from a large book, the missal, in the home of the saints. The writer recalls a festival when the priest did not appear when he was supposed to. The fiscal was highly agitated because the saint would be upset with the community for not properly celebrating his feast day and might punish the community. The fiscal emphasized that it was not his or the community's fault, but that of the priest who should be the one punished. Although the people do not attend the mass, they would be greatly upset if the cargo members and fiscales did not arrange for the mass and attend it, as this is their duty on behalf of the whole community.

The Mayordomos and Alfereces Entertain the Saints

Once the priest has left the mayordomos remain in the church, singing and dancing once again for the saints. Then they retire to their bench in front of the church and go through the same drinking round as the previous day. The alfereces also gather at their bench and spend the day singing, dancing, and drinking. About mid-afternoon the mayordomos reenter the church, remove the necklaces from the saint images to the accompaniment of their musicians, and return them to the coffers on their house altars.

The Moletik Gather in the Chapel

The moletik gather in the chapel of Señor Esquipulas whose image and altar have been decorated by the mayordomos reyes and mesoneros. The moletik sit at the chapel table where they are available for anyone who wishes to consult with them about cargo positions or any other matter regarding the organization and performance of community rituals.

The Two New Alfereces Are Formally Inducted

On the night before the first day of the fiesta the incoming alfereces took their oaths to be faithful in their performance of the duties of the cargo they were about to enter. Today in front of church the formal induction ceremony takes place via a double exchange of flags. The outgoing alfereces, holding their flags, kneel in the middle of a circle formed by all the other members of the cargo system and the civil officials. They hand over their flags to two kneeling regidores symbolizing the relinquishment of their burden of community duties after their year of service. The incoming alfereces then step forward, kneel, and receive the same two flags from the regidores, an exchange symbolizing their assumption of these duties in the coming year. During these exchanges stylized prayers similar to those of the preparatory ceremony are recited. The new alfereces then rise and individually greet all the members of the cargo system and the civil officials, offering each a shot of cane liquor. Following this, all the cargo members retire to the two houses of the new alfereces where they eat and drink as they did on the previous days at the houses of the outgoing alfereces. This ends the festival.

Church-Mountain Pattern

A description of the church-mountain pattern is included here by way of contrast with the festival patterns. Although the saints are invoked in part of the ritual, the priest plays no part in it. The main ritual specialists are the shamans (Early 1965: 322–25; Vogt 1969: 465–73). This ritual pattern, the Year Ceremony, occurs at least three times a year, usually in January, July, and December to mark the beginning, middle, and end of the year. The exact date is determined by the senior alcalde of the cargo system who acts as a host and helper of the ceremony along with the rest of the moletik, the mayordomos reyes, and the mesoneros. In the evening twenty shamans, two from each of the outlying villages, come to Zinacantán center to perform the ceremony. They gather in the house of the senior alcalde where many candles, flowers, and pieces of incense have been piled high on a long table. Several civil alcaldes from the town hall also arrive.

Throughout the night, five groups of four shamans take turns praying over the candles, flowers, and incense to be received by the protecting gods as supplication for their help during the year. At dawn a ceremonial meal is served. Then each pair of shamans takes candles, flowers, cane liquor, and incense, and sets off on pilgrimage to their assigned sacred places, either sacred mountains or crosses or waterholes. The four oldest shamans along with the alcaldes comprise the most important group. They visit the three churches to implore the protection of the saints. When each group finishes at its assigned places, all proceed to the sacred mountain, Kalvario, the meeting place of all the protective gods where more prayers are said and offerings made.

The Fiscal and Prayer

The preceding descriptions mention the many elements that comprise the celebration of the saint festivals. While candles, incense, cane liquor, song, and dance comprise a mosaic of things that saints like for the celebration, the prayers are also of great importance, the sine qua non of a ritual. The Zinacanteco cargo holders come from all over the municipio. This suggests that most have attended only the major festivals in Zinacantán center itself. Since there is no congregational worship during these festivals, the new cargo holders have had few occasions to observe the rituals of their predecessors. Their only previous experience is usually as an assistant while an older relative was serving in a position. Therefore when the cargo holders assume their duties, they are not familiar with the rituals they are to perform, especially the prayers. The importance of the fiscales is that as they know the prayers and frequently say them with the cargo members to ensure that they are properly recited. Sometimes if the cargo member is unable to recite a prayer, the fiscal will do it for him.

In some situations the fiscales are the designated prayer specialists. Zinacantán has had resident priests in the past. They have left their legacy as their residency enabled them to perform additional Catholic rituals such as the Good Friday service, Ascension Thursday along with its preparatory days, and Pentecost when a wooden dove is lowered from a ceiling rafter to symbolize the descent of the Holy Spirit. Festivals with such distinctive rituals in addition to the regular pattern are marked with a "D" in table 2.2. The common denominator of these ceremonies is the recitation of fixed prayers in Latin from a ritual or hymnal book by the fiscales in place of the priest. The fiscales, not realizing the prayers are in a different language, recite Latin as if it were Spanish. Comprehension is not necessary since the recitation of the words is deemed sufficient. The fiscales also perform the burial ceremony.

Variations

Ethnographic materials from Zinacantán have been used to illustrate the ritual patterns and the calendar of saint festivals. The main themes of the Zinacanteco materials are representative of traditional Maya postconquest culture. In other Mayan communities, however, these themes are embedded in a number of variations in both cargo structure and ritual patterns.

In addition to the church, in some communities there are saint houses with images where extensive ritual activity takes place. In Santiago Atitlán, a large Mayan town in Guatemala, some saint rituals are linked with shamanic rituals. The two major cofradías in Santiago require that the occupant of the major ritual role be a shaman (Carlsen 1997: 79–83, 152–57; Christenson 2001: 154–91). In Santiago and nearby San Juan Laguna important saints are also kept in the cofradía houses and are moved to the church during the festivals (Bizarro 1985: 266–75).

Summary

Chapter 2 listed the calendar of the saint festivals, and described the amount of time and resources involved. This chapter has described the three main types of festivals and the extensive ritual activity they involve for members of the cofradía/cargo systems. Within this structure of festival ritual, the Catholic mass and baptism administered by a Catholic priest are essential parts. The inclusion of these Catholic elements is the anomaly being investigated.

4

Mayan Insistence on the Mass Performed by a Catholic Priest

The previous chapter described the relatively brief appearance of the Catholic priest to celebrate the mass and perform baptisms during the multiday festival rituals. Is this brief appearance indicative of the priest's minor importance in the Mayan ritual matrix? To help answer this question, the present chapter probes historical and ethnographic materials to find indications of the strength and seriousness of the Mayan request for these Catholic elements.

Insistence on the Mass

Several historical incidents indicate the strength of the Mayan demand for the rituals of the Catholic priest.

A Drunken Crowd and the Demands of a King

In 1761 the town of Quisteil (Cisteil) in Yucatán became the center of a Mayan uprising against the Spaniards. It was led by Jacinto Uc who called himself

Canek. The town held meetings to plan the festival of the town's patron saint. Although supposedly preparatory, these meetings tended to turn into festive occasions accompanied by the heavy drinking characteristic of many festivals. A drunken group decided to continue the meetings and attempted to obtain more liquor from a ladino merchant but were refused. The crowd killed him in a rage. The next morning the visiting Catholic priest arrived. As he was celebrating mass, the intoxicated crowd jammed into the church intending to kill him. The priest stopped the service immediately, ran to his waiting horse, and began to depart. In spite of all this frenzy, "many Indians came up to him and begged him to stay with them to perform services for them" (Bricker 1981: 71). In such circumstances, this is insistence. Nonetheless, the priest fled.

Canek proceeded to crown himself king and declared the Maya free from the colonial authorities. He spoke of the many abuses suffered by the Maya: "Prominent among the grievances he listed in a speech made to rally supporters was the neglect that visita towns like Cisteil suffered from the clergy, who left them for weeks without hearing mass" (Farriss 1984: 314). Cutural revitalization took place.

> Adherents engaged in rituals suggestive of non-Christian ceremonies and came to believe that a Maya-controlled supernatural world would protect them from Spanish guns. . . . At the same time, the uprising was a nativistic movement. It intended to overthrow the colonial regime, and many adherents believed the movement would eliminate the Spaniards altogether. . . . Nevertheless the movement also chose to keep certain elements of foreign culture that accompanied colonialism. . . . Most important, aspects of Christianity were retained. . . . The cult of the Virgin Mary and of the saints were used to reinforce and legitimize the movement. Canek supposedly placed the Virgin's crown on his own head; the Maya used the buildings, the ritualistic paraphernalia—priestly vestments, the chalice, holy oils, the rosary—and sacraments of Catholicism for their own ceremonies. Canek himself proclaimed the continued legitimacy of the bulls of indulgence of the Santa Cruzada. (Patch 2002: 179–80)

Kidnapped Priests

The Caste Wars were a series of Mayan rebellions against Mexicans and the local government that swept the Yucatán Peninsula in the last half of the nineteenth century. The Maya initially gained the upper hand, but the Mexican forces rallied and captured a number of Mayan towns. The Maya retreated to unsettled areas, taking with them the saint images from their churches. This created a problem. Who was going to celebrate the masses for the saint festivals since there were no priests in these areas? If the saints did not have their masses, who would protect the rebels against the Mexican forces and natural disasters? Their solution was to capture Mexican priests and force them to celebrate masses. One of the rebel generals "had been using captured priests ... and the assembled loot of Valladolid to indulge his people in a magnificent series of fiestas and novenas. He entertained on a grand scale ... putting himself right with various village Santos, whose assistance he would need in the future." One of the captured priests, "the Vicar of Valladolid, Manuel Sierra, had been taken from village to village, celebrating fiestas and performing his religious functions. As a Dzul [ladino] he was hated, but as a priest he was necessary ... a fiesta wasn't complete without a mass, a cross nothing but wood until blessed" (Reed 1964: 89, 106, 107). This priest managed to escape, was recaptured, and escaped once more. Kidnapping priests and forcing them to celebrate masses for the saints is a striking example of the Mayan cultural dictates regarding the Catholic elements.

Insistence in Spite of Abuse

The insistence that these examples illustrate existed in spite of serious and not infrequent abusive behavior toward the Maya by Catholic clergy. The abuses were of such a magnitude that the Maya had strong incentives for completely rejecting Catholicism and its rituals. But they did not. The only thing they requested was an end to the abuse by removal of the guilty priest and substitution of another one to continue performing the Catholic rituals they so greatly desired. The data pose a question: What was the force driving this insistence? (It should be noted that the work of priests who helped Indian communities is lost in the silence of archival records concerned with complaints and transgressions. For some favorable Indian testimonies about such priests in the Nahua region, see León-Portilla 1974).

Cultural Abuse

Ignorance of Mayan culture and ethnocentrism permeated the treatment of the Maya by the Spanish colonial and later national governments. Initially the ethnocentrism resulted in the friars destroying many images and sacred books of the Maya religion believing them to be of diabolical origin. Bartolomé de las Casas (1958: 346) noted, "These books were seen by our clergy, and even I saw part of those which were burned by the friars, apparently because they thought [they] might harm the Indians in religious matters, since at that time they were at the beginning of their conversion."

Perhaps the most striking examples of cultural abuse occurred in Yucatán under Bishop Diego de Landa: "We found a large number of books using their manner of expression, and as they contained nothing but superstition and lies of the devil, we burned them all which they regretted to an amazing degree and [which] caused them much affliction" (Landa 1941: 78). In 1562, after a number of images were found in a cave among supposedly converted Maya, Landa began a campaign modeled on the methods of the Spanish Inquisition (Clendinnen 1987: 72–92). Bloody tortures were used both to extract confessions about image worship and child sacrifices and to punish the "confessed" offenders.

> More than 4,500 Indians were put to the torture during the three months of the inquisition, and an official enquiry later established that 158 died during or as a direct result of the interrogations. At least thirteen people were known to have committed suicide to escape the torture while eighteen others who had disappeared, were thought to have killed themselves. Many more had been left crippled, their shoulder muscles irreparably torn, their hands paralyzed "like hooks." (Clendinnen 1987: 76)

These early events in Yucatán appear to have been the worst of the cultural abuses that were to continue in various forms throughout the colonial and national periods.

A systemic manifestation of the rejection of Mayan culture was the exclusion of Maya from the Catholic priesthood. Any Mayan aspirant would have been rejected as lacking the necessary qualifications. As early as 1555 the synod of bishops from Mexico and Guatemala forbade the ordination of mestizos, Indians, and Negroes (Ricard 1966: 217–35). This attitude was the result of a number of factors. The Spaniards were wary of converts entering the priesthood as a result of experiences with Jewish and Islamic converts in Spain (Oss 1986: 161). In addition, the Maya were considered ignorant children by many Spaniards, and therefore not qualified for ordination.

The Franciscans attempted to found Indian schools that would turn out qualified candidates. But these efforts "met with violent opposition among the [secular] clergy and the public, for the greater part of the Spaniards in Mexico, to tell the truth, did not wish to see the natives elevated to the priesthood" (Ricard 1966: 228). In Yucatán "The Indians' status as perpetual neophytes . . . meant that they could not be trusted to undertake the duties of the priesthood, and the Spanish creoles and Peninsulares retained a near monopoly on the Catholic priesthood throughout the colonial period and beyond. A small proportion of mestizos and even a few candidates with some African mixture managed to infiltrate clerical ranks (over the protests of the creole elite), but no Indians" (Farriss 1984: 334). The same problems existed in Guatemala (Oss 1986: 160–64).

There were numerous other examples of cultural abuse. In 1763 a secular priest from a prominent ladino family in San Cristóbal Las Casas replaced a

Dominican friar in Chamula and served there for thirteen years. The priest described his attitude toward the boys who took weekly turns serving as porters for the priest:

> For we priests it is a serious business to have to treat . . . [in a familiar manner] these rustic boys, and their wild customs, endure their petty thefts, and other impertinences, that would become tolerable by the end of the week if these were not substituted by others who take their place who are so barbarous because they have just been pulled out of the woods . . . the service and familiar company of the porters is one of the insufferable jobs that we Priests of the Indians have. . . . Those whom I civilized, indoctrinated and taught to read and write for the utility of the Town have used and continue to use this skill to copy petitions against me. (Porrúa 1992 summarized by Laughlin 2003: 85–90)

This appears to have been the typical attitude of the ladino upper class.

Another case of cultural abuse occurred in 1950 in Santiago Atitlán (Tarn and Prechtel 1997: 15–28; Mendelson 1957: 332–52, 1965). A visiting priest came for the Holy Week services. He found Maximón, the local ancestral god-saint enshrined on the church porch with many Atitecos praying and making offerings to him. The priest became enraged and threw the image off the church porch. This in turn enraged the Atitecos, who physically threatened the priest. He went to his quarters, returned with a gun, and fired some shots in the air or at Maximón (versions vary). After discussion with the priest, Maximón was returned to the church porch but no one could approach him until the priest departed. Six weeks later the same priest with two others returned to Atitlán. With the help of some local Atitecos, they barged into the cofradía house of Maximón and made off with two of Maximón's masks. One wound up in a Paris museum and was not returned until 1979.

Economic Abuse

The colonial church faced the problem of financially supporting its priests. The crown exempted the Mayan population from church tithes to ease their acceptance of Christianity. This was intended to be a temporary measure until the Maya were Hispanicized, but the temporary measure became the custom. As an alternative to tithing, the Indian tribute to the crown was increased, and a portion of this (the *sínodo*) was supposed to subsidize the parishes. The crown collected the tribute and gave the subsidy to the bishops to be distributed to the parishes. But frequently the bishops and the cathedral chapters used the funds for their own purposes, and the subsidy seldom reached the parishes. As a result both friars and secular priests had to seek support directly from their parishioners in the form of rations; labor service; fees for masses sponsored by cofradías; first-fruit offerings; and fees for baptisms, marriages, and burials. The system created opportunities for abuse (Oss 1986: 79–108; Farriss 1984: 39–47).

The friars needed resources for the construction of churches and monasteries as well as for their own support. At the same time high mortality was decimating the Maya leaving a smaller population to provide those resources. For these reasons the friars developed large-scale food and cattle plantations. Excessive labor demands by the friars and later by secular priests caused much suffering in Mayan communities in Chiapas (Bricker 1981: 119; Rus 1983: 129–44; Wasserstrom 1983a), in Yucatán (Bricker 1981: 89; Farriss 1984: 40–44, 85), and in Guatemala (Ximénez 1973). An example of extreme abuse by a Father Quadrado is detailed in a formal complaint (O'Flaherty 1979: 177–78). Before the festivals he would demand that village leaders make an offering of a *tostón* (a Spanish silver coin), that male peasants under age forty offer two *reales* (smaller coins), that the women offer two hundred cacao beans, that young boys offer twenty such beans, and that men between forty and sixty offer according to their means. For the Holy Week and Easter services he demanded twelve thousand cacao beans. If this offering was not made, the priest would tie the offender to a post along with the church fiscal whose duty it was to collect the offerings and have them whipped. The women of the community refused to come to church because Father Quadrado reprimanded them for not bringing offerings they did not have. While the priest was away from the community, boys took care of his sheep, goats, pigs, and horses without any remuneration or the religious instruction they were supposed to receive.

Economic abuses became frequent and severe enough that official investigations were initiated and diocesan decrees with specific prohibitions promulgated. On an inspection tour Fray de la Torre reported,

Now the cleric, whether in a pueblo of Your Majesty, or of an encomendero, receives a salary as well as all the offerings . . . because the Indians have to provide all the food and services for these clerics, their servants and horses without them spending a penny, and in some pueblos the cost of taking care of the priest and his household for one day reaches sixteen reales of silver. The Indians are taxed by the bishop each day for two hens . . . . which in many pueblos is worth ten reales; would that the priests were content with that. Many Indians have complained to me that they take four hens each day and if they are not very fat, they throw them back in their faces. The Indians give the clerics three or four women to make bread (usually for a week) and some clerics do not want them if they are old. The Indians give them fruit and provide all the service which they need for themselves and their horses and from some I learned that the clerics have eight horses. . . . Above all there is hardly a cleric who knows the language and can hear confessions in it, nor preach except through a young servant and they do little more than say Mass on Sundays and baptize children. Would to God they would stop there and not give the example which they do. (O'Flaherty 1979: 180)

Bishop Marroquín held two diocesan meetings (synods) in Guatemala to correct abuses by the clergy. The documents from the synods are missing, but in 1558 the bishop issued regulations for the clergy of Soconusco which probably were similar to the prohibitions of the synods (O'Flaherty 1979: 183–84). In dealings with Indians priests were forbidden to sell or give to Indians the wine that was donated by the crown for mass; to conduct any business with Indians except for cacao beans; to demand or receive food beyond buying what was needed; to demand without remuneration feed for their horses; to have as a servant anyone over fifteen years of age; to say masses in addition to those freely requested by the Indians; and to wander from town to town seeking to say masses.

The church had a problem common to all bureaucracies: who was going to watch the watchers, in this case, the bishops? The bishop of a diocese periodically visited all the parishes to administer the sacrament of confirmation and to inspect their organizations, including the cofradías. During these visits the bishop collected a tax of six pesos from each cofradía to defray his expenses and an additional twelve or more pesos for his celebration of the mass (Ximénez 1971a: 240). One bishop made repeated visits for the sole purpose of collecting this tax, thereby diminishing the capital of the cofradías (Ximénez 1971a: 239). According to Ximénez this was one of the reasons for the Tzeltal uprising in 1712. This bishop was transferred to Guatemala, and trouble arose again because he founded new cofradías solely for the purpose of obtaining money from them (Ximénez 1971a: 365, 1971b: 9, 58, 112, 128). In addition to founding cofradías, a variant of this strategy was to increase the number of festivals a community celebrated and the cofradías consequently funded. Since the cofradías existed under the legal jurisdiction of the bishop, he also had the right to suppress them if he found any irregularities. In such a case, by law the possessions of the cofradía would pass into the hands of the diocese, and the bishop as head of the diocesan corporation could seize them. This gave the bishop another weapon: the threat of suppressing cofradías unless they increased their tax payments (Ximénez 1971b: 165, 167).

Sexual Abuse

Whereas cultural and economic abuse seem to have been most prevalent, sexual abuse also occurred. In the case of the infamous Father Quadrado, Friar de la Torre's inspection report further notes, "This witness said that it is public and well-known in the pueblo and spoken of among the macequales [peasants] that when don Antonio was out of the pueblo, his wife was very much asked for by said Quadrado and that the boys of the church acted as interpreters and that the said Indian woman, seeing herself bothered by the cleric, left the pueblo until her husband returned" (O'Flaherty 1979: 178). Collections of Mayan tales usually include some about sexual misconduct of priests. "The Zinacantec does not bear fools or priests lightly. . . . The vagaries of priests, their amorous adventures, are the subject not of humor, but outrage" (Laughlin 1977: 9). Two tales from San Juan La Laguna relate the seduction of Indian women by a Spanish priest. One was a parishioner who became an object of his intentions; the other a young bride at her wedding ceremony (Sexton and Bizarro 1992: 168–76, 176–85). Although sexual ridicule of public figures is commonplace in many communities, at times there is some basis for such tales.

A Typical Case of Maya—Catholic Priest Conflict

Although this dispute took place between 1985 and 1991, beyond the time frame of this study, it reflects many long-standing problems. San Juan La Laguna is a Mayan community of more than four thousand people located on the shores of Lake Atitlán in Guatemala. Nearby and with better road connections to the region is the larger Mayan town of San Pedro La Laguna that had a population of nearly 5,575 people in 1981. The residents of the two towns tend to be antagonistic because of forced land sales several decades ago and continued land disputes. Traditionally the Catholic priest resided in San Pedro but visited San Juan and several other nearby towns to administer the sacraments. On April 11, 1985, the bishop of Sololá assigned a new pastor to these parishes. The new priest attempted to initiate some changes in the accustomed routine of rituals. This led to a seven-year conflict between the priest and many in the community.

The conflict was recorded in a diary kept by a Mayan native of the town, Ignacio Bizarro Ujpán. Bizarro began to keep the diary in 1972 with the encouragement of the anthropologist James Sexton. The diary was written in Spanish, edited and translated into English by Sexton, and published in four volumes (Bizarro Ujpán 1981, 1985, 1992, 2001) along with two books of tales (Sexton & Bizarro 1992, 1999). Bizarro relates the dispute as it unfolded (1992: 192–209, 217–19, 233–49, 255–61, 2001: 64–70, 82–83, 124, 134, 184, 192–94). In providing a detailed account of the conflict and its many phases, his diary gives insight into many aspects and nuances of the relationship between the Maya and Catholic priests.

The Priest and the Cofradía

In San Juan in 1985 there were three cofradías, later expanded to four. The cofradías initiated the festivals of the saints by processing the images from the cofradía houses to the church and then processing them back to conclude the festival. The festival consisted of the usual ritual routine: burning candles, serving atole to visitors, and consuming liquor, all with the appropriate prayers. According to Bizarro (1992: 195), the cofrades "believe in the saints because the saints are very good friends of God. If someone serves as *alcalde, juez* or *mayordomo* devoted to the saint of the *cofradía*, they think that in the other life they will be forgiven for their sins because the saint is a very good friend of God and will intercede for them when they die so they will not suffer punishment in the other life." This understanding has been influenced by contact with Catholic doctrine.

The new priest forbade all use of liquor in the cofradías and mandated that cofrades attend one hour of instruction daily for twenty days on the meaning of the saints. Failure to comply with these demands would result in the priest banning the images from the church during the festivals. Bizarro wrote, "Those of the Church (the father and members of Catholic Action [orthodox Mayan Catholics]) said that the old *costumbres* are all abolished and that the *cofrades* only were able to participate in the mass and rosaries and bury the dead, nothing more. This did not suit the *cofrades*; it made them mad. But I think that the father and Catholic Actionists want what's good for them so that they will not spend their money. But the *cofrades* never reflect, they just think of what they have learned from our ancestors, that the old *costumbres* are beneficial for the community" (Bizarro 1992: 193).

Additional Changes

The new priest, an American, implemented additional changes designed to make the community conform to Catholic orthodoxy and to help meet their physical needs. Before being married, the engaged couple was required to attend one hour of instruction daily for twenty days about the meaning of the sacrament. Before a baptism, parents were also to attend daily one-hour sessions for twenty days about the meaning of the ritual as well as about infant health care and nutrition. The latter requirement was the result of a community survey that revealed poor health conditions in the community. The priest had raised money in the United States to help build dispensaries and latrines in several towns.

Finally, the priest informed the community that he would celebrate only a single mass on the festival days rather than the multiple masses that previously had been requested. The priest said, "Do not pay for any more masses; one is sufficient. Use the money you pay for mass to feed your children" (Bizarro 1992: 196). The community greatly disliked the education requirements. The priest's sermons further fueled the conflict. He repeatedly chastised the community for stealing, drunkenness, and adultery. Bizarro agrees that these were significant problems needing correction in the community, but the majority of the towns-people deeply resented the public denunciations.

The Priest and Catholic Action

In January 1986 the conflicts expanded to Catholic Action. This group had collected 1,300 *quetzales* for festival expenses. In the past some of these funds had been used to buy liquor. The priest found out about the money and the way it had been used. He demanded that the money be safeguarded in a parish account, a procedure mandated by church regulations for any parish assets. He also found out that the officers of Catholic Action had in their possession the land titles for the site of the church and some coffee land owned by the church. He demanded that these also be handed over for safekeeping in his office in San Pedro. Catholic Action leaders complied, giving him both the money and the titles. These actions enraged the community, including many other members of Catholic Action. In the minds of the community members and by long-standing custom, the local church, its properties, and the festival funds belonged to the community members who safeguard them and decide how they are to be used. The priest is a welcome visitor to the community, but is only a visitor whose diocesan regulations cannot supersede community custom. This situation is typical of the cultural conflicts that arise between Mayan communities and Catholic priests.

More Conflict with the Cofradía

Bizarro recounts that during the festivals the people of the town

> had become accustomed to all the *principales* [respected elders] being in-vited on behalf of the mayor for eating a succulent lunch, drinking their traditional *tragos* [shots of liquor], dancing some hours to the happy, regional sounds of the marimba, and remembering past times. But on this 25 June [feast day of the patron saint], the parish priest didn't permit the *principales* to go to the invitation. The same *padre* took them to the soccer field to watch the game. And they had to say yes, accompanied by the priest. It all seemed very well—the father wanted the best for the *principales* so they wouldn't get drunk, would avoid injuries and wouldn't spend money, because their bodies are very delicate due to their advanced

age and they are unable to earn money. It is known, however, that the old guys didn't like sports. Many of them just drank their *tragos* secretly and got very drunk. It's difficult for them to change their habits—they are old men, and they have lived many years with their old, traditional *costumbres*. To change their manners, one must have patience! (1992: 207–8)

In another section of his diary Bizarro writes about his own problems with alcohol and his overcoming it with the help of Alcoholics Anonymous. In his various cofradía positions he abstained from drinking, a radical departure from the usual custom. He gives his view of the cofradías, "there are good *costumbres* such as the processions of the images, drinking *atol* [non-alcoholic] in the *cofradías*, and the *cofrades* preparing food during the fiestas as gifts. The padre however wanted to completely cancel these activities, but this is what provoked the problems" (Bizarro 1992: 206). In 1994 Bizarro became a principal himself. He wants changes but within the traditional framework. While sympathetic to Catholic Action, Bizarro never became a member of the organization.

Another Dispute with Catholic Action

By now the vast majority of the community had turned against the priest. Only a small group within Catholic Action defended him. In December 1986 Catholic Action had collected two thousand quetzales and wanted to begin construction of a new church. The priest became aware of their intentions and the money. Once again holding to the principle that church funds should be put in the church account, he demanded that the money be handed over and that no work should begin on a new church until forty to fifty thousand quetzales had been collected. This time Catholic Action refused. The priest then removed the consecrated hosts from the church, locked it, and left town. Later he returned to San Juan to meet with the community. Once again, he explained the legalities of parish funds, demanded the money, and was refused. He left the church and as he approached his car was physically threatened by the enraged community.

The Search for a New Priest

The leaders of the opposition groups initiated a search for a replacement priest. In January they went to Guatemala City to demand one from the archbishop who referred them back to the bishop of Sololá who had jurisdiction over the San Juan parish. In February nine dissenters went to Huehuetenango to find a priest. A short time later they went to San Diego for the same purpose. The opposition groups did not fully understand the legal structure of the Catholic Church, namely, that only the bishop of a diocese can assign a priest to a parish. They appeared to equate the situation of Catholic priests with that of Mayan shamans who practice independently without the hierarchical structure of an organization.

Toward the end of February the bishop of Sololá visited San Pedro. While there, he met with the priest's supporters who requested that the liturgy be resumed. The bishop consented, and masses were again celebrated in San Juan. In March the opposition group went to the bishop of Sololá and demanded a new priest. The bishop rejected their request with the advice that they return and negotiate with the existing priest. As the wrath against the priest was intense, the dissenters refused and insulted the bishop for his inaction.

The Conflict Becomes Physical

On March 21 the priest arrived in San Juan, talked with the Catholic groups, said mass, heard confessions, and left the church to return to San Pedro. At this point,

> the first persons . . . seized him with the intent against his life. . . . When the majority saw that they had captured the father, they went to hit him with their hands, fists and stones, or perhaps kill him. Then some interfered to defend him, but since they were few in number, it was difficult. I too went to defend him, and we were able to rescue him from the claws of the enemies. We returned to the church. They also hit me hard. . . . A lot of people were shouting, "Kill him [the priest] once and for all! We don't want to see this man anymore!" When we were able to defend the father, the enemies captured a member of Catholic Action [from the faction defending the priest]. . . and nearly killed him. By God's grace, one of his sons-in-law and a son who is a student appeared. It was they who saved him. It's true that one of the *contras* [attackers] . . . a very tall, fat, wealthy man, was hit by Martin's son, but this was to defend his father. When the majority saw that one of its leaders was hit in the face and knocked down, they retreated. . . . A majority inside [the church] were able to leave for their houses. We could well have left, but to defend the life of the priest, indeed we stayed with him. . . . [A dissenter] went to the door to tell his supporters, "I counted these people; there are only 42 persons. They aren't able to do anything. If you want, we can show our strength. We can do what we wish." The people shouted "Let's go inside!" There were about 400 of them. (Bizarro 1992: 242)

A nun in the small group defending the priest faced down the leader of the dissenters and warned him that he would be responsible if any more violence should happen. The leader then told the crowd to back off. The priest left for San Pedro and the church was locked.

Failed Diplomacy

On March 25 the bishop invited the dissenting group to meet in San Pedro, but they did not come. On March 28 the dissenting group appointed a new set of church officials—president, vice president, treasurer, secretary, and two fiscales. They began to hold services in their homes. On the following days there was continued discussion about getting a replacement priest from Quetzaltenango, Panajachel, or Santiago Atitlán. On April 13 the dissenting group received a letter from the bishop saying that he would come to San Pedro in two days to see about reopening the church as long as the community would obey the laws of the church. This enraged the dissenting group who went to the church, broke the locks on the doors, and took possession of it. The governor of Sololá was informed. He sent a letter to the dissenters telling them that no one could go into the church until they discussed a solution with the bishop. The dissenters rejected the governor's directive. One of the leaders said "they were not going to respect either the governor or the bishop, that the church was built by their ancestors, not by the governor, much less the bishop" (Bizarro 1992: 258).

On April 15 a two-hour meeting with the bishop took place in San Pedro and ended in disorder. The dissenting group said the bishop and the governor meant nothing to them. They were the town leaders, and they could do whatever they wanted. On April 23 the group had an unsatisfactory meeting with the bishop in Panajachel. By this time news of the conflict had spread throughout Guatemala. It was carried on national television and reported in *Prensa Libre*, one of the country's leading newspapers. On May 11 the bishop summoned the dissenters to Panajachel for his decision. San Juan would have a new pastor who would live in San Pedro because of the lack of accommodations in San Juan. But the new priest would be appointed only if the dissenting group accepted the laws of the church and disbanded. "But the group in opposition did not want this," Bizarro noted. "They insisted on having a priest who would live in San Juan and who would be ordered by themselves on whatever they wanted him to do" (Bizarro 1992: 260). On May 23 a Mayan Indian was ordained a Catholic priest in Sololá. On June 13 this priest arrived in San Pedro as an assistant to the pastor, and one of his assignments was the parish of San Juan. In spite of his being Maya, the dissenting group rejected the new priest because he would be residing in San Pedro rather than in San Juan, and they feared that he would be manipulated by the hated pastor.

In July and August the small group loyal to the priest erected a shed where the visiting priest from San Pedro could hold services. Because of the ongoing dispute, it was feared any use of the church for mass or other services could become an occasion for violence. The dissenting group continued to agitate for a resident priest in San Juan.

On November 9 fifty-four members of the dissenting group went to Gua-temala City and occupied the cathedral. They demanded that the archbishop assign a priest to live in San Juan and announced that they would not leave the cathedral until he did so. This action brought widespread newspaper and television coverage. Three television stations carried interviews with dissent-ers who vilified the Sololá bishop and the pastor of San Pedro. The archbishop refused the dissenters' demands, and told them to vacate the cathedral, return to Sololá, and discuss the matter with the bishop there. If they refused to leave the cathedral, he said they would be removed by the civil authorities.

A Compromise

The following day a large group consisting of dissenters from San Juan and those returning from Guatemala City converged on Sololá to meet again with the bishop. As a compromise, the bishop said the priest assigned to San Juan would not live in San Pedro with the hated pastor. Rather he would visit from Panajachel, located across the lake. The bishop reiterated that the priest could not live in San Juan because there were no accommodations. From November to January the priest came weekly to San Juan. At some point in the interval, however, he became tired of the boat journey across the lake and began resid-ing in San Pedro again. In January the priest was transferred to Comalapa. According to Bizarro, he requested the transfer because of the ill will of the people of San Juan and their refusal to abstain from drunkenness, adultery, and stealing.

In February 1988 the bishop assigned another priest to say the weekly mass in San Juan. He came for seven weeks and then left for the same reasons as his predecessor. When the priest informed them of his decision to leave, the prin-cipales of San Juan replied "that they were elders of the town and that they were not dominated by a priest and that they were the ones who maintain order in the town and in the church" (Bizarro 2001: 70). To this the priest replied, "We are through with performing the mass. The principales can do it themselves." But neither they nor the shamans did so.

Bizarro is not clear on what happened in the next few months. In June the detested pastor of San Pedro was transferred to Panajachel and promoted to as-sistant to the bishop. A new priest became the pastor of San Pedro and appears to have resumed weekly visits to San Juan, celebrating mass in the shed for the group that had defended the priest. The church remained locked.

Reconciliation

Bizarro's diary is silent about the conflict from June 1988 to April 1991. During April and May of 1991 exploratory meetings about reconciliation took place between the Mayan leaders of the group who had defended the pastor and the dissenters. They agreed among themselves to end the conflict on one condition: The group loyal to the priest would tear down the shed and resume attending services in the church, to which they consented. From May to November the leaders of the two groups engaged in diplomacy within their respective groups to overcome objections to the reconciliation. Finally, on November 1, 1991, the two groups reconciled with a mass in the church celebrated by the bishop of Solalá and attended by the former pastor of San Pedro. The conflict had come to an end.

Cultural Differences

This is one of the few detailed accounts of cultural conflict between the Maya and the Catholic hierarchy. The conflict originated over cofradía practices; escalated over custodianship of parish assets; and reached a high pitch over the priest's denunciations of stealing, drunkenness, and adultery in the community. Both groups acted from ethnocentric positions, although people like Bizarro appear to have had some understanding of the cultural problems involved. They might have been able to act as mediators if they had not been forced to defend the priest when violence arose. The conflict involved more than cultural differences, however. The existential problems of alcohol abuse, degradation of marital relationships, and injustice were also present.

The Maya Demand for the Catholic Rituals

This incident shows that in spite of almost seven years of bitter conflict involving some physical violence, in spite of a battle between traditional Mayan customs and the non-Mayan culture, and in spite of the dissenting Maya's burning hatred for the parish priest, they still sought the ritual services of a non-Mayan Catholic priest. The dissenting group made repeated attempts to obtain a replacement priest. Bizarro remarks, "They spent a lot of money making other trips to Solalá, San Diego, San Luis [Santiago Atitlán] and Guatemala trying to contract a priest for the masses in San Juan" (Bizarro 1992: 261). Even the insertion of a Mayan Catholic priest into the fray had no effect on the dispute. In the midst of all the turmoil over the seven years, there was never any discussion of doing away with the rituals of the saints and the Catholic priest.

Conclusion: An Anomaly

This chapter has examined cases that dramatically illustrate the Maya's insistent demand that a Catholic priest celebrate mass for the saints. An enduring conclusion emerges from all the cases cited: In spite of Landa's inquisition in Yucatán, the idol smashings and book burnings by many early friars, and continuing conflict and abuse during the colonial and national periods, the

Maya always sought another non-Mayan priest instead of simply rejecting the priest and Catholic rituals. This is evidence of the great importance that the Maya continued to place on these Catholic elements. What was driving this insistence?

With regard to the saints, why did the Maya adopt the saints as divine protectors? Because the saints were originally imposed by the Spaniards, a historical perspective would suggest that their adoption by the Maya was not heartfelt, that it was done merely to placate the Spaniards and consequently that the saint divinities and all connected with them would be peripheral phenomena in the Mayan world.

With regard to the ritual of the mass, the Maya have shamanic rituals that invoke the saints for the same purposes as the mass. Why do they need the Catholic mass? With regard to the Catholic priest, why do the Maya insist that a non-Mayan priest perform the ritual instead of simply having their own shamans or fiscales add this ceremony to their ritual duties? The anomaly of the Catholic priest becomes even more pronounced when one considers the antagonistic relationship that has historically existed between the Maya and the colonial and national cultures surrounding them. This antagonism has been rooted in disputes with both civil and clerical authorities over land, taxes, and labor conditions including slavery. The priests come from this superordinate culture. Furthermore, Mayan culture, especially its religion, has traditionally been denounced or depreciated by the authorities in the historically Catholic countries within whose boundaries the Maya have lived.

Given these considerations, why have the Maya not rejected the Catholic priests, their gods, and their rituals and simply depended on the services of their own gods and priests to accomplish the same goals? Considerations of group pride, cultural ethnocentrism, and defensiveness would predict such a course of action. The fact that they have not yet rejected Catholic ritual does not mean that tendencies in this direction are absent. Rejection is a very human reaction and, given the opportunity, may rise to full consciousness and expressive action.

PART 3

Cultural Logics

This part begins the search for the reasons behind the Maya insistence on Catholic rituals. It examines the Mayan and Royal Spanish worldviews in chapters 5 and 6 respectively. Chapter 7 describes how the Conquistadors' worldview interpreted that of the king and how their military victories initially impacted the Mayan worldview. The examination of these worldviews constitutes a search for cultural logics.[1] Knowledge progresses from the known to the unknown. When confronted by a new situation, a group will perceive and evaluate the new situation in the light of their existing cultural logics formulated through their everyday experiences of seeking to understand the world around them. Cultural logics are based on a realization that the world is not composed of completely discrete entities, that there are relationships, seen and unseen, between these entities. These perceptions become concepts, and the relationships linking them become their internal logics. Being cultural, these logics are shared by many or all in the group. Cultural logics find expression in many different forms, including metaphors, parables, aphorisms, stories, religious beliefs, customary law, and observed behavior.

The cultural logics within a group's worldview do not constitute a perfectly linked system. Some aspects may coalesce into a sector or subsystem, but no cultural worldview attains complete logical consistency. This lack of overall unity means that the various components of a worldview can constrain and sometimes contradict one another. The operative logic for an individual or a group at any one moment depends on the circumstances of that moment and on the primacy given to any of the various cultural logics or to an idiosyncratic logic of an individual. During the moment when a particular cultural logic may define behavior, other cultural and idiosyncratic logics remain latent with the potential to become operative at another time.

The people living in a cultural group at any one time do not develop the cultural logics themselves. They are gradually formulated over time by various individuals and are passed down from generation to generation by older members of the community. Most people absorb them without reflection during the process of socialization. Consequently, cultural logics frequently function at a subconscious level and are unexamined. If an outsider probes for the logic behind a particular custom or way of thinking, a frequent response is the oft-repeated refrain that frustrates anthropologists: "it is our custom" or some variation such as "it has always been done that way."

The worldviews presented in the following chapters are constructs, ideal types in the Weberian sense. They are simplified abstractions from reality whose full complexity is impossible to conceptualize. They cannot be found as such in any Mayan or Spanish person, community, or historical period, but rather are mixed with the other contents of the human psyche. The abstraction is guided by the question being asked, namely, the reason for the Mayan insistence on Catholic ritual. The validation of the abstract construct is its explanatory power, its ability to give a rational explanation for a body of scattered facts that are independent of the data from which it was abstracted. This is the methodological function of parts 4 and 5 in order to answer the basic research question.

5

Traditional Mayan Worldview

This chapter formulates an abstract statement of characteristics of the pre-Columbian Mayan worldview pertinent to the question of the anomaly. The Maya have left records of their worldview in archaeological materials and in a few of their surviving books. These materials will be supplemented with early postconquest writings and ethnographic research depicting long-standing cultural patterns.[1]

Mayan Metaphysics

A cultural worldview is based on philosophical assumptions about the structure of reality, of all existence including the divine and human conditions. The Maya view ultimate reality as a power, a force, a god existing in itself and responsible for the coming into existence of all other beings. Several phrases have been used to designate this infinite entity, including "cosmic force," "spiritual force," and "sun-day-time." It is the divine principle of unity behind all existing things, an infinite god giving life force to all other gods and entities and continually sustaining them for their allotted time, and without which they would cease to exist.[2]

There is a structure to all existents. Traditionally, the Maya, as agriculturists, have lived close to nature. To them the world manifests itself as a series of cycles, small and large. Two related cycles are especially important: the solar cycle that gives rise to day and night and to the seasons of the year, the latter of which in turn gives rise to the corn cycle, the Mayan staff of life. In addition, all plant life and all fauna have their cycles.[3] Looking to the skies, there are astronomical cycles: the stars, the planets, and the cycle of the moon evolving through its various phases. There is the human life cycle and, within it, the female ovarian cycle and the embryonic gestational cycle. There is the intergenerational cycle of grandchildren replacing grandparents. All existence shows itself as a cycle of some kind. Therefore, the Maya interpret the cosmic force itself as a cycle that emanates into many lesser cycles.

All the emanated cycles have a common structure: birth, then death, leading to rebirth or regeneration and the beginning of a new cycle. Without death there can be no regeneration. Corn grows and is consumed, but its seed generates the new crop and another cycle begins.[4] The sun lives during the day, dies at night, and regenerates the next day. Human beings die at the end of their lives, but their souls can be regenerated in other beings.

Since a cycle goes through the pattern of birth, death, and regeneration, it has a duration, time. "Time permeates all and is limitless. Thus the priests computed millions of years into the past and as many others into the future. Time is . . . an attribute of the gods: they carry it on their backs. In a word, *kinh* [sun-day-time] appears, as the heart of all change, filled with lucky and unlucky destinies within the cyclic reality of the universe and most probably inherent to the essence of divinity itself" (León-Portilla 1988: 33).

The Two Worlds of the Cosmos

The cosmic force emanates out to form a cosmos that has been through various cyclical epochs. In the present epoch the cosmos is composed of two worlds, the visible world of humans' everyday experience and the invisible realm of the emanating forces, the creating and sustaining gods. The two worlds interact to form a single cosmos. This is a key aspect of Mayan thought. To distinguish the two worlds, Arias translates the Tzotzil terms as the "surface of sky-earth," the realm of everyday experience, versus "internal sky-earth," the realm of the gods. He uses the contrasts between "this sky-earth" and the "other sky-earth," and occasionally, "tangible" and "intangible" (Arias 1991: 38–39). There is a difference in the use of directional symbols between Mayan thought and some world religions. For the Maya the realm of the invisible world is contained within the surface of the sky-earth that is the world of everyday experience, whereas other religions symbolize this realm as "up there," "in heaven above," and so on.

The Emergence of Surface Sky-Earth

The Popol Vuh outlines the emergence of the visible cosmos inhabited by the ancestors of the Maya (D. Tedlock 1996: 64–70, 145–49).[5] It begins with a primal sea from which the earth and sky emerge.

> Let it be this way, think about it: this water should be removed, emptied out for the formation of the earth's plate and platform, then should come the sowing, the dawning of the sky-earth. But there will be no high days and no bright praise for our work, our design, until the rise of the human work, the human design. . . . Let's try to make a giver of praise, giver of respect, provider and nurturer. (D. Tedlock 1996: 65)

The Popol Vuh describes three previous epochs during which the gods attempted to obtain praise and nurturance. First, the gods made the animals, including deer and birds. They commanded them, "Talk, speak out. Don't moan, don't cry out. . . . Name now our names, praise us. We are your mother, we are your father" (67). When the animals failed to do this, they were condemned to live in the forests where they were to be hunted as food for humans.

The maker gods continued their efforts: "It must simply be tried again. The time for planting and dawning is nearing. For this we must make a provider and nurturer. How else can we be invoked and remembered on the face of the earth? We have already made our first try at our work and design, but it turned out that they didn't keep our days, nor did they glorify us" (68). The gods began experimenting with human figures made out of several materials. They tried mud, which quickly crumbled. The divine makers were disappointed and asked themselves, "What is there for us to make that would turn out well, that would succeed in keeping our days and praying to us?" (69).

Next they made the human figures out of wood. Again, they were disappointed because "there was nothing in their hearts and nothing in their minds, no memory of their mason and builder. They just went and walked wherever they wanted. Now they did not remember the Heart of the Sky" (70). Since the wooden figures could not praise their makers, they were killed in a great flood and turned into monkeys. These three earlier epochs were cycles of birth, death, and rebirth. The end of each cycle occurred due to the failure of its creatures to fulfill the purpose for which they were created, the praise and nourishment of the creator gods.

On the fourth attempt the maker gods made the human figures out of corn and water. This time they were successful. "They talked and they made words"

(146). These were human beings, the Mayan ancestors. Earth and sky exist for the praise and nurturance of the gods, but this praise and nurturance is funneled through human beings in the form of the praise and food offered to the gods during rituals.

Internal Sky-Earth

A plurality of emanated Mayan gods live in the internal sky-earth. They are identified with the power cycles of nature, such as rain, wind, and fertility. They are manifestations or emanations of the unitary cosmic force, not simply a polytheistic pantheon. However, some Mayan fundamentalists appear to give a literal interpretation to the separate names or functions of these gods and may interpret them in a polytheistic sense.

The dynamics and cultural logics of internal sky-earth are different from those of surface sky-earth. Arias suggests the dynamics of dream activity as a helpful analogy to understand these logics. For the Maya, when humans dream, their souls leave their bodies and journey to the internal sky-earth. There humans can morph into nonhumans and vice versa. Upon their return to their bodies, the souls' experiences in internal sky-earth can influence people's judgments and actions in everyday life. Arias emphasizes that understanding the existence of the internal sky-earth is essential for comprehending the Mayan worldview.

Points of Linkage between the Surface and Internal Sky-Earth

The beings of surface sky-earth, all the heavenly bodies and earthly entities, are animated and sustained by the cosmic force and its emanations from internal sky-earth. Mayan thought sees certain places as homes of the gods and portals through which the cosmic forces flow from internal sky-earth to the beings of surface sky-earth. Caves are both intrusions into internal sky-earth and extrusions into surface sky-earth. They are seen as important points of contact between the two sky-earths (Bassie-Sweet 1991; Sharer 1994: 524). Corn, from which the Maya were made and sustained, was found in a cave. Its propagation depends on rain, wind, and fire, all of which are kept by the gods in their cave-homes. The physical characteristics of caves in the Mayan area lend themselves to this interpretation.

> The cave was thought to be the source of surface water because most of the caves in the Maya region are wet and many contain springs, streams, rivers, waterfalls, pools of water and small lakes. The Maya also believed that rain, mist clouds, thunder, lightning and wind were produced in caves. There is often a cool or even cold wind blowing from the open-

ing as the warm air of the outside draws the cool air from the cave. This natural observation surely led to the conclusion that wind was created in caves. Moist environment and temperature changes often create mist. It is not unusual to find clouds of mist at the mouth of the cave and at vertical openings. In addition, clouds form on the slopes and tops of mountains. These phenomena have been used to explain why clouds and rain were thought to be formed in caves. . . . During storms, lightning bolts flash around the mountain tops, giving the impression that lightning, a natural source of fire, originates there. (Bassie-Sweet 1996: 10)

The Maya perceived mountains as the outer shells of large interior caves (see figures 5.1 and 5.2). The gods lived in the recesses of these caves, the internal sky-earth. "For the Maya, the cave acted as a passage of transition between the real and invisible world. . . . The archeological record suggests that caves as sites of ritual activity were important as far back as the Preclassic" (Bassie-Sweet 1991: 240). The Maya also erected pyramids conceived in much the same fashion as mountain caves. Several symbols were used to depict these points of linkage: the serpent's throat, a cracked turtle shell, the jaw of a jaguar. From them flowed the sustaining powers of the emanating gods.

Figure 5.1. One of the sacred mountains whose cave-like interior is a home of an ancestral god.

Figure 5.2. A typical altar on top of a sacred mountain.

The Divine Condition

The Maya do not see their gods as perfect or self-contained. As indicated by their frustration during the first three epochs described in the Popol Vuh, the emanating gods need human beings to feed, praise, and thereby sustain them. If these needs go unfulfilled, the emanating gods, being themselves cyclical, will decay and die. The gods demand food in the form of candles, fermented drink, incense, animal blood, and human blood, and in some historical periods this logic was taken to the extreme of offering them decapitated heads and beating hearts.

> In the Maya scheme of things, man's existence depended on a host of sacred beings who controlled the universe and everything in it. . . . Their whims could be manipulated because they in turn were dependent on human attention for their welfare, if not their very existence. Mesoamerican gods were like extremely powerful infants . . . likely to go into terrible tantrums and eventually expire if neglected. They had to be housed and cared for, diverted with music, dance, and colorful paintings and—most especially—fed. (Farriss 1984: 286)

But the gods themselves are mortal. "In Atiteco theology, Martín is the deity who embodies the positive, life generating aspects of the world. Although

Martín is a powerful deity, he also has his limits. Like other Maya gods, he ages, falters and dies on an annual basis. No single god . . . has the advantage of omnipotence. In the end everything, including gods in all their manifestations, must periodically give way to darkness and chaos before they can be reborn to new life" (Christenson 2001: 157). In other words, every emanated god cycles through a pattern of birth, death, and rebirth as part of the endless cycles of existence.

The Human Condition

The situation of humans has two aspects: the individual person and that person as a social being living with others in a community.

The Individual

Humans are composed of a corporeal body and an invisible soul. At birth the cosmic force emanates as a soul and is incarnated in or near the body of a human being.

> The body primarily belongs to the visible world, but the abode of the soul is mainly in the invisible world. . . . While the body lives, the soul remains in it as a transient who will emigrate to the other world when it leaves the body. The soul comes from the other world and should return to it. In addition, the soul can easily escape from the body and frequently get lost . . . [due to] anything that lessens self-consciousness; fright, abstractedness, or concentration on something foreign to the ego, even distraction, that is described in terms of the soul abandoning the body. (Arias 1991: 40–41)

At birth the soul is near but not yet in the body. Over time it needs to be securely implanted.

> Education is a long process that begins with the birth of the child and lasts until the last moments of life. Education is the slow but constant, step-by-step acquisition of a soul (*ch'ulel*). . . . Tzotzil and Tzeltal communities consider the formation of a personality as the constant and diligent building of what is culturally considered to be the ideal man and the ideal woman. . . . Since the *ch'ulel* does not immediately possess this ideal, it is the duty of each person to orient himself or herself toward the ideal world formed by the ancestors and living elders because only they are in full possession of their souls. . . . The childish and unproductive activities of six- or seven-year-old children are attributed to the fact that their souls have not yet arrived; it is the age of games and trivia. (Arias 1991: 28–29)

The individual person goes through his or her life cycle from birth to death with a destiny, an allotted number of days to live as determined by the conjunction of cosmic forces on the day of birth. Whether this destiny unfolds in a favorable or unfavorable manner can be influenced by the person's dealings with the gods. Regeneration after death is vague in Mayan thought, and there is no unanimity about it. Essentially, the soul is absorbed back into the cosmic force and can be recycled in various ways. Some see the freed souls later becoming the souls of future infants. A Mayan shaman expressed his view in this manner: "The Maya religion is not like all the other religions where you return to God when you die. The Mayan religion is to hope that, after death, one returns so as not to appear dead. Simply put, death is a journey, or a change of clothes, because the spirit never dies. We pass to a star of the firmament. The spirit retains its existence and power and immortality" (Pieper 2002: 56).

The Mayan Community

Mayan thought does not abstract the individual from the Mayan community. Education consists in teaching and living up to the norms of the ideal man and woman as defined by the community. At the beginning of the present epoch, the founders of the different Mayan groups were great ancestral shamans whose powerful souls conversed with the gods in internal sky-earth. From them they learned the divine purpose and design of the present epoch, including the templates to follow in molding their communities physically, culturally, and morally.[6]

When the Maya follow these templates, surface sky-earth is in harmonious balance, an equilibrium that should be continued without change by every generation until the end of its allotted cycle. In this sense, the "is" of the template becomes the "ought to be" for all generations. The Popol Vuh describes an ordered linkage inherent in this harmonious balance. Plants are seen as the food of higher creatures; animals are to be food for humans, and humans exist to praise and feed the gods. In philosophical language, human beings, their community, and the surface of sky-earth are teleological, a hierarchy of finality (Arias 1991: 36).

A Mayan community has a history passed down from its ancestors. The Maya chronicled their history in terms of cycles of their respective gods. This can be seen on various stone monuments and in the *Book of Chilam Balam of Tizimin*, a compilation of Yukatek Mayan historical writings from both preconquest and postconquest periods (Edmonson 1982). The Maya realized that if they could quantitatively describe the cycles, they could understand the cosmic forces of the future since these would repeat analogous cycles in the past. This led to their development of mathematics and of the sophisticated calendars that served as the basis for the activities of shamanic diviners and ritual specialists. When the Maya encountered a new situation, they would attempt to interpret it in terms of logics drawn from an appropriate cycle.

The surface of sky-earth is a dangerous place. There are many threats against the allotted life cycle of both the individual and the community. These threats can be unleashed by rejected or ambivalent gods and include the withdrawal of protection from evil demigods.[7] These demigods inhabit both the interior and surface sky-earths, constantly threatening the lives of Mayan families. This is the significance of the references to demons in the mayordomos' prayers during the flower changing ceremony (see chapter 3). The forms of punishment are many: the food supply may be damaged or destroyed by disruption of the normal cycles of nature through droughts, floods, winds, or insects; or deadly disease may strike at any time. Humans can turn against their community through kin disputes, stealing, or murder.[8] People and their communities need protection in order to survive their allotted time as they traverse through their dangerous cycles of existence.

The Mayan Covenant of Reciprocity

Given the human and divine conditions, human beings and the gods need each other for survival. In order to continue to exist, the gods need to be praised and nurtured by humans. Praise means not only ritual words, but the offering of lives conducted in conformity with the divine template given to the ancestors.[9] Human beings, in turn, need the protection of the gods to survive their allotted time in the face of all the dangers that beset the human life cycle. Because of these mutual needs, the gods and Mayan communities enter into a sacred covenant of mutual support. By the Mayan covenant the gods will protect and sustain humans in return for humans praising and nurturing them.

The covenant is modeled on reciprocity agreements, a common mechanism for the exchange of goods and services in many nonmarket societies.[10] This is a personal agreement based on kinship or friendship, in which a good or service is given with the expectation of some kind of future return, although usually there is no strict accounting. If a receiver does not eventually reciprocate, especially when the giver is in need, the pact is broken. This kind of social interaction is a way of spreading the risks of the life cycle, a type of insurance. It is an important part of daily Mayan life, and they use it to express their view of the god-human relationship.

The founding shamans continue to live in mountain caves as assistants to the gods, or sometimes fused with them. They are the sacred ancestors, the Mayan saints. They sustain Mayan communities and monitor the latter's observance of the divine templates, frequently expressed by the oft-repeated phrase "tradition of the ancestors." Arias constantly emphasizes the teleology of the Mayan community, its covenant, and the role of the ancestors through the use of such phrases as "given order," "destiny of the world," "established order," "norms of tradition," or "transgressions of the rules linked to tradition" (Arias 1991: 38, 42, passim).

In the Mayan worldview, observance of the covenant obligations results in harmonious balance, a condition to be actualized in this world. There is an important difference between Mayan thought and those worldviews that have a preoccupation with "the saving of one's soul" or "going to heaven" or "one's spiritual perfection." In such views, the soul is the center of attention, and the body is devalued. Daily life in a community is a means to an afterlife. In contrast, in Mayan thought "the interaction . . . with the world and its surroundings is not considered a means but an end in itself; interaction with the invisible world is oriented toward the maintenance of harmony in the tangible *habitat* of humanity" (Arias 1991: 52–53). Arias is echoing what Landa (1941: 129) found in Yucatán in the sixteenth century: "This people had a great and excessive fear of death, and they showed this by the fact that all the services, which they performed for their gods, were for no other end nor for any other purpose than that they should give them health and life and sustenance."[11]

Covenant Rituals

The offerings made during rituals nurture the gods while the accompanying prayers and songs praise them. Consequently, rituals are an essential ingredient of the covenant. Their structures, the kinds of foods offered, and the exact words of the prayers and songs were originally learned from the gods themselves by the first ancestors in internal sky-earth (Arias 1991: 35, 38, 43). "A spiritual contract between the people of the village and the Gods said that they would keep life coming to us if we promised to send them remembrance. The fruit of our remembrance was this earth and our lives, and we had to send them some of its deliciousness by means of ritual" (Prechtel 1998: 106).

For the Maya ritual is not just a request for a desired result, but by the logic of the covenant, the performance itself actually sustains or regenerates the cycle that is surface of sky-earth. "When a Maya priest-shaman performs a ritual at the proper time and in the proper manner, he is able to recreate the world just as it was at the first dawn of time." "Traditionalist Atitecos believe that the regenerative nature of the earth is controlled through ritual first established by the ancestors of the community" (Christenson 2001: 24, 78).

Figure 5.3. The gathering on Mount Kalvario in Zinacantán for the final part of the traditional Year Ceremony. The two kneeling men in the right foreground are the two alcaldes with their silver-tipped staffs and their distinctive head wraps. Beyond them are the four regidores, two of them bent over in the act of obeisance. The remaining bent-over figures to the left are shamans in their act of obeisance to the ancestral gods living in Kalvario. The lone figure in the background is a drink pourer. In the left foreground can be seen the head of a guitar. Seated to the left out of the picture are the musicians: a violinist, harpist, and guitarist.

Types of Rituals

"The Indians of Guatemala have two types of sacrifices. One is general inasmuch as the whole town together offers sacrifices during the festivals that they celebrate. The other type consists of the private sacrifices that . . . a private person offers according to his own devotion and for whatever necessity he has" (Las Casas quoted in Ximénez 1965: 70–72).

Community Festival Rituals

A pre-Columbian K'iche' [Maya] town had a central plaza containing a four-sided pyramid of stone. On top of the pyramid the K'iche' erected a small chapel where they placed an image of their god, Tojil. On and around the pyramid the community festivals to fulfill their covenant duties took place (see figure 5.3).

The community sacrifices are usually offered during the festivals that are held five or six times a year in some provinces or at any time if a particular necessity should demand it. [Further on, Las Casas specifically mentions lack of rain, sickness, and war.] For each sacrifice a meeting is held by the caciques of the town or province together with the elders, the high priest, and other priests of the forthcoming festival. There, they decide what sacrifices are to be made and what must be done. As for the time of the sacrifice, they do not decide this nor would they even think of doing so. Rather, a divination must be performed and this alone dictates the time. They call a diviner and inform him of the festival or problem and the required sacrifices. They request him to perform divinations to find out what day would be the most propitious to make the sacrifices. The diviner insists upon the results of his divination being strictly followed.

With the date of the festival determined, the priests of the festival begin their vigil. During this period both the young and old married men withdraw from their women. The vigil lasts seventy-eight days and at times one hundred according to the urgency of the petition and the type of festival. Each day during this period everyone draws blood from their arms, feet, thighs, nose, ears, tongues, and all parts of their bodies. This is done twice a day. During the night they burn incense for their gods. Afterwards, the priests wash and continue their penances in preparation for the festival. Other men draw blood and smear themselves with it; they do not wash but wear the sprinkled blood as a hair shirt, a symbol of penance. Everyone faithfully keeps the required discipline because if anything is omitted, they would be punished. They also have a great fear of being killed by their gods or suffering some misfortune. . . .

They adorn their images for the festivals with much gold and precious stones. They wrap them with an infinite number of richly decorated cloths. They put them on stands and with great reverence carry them in procession, accompanied by the music of drums and other instruments. After processing around the town, they put the images in the major squares that are used for ball games. There, the caciques and town officials play ball before the gods.

In some towns they carry the images from the temples, where they have been kept since the beginning of the penance period, to plazas where small sacrifices such as birds and incense are offered. In other towns they only perform sacrifices in caves where the images are hidden. (Las Casas quoted in Ximénez 1965: 52–53, 70–71)

The divinations were based on calendric readings which are discussed later.

A table in Sharer (1994: 541–49 based on Landa and other early sources) shows the rituals and their specific purposes for seventeen of the nineteen Mayan months comprising the cycle of the solar year. Some ritual elements were reciting prayers; burning incense; drinking fermented beverages; offering food, ornaments, valuables, and blood; and performing dances during the major festivals, all ending with feasting that usually culminated in drunkenness. A number of these ritual elements and those previously mentioned by Las Casas were seen in the descriptions of Zinacanteco rituals in part 2.

Private Rituals

The Maya had statues of their gods and were attentive in their care of them. With great reverence they placed them on altars and in sacred places such as caves, springs, hilltops, certain large trees, and crossroads. There they performed rituals in which they burned incense, killed birds and other animals, sprinkled blood drawn from various parts of their bodies, and made offerings of cotton, cacao, salt, red pepper, or some other valuable gift (see figures 5.4 and 5.5). By these rituals they had recourse to the gods for protection or provision of their necessities for any important event: for building a new house, for protection from danger while traveling or searching for feathers used in orna-

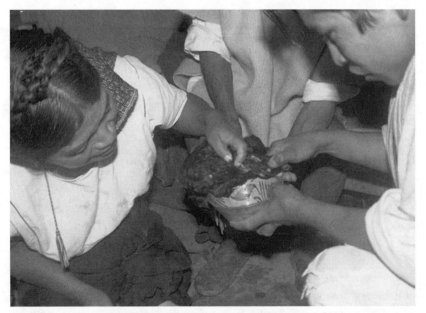

Figure 5.4. During a curing ceremony in Zinacantán, a shaman (at left) has made an incision in the neck of a chicken to obtain sacrificial blood. The chicken is later sacrificed and left in a mountain cave as food for the gods, as shown in figure 1.1.

Figure 5.5. The chicken blood in the bowl is used to anoint a sick patient. Later she will consume it.

mentation, for any kind of planting, for guarding fruit orchards, when weeding their grain fields, at harvest time, at times of sickness, when wanting to have children, at the birth and weaning of a child, when the child begins to crawl on all fours, when it begins to talk, when it has its first haircut, on birthdays, and when young girls around age eight leave to live in the temple until married (see Las Casas in Ximénez 1965: 83–90, 715).

The Words of Ritual Prayers

Prayers following fixed formulas were an integral part of Mayan rituals. The efficacy of the rituals depended on the recitation of the exact words of the prayer formula as learned by the first generation of shamans from the gods in internal sky-earth (Arias 1991: 38). The importance of specific words is recorded in the Popol Vuh. Emanation itself was accomplished by saying the proper words. "The earth arose because of them, it was simply their word that brought it forth. For the forming of the earth, they said 'Earth.'" In describing the making of the wooden figures that became the first humans, the Popol Vuh says "the moment they spoke, it was done." When the gods changed from making animal to human forms, the Popol Vuh states "we have changed our word" (Tedlock 1996: 65, 70, 67). Chamulan tradition also sees words bringing forth the first world (Gossen 2002: 21, 221). These passages imply that the utterance of a word brings forth the specific thing that the word signifies. This conception of the power of words is restated in Chilam Balam books from prior to and after the conquest (Edmonson 1986: 31). It is also echoed in the Santiago Atitlán version of the Popol Vuh account: "Two Deities, an Old Man and an Old Woman, sat in each of these [five] creation layers, and they were the ones who assembled you. . . . As each pair of Old People did this . . . , they uttered special magical words and phrases. These words became the very things they described. The Gods spoke the world into life by continuously repeating their names. When they reach the fifth creation [surface sky-earth], the Deities' names take on physical form and function. . . . We are made of words, and those words are places in our bodies and on the earth, too. The fifth world gave all these Old People's words a place to have form and run around, happy to be alive and eating together" (Prechtel 1998: 105–6).

In Santiago Chimaltenango the power implied in words is the soul of the word. There *naab'l* has "soul" as one of its meanings, used only in reference to human beings. But there is one exception. "Significantly, words are the only non-human beings possessing *naab'l*, *tnaab'l yoal* meaning a word's 'meaning'" (Watanabe 1992: 82).

Comparing pre-Columbian glyphs on a stela with the Popol Vuh, Freidel has noted, "As the opening quote from the Popol Vuh explains, Creation began with the utterance of a word and the appearance of the thing embodied by the word. The ancient Maya apparently thought of the process in the same way." Later, he continues, "words are a fundamental medium for Maya communion between this world and the Otherworld. They are not merely preamble to some magical action or a way of describing things that are manifested through tangible supernatural and natural forces like rain, lightning, and thunder. They are, rather, an essential conduit of those forces" (Freidel, Schele, and Parker 1993: 65, 179–80). The cosmic force emanates to become the souls of words so that, when they are spoken, it extends existence to the entity they signify. This cultural logic explains the necessity of the recitation of the exact words of a prayer formula for the effectiveness of ritual and the consequent fulfillment of the covenant.

Failure of Reciprocity

If the Maya constantly fail in their covenant obligations, either deliberately or accidentally, the covenant is broken. Because of their mutual dependence on each other, both the gods and the humans will end their cycle of existence. In the Atiteco version, "A forgotten God was an angry God, or a dead God. In either case, the life sap [cosmic force] would stop flowing, and all this life would be as if it had never existed. We would cease. All of our rituals in the village, whether personal or public, were memory feasts for the spirits. Being remembered was their food" (Prechtel 1998: 107). For occasional instances of neglect the Maya are punished by the angry gods letting loose some of the previously described threats to the life cycle, inflicting great suffering on the community. These serve as warnings to prevent further deterioration of the covenant.

The Tension of the Covenant

The Maya fully realize their shortcomings with regard to the covenant, that their community is not always in harmonious balance, that daily life frequently does not mirror the "ought to be" of the template of the original emanation. Studying the themes of numerous traditional Zinacanteco tales, Laughlin (1977: 2) finds "despite the Zinacantecs' lack of compulsion to recall an origin for every aspect of the present world, to an extraordinary degree their tales reveal the Zinacantec musing over his cosmic journey. . . . In tale after tale the Zincantec wrestles with the problem of his fall from grace. 'Where does the responsibility lie?' he asks. His answer is contradictory, as many-angled, as the historical facts warrant. 'It is the Ladino, the wenching priest, who brought divine punishment upon our town. But, too, the negligence of the elders—or was it the shamans, or even the entire town which shares the guilt?'" The "wrestling with the problem of a fall from grace" creates tensions in Mayan lives.

Coping with the Tensions

The unfolding of one's destiny as a member of the covenant can take place in various ways, some good and some bad. Ritual performances not only praise and feed the gods, but also are a means to cope with these tensions. Shamanic diviners and curers are asked for assistance in obtaining a favorable unfolding of one's destiny. "The time universe of the Maya is the ever-changing stage on which are felt the aggregate of presences and actions of the various divine forces which coincide in a given period. The Maya strove by means of computations, to foresee the nature of these presences and the resultant of their various influences at specified moments. Since *kinh* [the cosmic force] is essentially cyclic, it is most important to know the past in order to understand the present and predict the future" (León-Portilla 1968: 54).

The Maya observed and measured the cycles of their epoch, especially those of the sun and moon. They formulated cyclical, interlocking calendars of days, months of twenty days, years, and groupings of twenty years. The days and gods were also assigned numbers from one to thirteen, each day with its corresponding god. Each of these units also had an astrological connotation. Therefore, each day could be defined by the multiple divine influences comprising it. The diviner used the calendars to understand the forces impinging on an individual or community. Then the diviner had to decide the result of the forces and choose a day favorable for corrective action, usually a ritual in which the shaman intercedes for his or her worried client. "Once the original order, or balance, of the cosmos has been broken, it is the function of the shamans to restore it by their ceremonies. Their shamanic power enables them to enter the internal sky-earth and plead directly with the gods to remove the punishment and to restore order and harmony. Some ceremonies may include confession of wrongdoing, either to the gods or to the person offended" (Arias 1991: 43–44).

Plurality of Covenants

The Popol Vuh narrates the epic of the K'iche' Maya, although the underlying thought patterns were common to many Mayan and other indigenous groups. The term *Maya* can be misleading as it implies a unity among the Mayan people that never existed. Consequently, there is not one but many covenants between the gods and the Mayan people. Elements of the worldview described here appear to be common to most groups, but there are differences in specification arising from differences between and within various Mayan groups.

Independence of Mayan Groups

In Mayan thought there was a close unity between the physical place where one lives, the gods who dwell in and watch over that place, and the community that resides there. Most Mayan groups saw themselves as emanating from internal sky-earth at the center of their portion of surface sky-earth. Their survival and self-identity as corn farmers depended on the land occupied by their own and other descent groups. They had little sense of belonging to a broader community. For these reasons, each Mayan group looked upon their gods and images as tribal, belonging only to their own community. Other Mayan communities had their own covenants with the gods, but their gods were different.

> In some areas they have the custom of guarding the images in very hidden places. This creates greater reverence because if the images are viewed many times, the people lose their reverence and respect for them. This is also done so that neighboring groups will not steal them. These people become very envious when they think there are stronger images in some areas than others. People would risk their lives to steal them. The priests have for assistants the sons of nobility and relatives of the town leaders who are young and unmarried. These alone know where the images are concealed, and they have the responsibility of guarding them and bringing them the offerings of the faithful. When it is decided to bring out the images from the ravines and caves and to have a proces-

sion through town, the young nobles carry them. Stopping from time to time, they sacrifice the offerings made during the procession. The boxes in which the images are carried are lined with branches and flowers so as to make them as beautiful as possible. (Las Casas quoted in Ximénez 1965: 72–73)

The residents of one Mayan community often boasted that their god was good and that the god of another community was not worth anything, meaning unable to deliver what was asked for (Ximénez 1965: 714). The different Mayan groups with their tribal gods waged war against each other to obtain a vassal group that would supply tribute and slaves to the conquering group. Some of the slaves would be used for ritual sacrifice. Such warfare was seen as a clash of gods as well as men because of the tribal nature of the gods.

Social Strata within a Mayan Group

There was a Great and a Little Tradition for interpreting a group's covenant. Mayan communities were composed of one or more descent groups, who would compete to occupy the administrative offices of the community.

Elites and the Great Tradition

An elite would be formed by one kin group occupying the ruling offices and arranging for members of their group to succeed them. Among the high offices was that of the high priest, the carrier of the Great Tradition. In Yucatán,

they had a high priest who was called Ah Kin Mai, and by another name Ahau Can Mai, which means the Priest Mai, or the High-Priest Mai. He was very much respected by the lords and had no *repartimiento* of Indians, but besides the offerings, the lords made him presents and all the priests of the towns brought contributions to him, and his sons or his nearest relatives succeeded him in his office. In him was the key of their learning and it was to these matters that they dedicated themselves mostly; and they gave advice to the lords and replies to their questions. He seldom dealt with matters pertaining to the sacrifices except at the time of the principal feasts or in very important matters of business. They provided priests for the towns when they were needed, examining them in the sciences and ceremonies, and committed to them the duties of their office, and the good example to people and provided them with books and sent them forth. And they employed themselves in the duties of the temples and in teaching their sciences as well as writing books about them.

They taught the sons of other priests and the second sons of the lords who brought them for this purpose from their infancy, if they saw that they had an inclination for this profession. (Landa 1941: 27)

The priestly worldview was more developed and sophisticated than that of the commoner. "The sciences which they taught were the computation of the years, months and days, the festivals and ceremonies, the administration of the life cycle rituals, the fateful days and seasons, their methods of divination and their prophecies, events and cures for diseases, and their antiquities and how to read and write with the letters and characters, with which they wrote, and drawings which illustrate the meaning of the writings" (Landa 1941: 27–28).

Commoners

The worldview of the commoners was dominated by their role as producers of corn that was *el cuerpo y la emanación de nuestro Señor*, "the body and emanation of our Lord" (Arias 1991: 23). Arias' explanation of the Mayan cognitive world shows that furnishing corn was a basic necessity for fulfilling the covenant. In San Pedro Chenalhó corn comprises 80 percent of all consumed food and without it, there would be starvation. The prestige required for community service was based on the amount of corn one cultivated as it supplied the resources to obtain the ritual offerings. The intricacies of corn farming comprised a large part of a boy's education. A boy was not considered a man until he had shown he could produce a crop on his own. Corn, the local community, and performing service for it were at the heart of the commoner's worldview along with the two main threats to their successful accomplishment: crop failure from any source and disease. In learning and fulfilling these duties, a person's soul entered more fully into the body.

Physical Representations of the Gods

In Yucatán Landa reported that the god images used during a sacred ritual were made of wood, clay, and stone.

One of the things, which these miserable people regarded as most difficult and arduous, was to make idols of wood, which they called making gods. And so they had fixed a particular time for this . . . [having] consulted the priest first, having taken his advice, they went to the workmen who engaged in this work. And they say the workmen always made excuses, since they feared that they or someone of their family would die on account of the work, or that fainting sickness would come upon them. When they had accepted, the *Chacs* whom they had also chosen for this purpose, as well as the priest and the workman, began their fast-ings. While they were fasting the man to whom the idols belonged went in person or else sent someone to the forest for the wood for them, and this was always cedar. When the wood had arrived, they built a hut of straw, fenced in, where they put the wood and a great urn in which to place the idols and to keep them under cover, while they were making them. They put incense to burn to four gods called Acantuns, which they located and placed at the four cardinal points. They put what they needed for scarifying themselves or for drawing blood from their ears, and the instruments for sculpturing the black gods, and with these preparations, the priest and the *Chacs* and the workmen shut themselves up in the hut, and began their work on the gods, often cutting their own ears, and anointing these idols with the blood and burning their incense, and thus they continued until the work was ended, the one to whom [the idols] belonged giving them food and what they needed, and they could not have relations with their wives, even in thought, nor could any one come to the place where they were.

. . . When the idols were finished and perfected, the owner of them made the best present he could of birds, game and their money in pay-ment of the work of those who had made them; and they took them from the little house and placed them in another arbour, built for this purpose in the yard, where the priest blessed them with great solemnity and plenty of fervent prayers, he and the workmen having first cleansed themselves of the soot with which they had anointed themselves, since they said that they fasted while they were making them, and having driven off the evil spirit as usual, and having burned the blessed incense, they placed the new images in a little hamper, wrapped up in a cloth, and handed them over to their owner, and he received them with great devotion. The good priest then preached a little on the excellence of the profession of making new gods, and on the danger that those who made them ran, if by chance they did not keep their abstinence and fasting. After this they ate very well and got drunk still more freely. (Landa 1941: 159–61)

In this account the image was being made for a private individual, not the community. While some idols were kept in the temples, more appear to have been kept in numerous private residences. "They had a very great number of idols and of temples, which were magnificent in their own fashion. And besides the community temples, the lords, priests and the leading men had also orato-ries and idols in their houses, where they made their prayers and offerings in private" (Landa 1941: 108).

Landa's description says that the god images were "placed in a little hamper and wrapped up in a cloth." A Kaqchikel shaman, Apolinario, gave a further description. "In the classic epoch of the Mayans . . . the forms of our ancestors . . . were made of tied-up leaves, wood, or bark. . . . In the beginning it was made out of *sacate* [weeds], with a relic or a bone of the person inside. It was called *grandesa*. . . . That is what we call the relic that contains all of your inheritance, your power. . . . No one is ever allowed to see or know what is inside. Inside it has many things. It is the power of the ancestors. Later they began to make it out of wood, from a special Mayan tree" (Pieper 2002: 54, 58). According to Landa's account, small statues were one of the items in the sacred bundles.

Confirmation: The Covenants with the Mexica and Tlaxcalan Gods

The research materials about Nahuatl-speaking cultures are more plentiful and richer in content than those for the Maya. The two cultures sprang from the same roots and had many cultural logics in common. An examination of some Mexica materials both confirms and enriches the description of the Mayan worldview.

The Spaniards entered Mexico City without violence and were treated as guests by Montezuma. The Spaniards took Montezuma hostage, but initially treated him well. During this time there were exchanges of viewpoints. The Spaniards constantly requested that Montezuma and his people do away with their statues (idols) and the sacrifice of humans as food for their gods. To Cortés' pleas Montezuma replied, "We consider them [the Mexica gods] to be very good, for they give us health, rains and good seed times and seasons and as many victories as we desire, and we are obliged to worship them and make sacrifices, and I pray you not to say another word to their dishonor" (Díaz 1928: 305). Montezuma's reply shows that the Mexica covenant had the same cultural logic as the Mayan covenant: The gods, in return for being fed by ritual, send all the necessities for survival: health, rain, good crops, and victory in warfare (León-Portilla 1993: 41–64).

The cacique of the Tlaxcalans explained their covenant to Cortés in reply to his entreaties to forsake their gods.

Malinche [the Nahuatl name for Cortés' interpreter], we have already understood from you before now and we thoroughly believe this God of yours and this great Lady [the Virgin Mary] are very good, but look you, you have only just come to our homes, as time goes we shall understand your beliefs much more clearly, and see what they are, and will do what is right. But how can you ask us to give up our Teules [gods] which for many years our ancestors have held to be gods and have made sacrifices to them and have worshipped them? Even if we, who are old men, might wish to do it to please you, what would our priests say, and all our neighbors, and the youths and children throughout the province? They would rise up against us, especially as the priests have already consulted the greatest of the Teules [gods], and he told them not to forget the sacrifice of men and all the rites they were used to practice, otherwise the gods would destroy the whole province with pestilence, famine and war. (Díaz 1928: 225)

Following the conquest of Mexico, twelve Franciscan friars arrived and began their program of evangelization by dialoging with Mexica priests. The friars repeatedly told them that their gods were false and that they should forsake them, their idols, and their sacrifices to them. The Mexica priests replied,

You have told us that we do not know who it is by whom we live and exist, this master of heaven and earth. Likewise, you have said that those whom we adore are not gods. This kind of discourse is completely new for us, and because of it we are very upset and disturbed. We are frightened to hear such things. Indeed our ancestors, who have experienced this earth and lived their lives here, never spoke like this. To the contrary, long ago our ancestors bequeathed us the cult of honoring the gods. All the ceremonies, all the sacrifices we make, they are the ones who taught them to us. Our ancestors always told us that it is by the favor of these gods that we live and exist, that these gods are very deserving of our being faithful to them since they have existed longer than anyone knows, long before the sun began to shine. Our ancestors taught us that our gods, whom we adore, provide us with all the nourishment we need for our bodies: maize corn, beans, and wild herbs for seasonings. And finally from these gods we seek rain to let the earth bring forth its bounty. . . . And now, why should we destroy what has been our whole way of life? . . . We are born with faith in these gods; we have been brought up with their cult. We are familiar with them and hold belief in them in our hearts.

Oh, very distinguished noblemen, you need to be careful that you do not stir up the people and provoke your subjects to bad things. [This group had submitted to the Spanish king.] How can elderly men and women abandon that which they have believed in all their lives? Likewise, be careful that this community does not rise up against us if we should say that what we have always believed to be gods now are not gods. (Sahagún 1990: 83–85; also León-Portilla 1974: 22–23)

The Nahua gods were also tribal: "It is a laughable matter that every province had its Idols and those of one province or city were of no use to the others, thus they had an infinite number of Idols and they made sacrifices to them all" (Díaz 1928: 310).

These passages show how deeply rooted the indigenous covenant was in the psyches of the people. Their basic argument to the Spaniards was, Why should we give up what we know to be certain for an unknown that the conquistadors and friars talk about? The gods of the Spaniards provide salvation in a unknown life to come at the expense of renouncing our proven gods who provide survival in the here and now.

Mayan Religion: A Comparative Perspective

The Maya were not unique in their metaphysical views. Analogous systems exist among a number of groups, especially those associated with Hinduism and Buddhism. This is not surprising since American indigenous groups came from Asia. Eliade's book *The Myth of the Eternal Return* (also published as *Cosmos and History*) contains many examples: "This book undertakes to study certain aspects of archaic ontology—more precisely, the conception of being and reality that can be read from the behavior of the man of the premodern societies. . . . the metaphysical concepts of the archaic world were not always formulated in theoretical language; but the symbol, the myth, the rite, express, on different planes and through the means proper to them, a complex system of coherent affirmations about the ultimate reality of things, a system that can be regarded as constituting a metaphysic" (Eliade 1959: 3).

In regard to the cosmic force, "If we observe the general behavior of archaic man, we are struck by the following fact: neither the objects of the external world nor human acts, properly speaking, have any autonomous intrinsic value. Objects or acts acquire a value, and in so doing become real, because they participate, after one fashion or another, in a reality that transcends them" (Eliade 1959: 3–4).

Eliade describes the cyclical nature of the cosmic force as follows: "Belief in a time that is cyclic, in an eternal returning, in the periodic destruction of the world and mankind to be followed by a new world and a new, regenerated mankind—all these beliefs bear witness primarily to the desire and hope for periodic regeneration of the time gone by, of history. A cosmic cycle includes a 'creation,' an 'existence' (or 'history,' wearing-out, degeneration) and a 'return to chaos' . . . hope of a total regeneration of time that is evident in all the myths and doctrines involving cosmic cycles" (Eliade 1958: 407).

Eliade has also shown how widespread is the view that the structure of ritual, including the words, must follow a template associated with the emanation of surface sky-earth. "Rituals and significant profane gestures acquire the meaning attributed to them, and materialize that meaning, only because they deliberately repeat such and such acts posited *ab origine* by gods, heroes or ancestors" (Eliade 1959: 6–7). Also "*in illo tempore*, in the mythical period . . . the creation and arranging of the cosmos took place, as well as the revelation of all the archetypical activities by gods, ancestors, or cultural heroes. . . . From the point of view of primitive spirituality, every beginning is *illud tempus*, and therefore an opening into the Great Time, into eternity. . . . Every one of these "religious things" indefinitely repeats the archetype; in other words, repeats what took place at the "beginning," at the moment when a rite or religious gesture was, being revealed, at the same time expressed in history" (Eliade 1958: 395–96). These passages place the Mayan worldview in the context of the panorama of world religions.

Mayan Religion: Its Theological Context

The previous descriptions of the emanation of surface sky-earth and human beings raise one of the oldest philosophical problems of pensive people: how do the many come from the one? Historically, religions have tended to answer this question by viewing divinity in one of two ways: either as a distinct being apart from created entities (creation view), or as an entity that expands itself out by bringing into existence and continually sustaining entities, and by this very fact being a part of them (emanation view). These differing positions are sometimes labeled as *classical theism* versus *pantheism*. As a result of their differing assumptions, the internal logic of these systems differs.

In this dichotomy of classical theism versus pantheism, the Mayan system is pantheistic, whose simplistic definition is "god in all things." But there are different types of pantheism that become submerged by such a definition. Because of its emphasis on cycles and time, León-Portilla (1968: 55) suggests the system is "a peculiar type of pantheism which could be designated by a new term: panchronotheism." *Encyclopaedia Britannica* (15th ed., 550–51) distinguishes seven forms of pantheism: hylozoistic, immanentistic, absolutistic monistic, relativistic monistic, acosmic, identity of opposites, and Neoplatonic or emanationistic. In terms of *Britannica's* definitions, this writer sees the Maya system as either immanentistic or emanationistic. In immanentistic pantheism, "God is part of the world and immanent in it. Though only a part, however, his power extends throughout its totality." In Neoplatonic, or emanationistic, pantheism "God is absolute in all respects, remote from the world and transcendent over it. This view is like classical theism except that, rather than saying that God is the cause of the world, it holds that the world is an emanation of God, occurring by means of intermediaries. God's absoluteness is thus preserved while a bridge to the world is provided as well. In Plotinus . . . the foremost Neoplatonist, the Nous (Greek, "mind"), a realm of idea or Platonic forms, serves as the intermediary between God and the world, and the theme of immanence is sustained by positing the existence of a World-Soul that both contains and animates the world." Since the theological basis of the Mayan religion is seldom expressed and many variations of its basic ideas exist, there is no ideal type represented in the preceding definitions that exactly fit it, but they do help us to understand the system.[12]

Anthropologists have used various terms to describe Mayan metaphysics: "deep, generative roots" (Gossen 1986: 4–5); "underlying foundation," "cognitively deep" (Fischer 2001: 17–20); and "durable transposable dispositions" (Bourdieu 1977: 22, quoted in Fischer 2001). Christenson (2001: 15) has observed, "I have found that a cycle of mythic tales concerning revered ancestors and divinities is widely known in Santiago Atitlán and repeated often, although not codified in any known written text. Such tales are never told the same way twice, even by the same person; however, the basic core concepts embedded in each vary little."

Summary

This chapter has presented a synthetic construct of the pre-Columbian Mayan worldview and some of the cultural logics contained within it. It has focused on the metaphysical viewpoint from which to understand other aspects of Mayan thought and behavior. The chapter is a preparation for examining what happened to these cultural logics and some of their implications after the Maya encountered the Spaniards with their Catholic saints and rituals.

The Worldview of the Spanish Crown at the Beginning of the Sixteenth Century

The Spanish presence in the Mayan regions involved three different entities: the king who initiated the conquest and was ultimately responsible for the colonies; the conquistadors who carried out the conquest and many of whom remained as *encomenderos* and settlers; and the friars who attempted the evangelization and conversion of the Maya. To the conquistador group should be added Spanish settlers who arrived after the conquest. While the worldviews of all three were in agreement on basic propositions, there was disagreement about their applications. The cultural logics of the crown are examined in this chapter. The application of it by the conquistadors is described in the following chapter, and that by the friars in chapter 8.

The Spanish worldview had its origin in the Bible, which continued to be the basis of its legitimation. In the Western world at the beginning of the sixteenth century, there was an intellectual assumption that the Bible contained most of the knowledge attainable by the human mind (Phelan 1970: 6–7). Consequently, the Spanish worldview during this period was based on interpretations of cultural logics from the Bible as colored by later Spanish historical experience. The Spanish king saw himself as the inheritor of both the Jewish and Christian covenants.

Biblical Covenants: A System of Cultural Logics

The Spaniards were not the only group to base their worldview on the Bible. Among the world religions, Judaism and Islam also had a foundation in whole or part on biblical covenants. Like the Mayan covenant, these religions used the reciprocity relationship as their guiding principle. Smith (2003: 50) in tracing the roots of modern nationalism, has abstracted six ideas comprising the common elements of biblically based covenants.

1. The first idea is that of choice, God chooses a community, and/or individuals, to fulfill His design for the world. It is God who chooses and the people respond. God is the initiator of the relationship, but the people are not passive. They agree to enter into the relationship and be His partner. [source of legitimation]

2. The second is that of divine announcement or promise. God's choice is expressed by a promise to His chosen people, usually in the form of land, prosperity and/or power. This may also include a promise to make the chosen people a source of blessings to other peoples. The promise may be absolute or conditional, and sometimes both kinds of promises coexist; and are understood to do so. [reciprocity: God to human]

3. The third is that of sacred law. God seeks out families and a community that will do His will by keeping His commandments and laws—that is by adhering to His code of morality, law and ritual practices, and by observing the things He has sanctified and separated, from the everyday world. [reciprocity: human to God]

4. The fourth idea is the drive to collective sanctification. The people are commanded to be holy as God is holy; they thereby agree to be adherents, even priests, of the true faith and members of a holy community, set apart from all others. [group superiority]

5. The fifth is a corollary of the fourth, the idea of conditional privilege. God will favor and bless the community provided they keep His com-

mandments and obey His law. This significantly qualifies the original promise of blessing and possession. If they fail in their witness and adherence, they will be punished by God withdrawing His favour from the people. [punishment for violation of reciprocity]

6. The sixth idea is that of witness. God reveals Himself to the community and/or its leaders through signs and miracles witnessed by the community as a whole; and it is as witnesses and recorders of God's promise and theophany that the community establishes its unique claim and justifies its role in the covenant. [criterion of recognition]

These six ideas form a system of cultural logics that manifests itself in the actions of groups who see themselves as having a biblically based religion. The logic of the system has many points in common with the non-biblical Mayan covenant.

In light of the question about the Mayan anomaly, a seventh idea should be added, that of mission "on behalf of the deity or his earthly representatives. They therefore see themselves as 'instruments' of God's plan, executing His will on earth and hastening the day of salvation" (Smith 2003: 49). Smith sees this as an alternative to covenant because mission without covenant occurs in building nationalism. But the concept of mission is implied in his second idea, "to make the chosen people a source of blessings to other peoples." Once a group sees itself as divinely chosen "to fulfill His design for the world," mission is a frequent corollary. The exception was Judaism, which in contrast to Christianity and Islam, was seldom proselytizing.

The second idea describes what humankind receives from God: land, prosperity or power. These rewards have been understood in either a literal or metaphorical sense and sometimes in both senses. If taken metaphorically, these promises are seen as rewards in a life after death for observance of a moral code, rather than as literal promises to be fulfilled in this life. Biblically based groups have used both kinds of interpretations.

The third idea describes what God receives from humankind in the reciprocity relationship: adherence to a "code of morality, law and ritual practices." Given the difficulties of practicing morality and its specification in law, there is a tendency to give priority to mechanical ritual observance over morality. Theoretically, ritual should be an aid to and an expression of morality rather than an end in itself.

There is a latent intolerance in the logic of biblical covenants. Once a group sees itself as chosen by God in preference to all other peoples, this belief can easily lead to a sense of superiority that can and has resulted in a continuum of derogatory acts against other peoples, ranging from discrimination to murder

Figure 6.1. The Spanish king as portrayed by the Maya in their Dance of the Conquest.

and genocide, all done in the name of God and religion. Landa's inquisition in Yucatán was just one example.

Biblical Roots of Spanish Kingship

The conquest and evangelization of the Maya took place under the authority of the Spanish king (see figure 6.1). This raises two questions. What was the basis of the Spanish king's legitimacy as the supreme ruler of Spain and the Spanish church? How did this, in turn, legitimate the Spanish intrusion into the New World and their consequent conquest of the Maya?

The *Requerimiento*

After seeing how the Spaniards mistreated the Indian populations in the early colonies of Hispaniola and Cuba, some Dominican friars challenged the crown about its justification for such actions. In 1512 the crown turned to the Spanish jurist Juan López Palacios Rubios to formulate a legitimation for its presence and actions. He produced a document entitled the *Requerimiento*. It was a juridical hybrid based on some of the logics described previously and on some drawn from an Islamic school of jurisprudence that insisted on a legal ritual before the initiation of a *jihad*, a holy war (Seed 1995: 69–99; Las Casas 1986: 213–16). To maintain the legality of its actions, the crown decreed that this document was to be read to indigenous populations on their first contact with Spaniards. It contains five parts, the first of which summarizes in a highly condensed form the main points of legitimation in the royal worldview.[1]

> On behalf of the King, Don Fernando, and of the Queen, Doña Juana, his daughter, Queen of Castile and Leon, civilizers of barbarous nations, we their servants notify and make known to you, as best we can, that the Lord our God, Living and Eternal, created Heaven and Earth, and one man and one women, of whom you and I, and all the past and present peoples of the world are their descendants, as will be all those who come after us. But, on account of the multitude which has sprung from this man and women in the five thousand years since the world was created, it was necessary that some groups should go one way and some another, and that they should be divided into many kingdoms and provinces, for in one alone they could not have been sustained nor survived.
>
> Out of all these people, God our Lord placed in charge one man, called Saint Peter. By this authority Saint Peter became the lord and superior of all the peoples in the world. As the head of the whole human race, he should be obeyed by everyone no matter where they may be living or under what kind of law or community, or what belief they should have. Peter was given the world for his kingdom with the right of governance.
>
> And God commanded him to establish his seat in Rome, as the place most fitting from which to rule the world; and in addition allowed him to establish his seat in any other part of the world as the judge and ruler of all peoples, be they Christians, Moors, Jews, Gentiles, or any other type of community or belief there may be. Saint Peter was called Pope, which means Admirable Great Father and Governor of Men. The people who lived at that time obeyed Saint Peter and held him to be the lord, the supreme king of the universe. They have regarded all those succeeding him as elected popes in the same way, just as those living do today and those living in the future will continue to do until the end of the world.

One of the past pontiffs who succeeded Saint Peter in the dignity and seat of the Lord of the universe, as I have just mentioned, handed over the sovereignty of these [Caribbean] islands and the main land of the Ocean Sea [New World] to the king and queen mentioned in the beginning of this document, and to their successors, our lords, with everything there is in these territories, as is set down in certain writings about this matter, which you can view if you should wish.

This extract explains the Spaniards' sixteenth-century hierarchical view of the universe: God to Saint Peter, to the popes of the church, to the kings and queens of Spain.[2] (The remaining sections of the *Requerimiento* will be discussed in the next chapter.)

The Jewish Covenant

The very summary account of history given in the *Requerimiento* omits the foundation of Spanish legitimation in the Jewish covenant and its kings, as well as the evolution of the Jewish covenant into the Christian covenant through the sacrificial blood of Jesus as explained by Saint Paul in the Epistle to the Hebrews.

No king of Spain aspired to be anything but a Christian monarch. All inherited the ancient tradition of the covenant, enshrined symbolically in the temple of Jerusalem built by Solomon, and perpetuated by a long line of medieval kings and emperors. Many dreamed of a New Jerusalem to crown their reigns. When Braulio (bishop of Zaragoza, 631 to c. 651) wrote to the Visigothic King Chindaswith, he took care to hold before him the examples of Joshua, David and Solomon. The Spanish hymn "In profectione exercitus" referred to Moses, the defeat of Amalec, and David as models for the subjection of Iberia's barbarians by the Visigothic king of a New Israel. In 798, Alcuin wrote to the future Holy Roman Emperor, expressing the wish "to see you in Aachen, where the temple of the very wise Solomon, with the help of God, is being built." Charlemagne indeed took the temple of Jerusalem as his inspiration. He had his throne in the Palatine Chapel assembled according to the measurements of Solomon's throne, and in his court academy he allowed himself to be called by the name of David. Charlemagne's namesake, Charles V, inheritor of the Holy Roman Empire and king of Spain [as Charles I], also inherited the medieval ideal of the covenant and the New Jerusalem. (Oss 1986: 2)

A more complete summary of the Spanish logic of legitimation would be God to the Jewish people and their covenant, to Jesus and the new covenant, to Saint Peter, to the popes, to the Spanish monarchs.

Spain stumbled upon the New World in its search for prospective riches from trade routes to Asia. Consequently, it was included in the Spanish hierarchical view of the universe and legitimated the Spanish presence in the New World. The Spanish presence included an obligation to "civilize" the indigenous population, interpreted as Hispanicizing them and converting them to Christianity. These two functions formed a conceptual unity in Spanish consciousness that did not permit any distinctions.

Historical Experiences that Colored the Spanish Covenant

In 711 the Muslims invaded Spain from North Africa. In a few years they captured most of the Iberian Peninsula and pushed into southern France. Independent Christian remnants were driven into the mountains of far northern and western Spain. The Muslims and their culture ruled most of Spain for five centuries, until 1212, and retained Grenada until 1492. Although the Muslims granted a measure of religious tolerance to Christians and Jews and made important contributions to Spanish culture, they were deeply resented. Their presence was considered an affront to Spanish culture and religion.

Shortly after the initial invasion of the Muslims, various Spanish forces initiated the Reconquista, the attempt to regain the lost territories and reestablish Spanish culture and Christianity. This effort lasted several centuries and drew on Christian mythology for its inspiration, especially on Saint James (Santiago), one of the original twelve apostles. According to unverified tradition, after founding a number of Christian communities in Spain, Santiago returned to Rome, where he was arrested and put to death by Herod in AD 44. His remains were secretly transported back to Spain and buried in Galicia. Due to wars and migrations, the place of Santiago's tomb was forgotten. In 813 the tomb was rediscovered by a hermit, and King Alfonso of Asturias ordered a church built to house the relics. This became the site of the famous pilgrimage shrine of Santiago de Compostela.

The early Christian resistance against the Muslims was weak and disorganized. According to unverified tradition, a turning point came at the battle of Clavijo in 844:

> The Moslem princes from their capital at Cordoba had been in the habit of demanding and receiving one hundred Spanish virgins as an annual tribute. Ramiro I, king of Galicia, at length refused to comply with the infamous exaction and assembled an army, which numbered in its ranks an archbishop and five bishops, to face the Moorish legions that speedily marched against him. In their meeting at Clavijo, Rodrigo and his Christian partisans suffered a severe mauling and were driven from the

field. In disarray, they fell back to cliffs at the edge of the valley and went into camp.

During the night, the king had a dream in which Santiago visited him. The apostle promised that the Christians would be victorious on the following day, their casualties minimal, and he himself, as protector of Spain, would participate in the battle. He even imparted instructions on strategy. At dawn, Rodrigo summoned his men. When he revealed his dream, they were fired with new zeal and courage. Returning to the field, abandoned the previous day, the enspirited Christian army hurled itself against the Moslem armies. Sure enough, in the midst of the fray, Santiago galloped out of the clouds on a pawing white stallion to lend assistance to the allies of the Lord.

Taking the lead, he swung a mighty sword and slew the warriors of Mohammed to the number of 60,000 or more. Evidently, many of his victims were decapitated. At least Church artists and sculptors have always thought so, for they consistently depict severed heads, turbaned and bloody, scattered at the feet of the raging steed. . . . Heartened by the sight of their patron saint knee-deep in blood, Ramiro's soldiers rushed in to complete the rout and claim the spoils. In so doing, they shouted the name of Santiago, using it for the first time as a battle cry. From then on the cry was voiced in every engagement with the Moors, and in time the Indians of the New World would hear it from the throat of the conquistadors. (Simmons 1991: 9; see figure 6.2)

The centuries of combat against the Muslims under the patronage of Santiago helped to form the Spanish national character. "The war had produced a hardening of the faith and an intolerance toward others, leading to the widespread notion that Spaniards were the new chosen people of God. . . . As a result, pride and arrogance characterized the ruling classes of Spain, as well as the conquistadors who opened a new kind of crusade against the pagan inhabitants of the Americas" (Simmons 1991: 15). "The history of the Spaniards would not, in truth, have taken the course it did without the belief that there reposes in Galicia the body of one of Christ's companions and disciples" (Castro 1971: 381).

The Spaniards in the New World: Legitimation and Motivation

It was during the reign of King Charles I of Spain from 1516 to 1556 (who was also Emperor Charles V of the Holy Roman Empire) that the intrusions into the Mayan areas of Mexico and Central America took place. The preceding discussion does not mean to imply that just because the Spaniards had cultural

Figure 6.2. Santiago riding to the aid of the Spaniards during the Reconquista. Note the slain Moors at the bottom of the picture. The cross on the flag resembles the Santiago cross.

logics of legitimation for their intrusion, this was the only reason it took place. The situation was more complex.

European Wars

During the sixteenth century the Christian kings of Europe were brawling with each other over territory and alliances. King Ferdinand was at war with France from 1500 to 1505, with the Muslims in North Africa from 1509 to 1511, and again with France in 1511. King Charles I was at war with France from 1521 to 1529, 1535 to 1538, 1542 to 1544, and 1551 to 1556. King Philip II continued the war with France from 1556 to 1559, then fought with the Turks in 1576, and with England from 1588 to 1603, a conflict that also involved the French from 1589 to 1598. King Philip III brought Spain into the Thirty Years War from 1618 to 1648.

These wars were costly and the monarchs hard-pressed to finance them. The explorations that led to the discovery of the New World were undertaken to find new trade routes that would enrich the kings and finance their costly undertakings. Hence came Columbus' first voyage and his false hope that he had reached India, a densely populated country that held great prospects for trade. When unknown lands were discovered instead, the crown hoped to obtain riches by conquest followed by taxation of its inhabitants in the form of goods and labor. But if conquest was to take place, then the logic legitimating Spain's intrusion into the New World also required evangelization of its non-Christian populations.

The Spaniards and Their Religion

The early Christian communities, once they had definitively broken with Judaism, became missionaries of their new faith based on Jesus' words: "Go therefore and teach all nations, baptizing them in the name of the Father, and of the Son and of the Holy Spirit" (Matthew 28:19). This concept is part of Smith's first idea of covenant, that God chooses a people "to fulfill His design for the world." Initiated by the dispersal of the original apostles from Jerusalem and expanding throughout the Roman Empire, missionary activity gradually spread to most of the Hellenized world, to North Africa, to the Balkans and Russia, and to northern and western Europe, including Spain.

It might appear that the Spaniards' religious beliefs were superficial, that their use of religion was simply pragmatic or illusory in a Machiavellian or Marxian sense. Such views fail to recognize the complexity of the Spanish worldview and the differences between contemporary and medieval times. The Spaniards took religion seriously in evaluating the morality of their actions, not in the sense of external propaganda, but rather in an internal search of their consciences. For the Spaniards religion was an intrinsic ingredient of both the identity of their psyche and the worldview of their culture. Its demands merited serious consideration. The conclusions they reached may be open to question and may have been extremely self-deceptive, but the seriousness with which the Spaniards attempted to justify their Christian consciences is not. The tragedy was the immense suffering their self-deception inflicted on human beings in the name of religion.

The Question of Forcible Conversion

Does the king's jurisdiction over Spain, part of the New World, and the church legitimate the use of force in dealing with indigenous populations? The question of the methods used to carry out the mandate of the Christian king arose early in the conquest period. Because of Spanish activities in Hispaniola and Cuba, the morality of the use of armed force and slavery were burning questions before the Spaniards encountered the Maya. As previously noted, a basic assumption of this historical period was that the Bible contained most of the knowledge that could be attained by the human mind. Therefore, the intellectual debate concentrated on the interpretation of biblical metaphors and parables. The debate about the use of force centered around the parable of the great supper. Its interpretation reveals some of the twists and turns taken in logics drawn from biblical passages.

> There was a man who gave a great supper, and sent out many invitations. And when the time came for his supper, he sent one of his own servants, telling the invited guests to come, for all was now ready. All of them with one accord began making excuses. I have bought a farm, the first said to him, and I must needs go and look over it; I pray thee count me excused. And another said, I have bought five pair of oxen, and I am on my way to make trial of them; I pray thee, count me excused. And another said, I have married a wife, and so I am unable to come. The servant came back and told his master all this, whereupon the host fell into a rage, and said to his servant, Quick go out into the streets and lanes of the city; bring in the poor, the cripples, the blind and the lame. And when the servant told him, Sir, all has been done according to thy command, but there is room left still, the master said to his servant, Go out into the highways and hedgerows, and give them no choice but to come in, that my house may be filled. I tell you, none of those who were first invited shall taste of my supper. (Luke 14: 16–24 from Phelan 1970: 7)

At that time the accepted interpretation of this parable saw Christ as the host and the invitation to the feast as preaching the message of Christianity to non-Christians. The host's reactions to the refusals of the invitations became the basis for the various positions on the methods of extending the Christian message in the New World. Phelan (1970: 5–11) sums up the debates of the period using the positions of Sepulveda, Mendieta, and Las Casas.

Sepulveda emphasized the Spanish mission of civilizing the indigenous peoples. He "suggested that the servant's first invitation . . . corresponded to the Primitive Apostolic Church . . . before the reign of the Emperor Constantine (AD 311–77). Coercion was not used. The servant's third invitation . . . corresponded to the Church after Constantine. During the reign of that emperor there emerged for the first time one unified Christian society. . . . This union meant that the Church acquired a secular arm, which under the legitimate authorization of the spiritual power could employ force to convert the heathen" (Phelan 1970: 9). This was the intellectual expression of the experience with the Muslims during the Reconquista and the position taken by the crown legitimating the use of force by the conquistadors.

The rejected positions were those of Mendieta and Las Casas. Mendieta saw the three invitations as representing methods of making the adherents of non-Christian faiths members of the community of the Christian covenant before the final Judgment. The Jews and Muslims already had contact with the Holy Scriptures. Therefore, only preaching to the Jews was required, and for the Muslims, examples of right living and good works would suffice. For Gentiles lacking contact with the Scriptures, such as the Maya, more forceful means were required, similar to those employed by a father in disciplining his children. Although rejecting harsh treatment, this position does not exclude the use of force befitting the punishment of a stubborn child. This was the policy adopted by the friars to enforce their program of evangelization (outlined in chapter 9). Las Casas rejected any use of force. He based his argument on the methods of Jesus, Saint Paul, and the early Christian church.

Conclusion

Through the actions of the papacy, the Spanish elite perceived that the Christian covenant had been entrusted to them. This made the Judeo-Christian God a quasi-tribal god of the Spaniards, legitimating, in turn, the Spanish entrance into the New World, the subjugation of the indigenous populations, and the attempts to convert them to Christianity. The intolerance latent in this biblically based covenant would be actualized in one of many examples of the immorality of western colonialism.

Spanish Victories and Their Impact on the Mayan Worldview

Early in the sixteenth century the Spanish and Mayan views of the world met when the Spanish conquistadors from their Caribbean outposts invaded Mexico and Central America. From 1524 to the late 1530s Pedro de Alvarado with a small band of Spaniards and many Tlaxcalan allies conquered and pacified Guatemala. In 1524 Luis Marín conquered Chiapas, and in 1527–28 Diego de Mazariegos founded Spanish settlements there. From 1527 to 1547 Francisco de Montejo and his family along with Tlaxcalan allies subdued parts of Yucatán. The Spaniards claimed these regions in the name of the Spanish king and set about imposing their control over the conquered territories.

Who were these Spanish conquerors of the Maya? Called conquistadors, they were men who accepted the crown's worldview, described in chapter 6, as legitimating their own presence in the New World. They were not a Spanish army dispatched by the crown to gain new territories, but private individuals with their own self-interests. This chapter describes the conquistadors' version of the Spanish worldview and how the Maya interpreted their first encounters with them.

The Conquistadors

The conquistadors were a group of Spanish adventurers intent on acquiring a fortune by coming to the New World and taking advantage of its material and human resources.

The Strategy

The plan of the leading conquistadors was to buy licenses from the king to explore and conquer an area of the New World that had been ceded to Spain by the pope. They were required to arrange private financing for recruiting and outfitting an armed force, which was composed of other men seeking their fortunes in the New World but lacking the resources to obtain their own licenses. For the most part, these recruits were not professional soldiers, much less a Spanish army (Restall 2003: 27–43). Once indigenous groups submitted to Spanish authority by force or peaceful submission, the highest ranking conquistador was usually rewarded with the governorship of the region. This, in turn, gave him the power to acquire *encomiendas* for himself and his followers. An encomienda was the right to exact tribute and labor from specified indigenous groups in the conquered areas, thereby providing the means to support the lifestyle of a wealthy Spanish nobleman. This method of intrusion into the New World not only saved the king the expense of dispatching an army, but also raised funds from the sale of licenses.

Initiating the Plan that Led to the Mayan Conquest: The Cortés Model

The four voyages of Columbus took place under the patronage of Ferdinand and Isabella, who granted him licenses to explore and conquer territory in their name. Columbus founded a settlement at Santo Domingo, which became a royal colony in 1499. In the name of the king, Velasquez conquered Cuba in 1511, and in exchange, the king gave him that governorship. Santo Domingo and Havana became centers for Spanish exploration and expansion into Mexico and Central America.

The governor of Cuba, as a private citizen, raised money and recruited Spaniards who "should try our fortune in seeking and exploring new lands where we might find employment" (Díaz 1928: 45).[1] After some secret agreements about dividing the wealth to be acquired during the expedition, Cortés was placed in charge. The governor "secretly . . . was sending to trade and not to form a settlement, . . . although it was announced and published that the expedition was for the purpose of founding a settlement" (Díaz 1928: 76). Cortés commissioned two banners to be made. One had a cross worked in gold and the legend "Comrades, let us follow the sign of the Holy Cross with true faith, and through it, we shall conquer" (Díaz 1928: 77). This may have been the cross of Santiago, in which the lower part of the vertical piece is shaped like a sword blade and both the transverse piece and the upper part of the vertical piece, like the hand grip of a sword. The other banner had the royal coat of arms on one side and an image of the Virgin Mary on the other (Ricard 1966: 15). Cortés, accompanied by drums and trumpets, made a proclamation that "whatsoever person might wish to go in his company to the newly discovered lands to conquer them and to settle there, should receive his share of the gold, silver and riches which might be gained, and an *encomienda* of Indians after the country had been pacified, and that to do these things Diego Velásquez [the governor of Cuba] held authority [a license] from his majesty" (Díaz 1928: 77).

Cortés recruited 508 men plus approximately 100 shipmasters, pilots, and sailors in eleven ships (Díaz 1928: 89). They set out from Cuba and landed first at Cozumel. Then they made their way around the Yucatán Peninsula; visited and fought with indigenous groups along the eastern coast of Mexico; started a small settlement at Vera Cruz; and proceeded inland, meeting and fighting with various Nahuatl-speaking groups until they arrived at Mexico City. At first, they entered peacefully and dialogued with Montezuma. But relations worsened and a hard-fought campaign ensued, with the Spaniards finally taking Tenochtitlán (now Mexico City) in 1521. Next the Spaniards set their sights on the Maya. Cortés dispatched one of his captains, Alvarado, to conquer Guatemala and El Salvador. Another captain, Montejo, who had been in Spain on Cortés' behalf, obtained a license to explore and conquer Yucatán.

The Worldview of the Conquistadors: Folk Christianity

Accepting the royal view of the world, and in spite of their personal goals of acquiring wealth and power, the conquistadors took their religion seriously. As with all religious systems, Christianity evolved over the centuries and developed variant forms. By the early sixteenth century, it had in many places become a folk religion focused on popular devotions involving vows to saints in return for protection or magical gifts and powers. In the popular religion of the period, Jesus was de-emphasized in favor of saints as patrons of various forms of security or magical powers. The orthodox intercessory link between the saints and God was frequently pushed aside, and the saints were divinized in their own right with many unorthodox practices in the devotions to them.

In the sixteenth century . . . the core of devotion [was] the vow and the patron [saint]. For at the root of these devotional acts and relationships is a defenselessness in regard to epidemic disease, plagues of locusts, vine blights, hail, and drought that remained unchanged. Religion in the form of bargains with the gods provided a means of control over these disasters. How was *devotion moderna* [a reform reaction against popular religion] to keep hail away? Cure the crippled? Bring back the dead? . . . The local landscape, urban and rural, had a sacred overlay; special places for contacting the divine were known to everyone. . . . In each place a small band of people were professionally dedicated to maintaining and keeping holy the sacred places, and circulating the power of the saints. But everyone, especially town officials, knew that it was a collective responsibility going back in time and ahead into the future to observe the sacred contracts, and that dire consequences could follow lapses. (Christian 1981: 175–77)

Christianity had been transposed into a cult focused on covenants with divinized saints. Contrary to orthodox Christianity, Christ and the Virgin were looked upon as especially powerful saints. The reciprocity agreements between folk Catholics and their saints were a means of physical protection against disease and the ravages of nature rather than a means to foster the internal spirit required for moral action. In some instances the requests were for magical or immoral rewards. This Catholicism of popular devotions had much in common with the Mayan worldview described in chapter 5. The symbolic expressions of the religions were quite different, but the underlying logic was similar if not identical. Given that most conquistadors were poor and uneducated soldiers of fortune, they were influenced in whole or part by this type of Christianity.

Prior to Combat: Cultural Logics of the Conquistadors

Through their invasion of Mayan territory, the conquistadors saw themselves as implementing the king's obligation to bring the New World under his Christian rule.

The Demand for Acknowledgment and Submission

Upon encountering a Mayan group, the conquistadors were required to proclaim the *Requerimiento* and to carry out its anathemas against those groups who refused to submit. The second part of the proclamation cites examples of indigenous populations who had previously submitted to the crown. It is omitted here because much of it is repeated in the third part of the mandate:

To make certain that you clearly understand what we, to the best of our abilities, are telling you, we request and even insist that you take as much time as needed to comprehend and deliberate about the following points: that you recognize the Church as the lord and ruler of the universe as well as the supreme pontiff, the pope; and in his name you recognize the king and queen, Doña Juana, our lords, who act in his place as the superiors, lords and kings of these islands and mainland by the power granted to them in the pope's decree; and that you consent and allow friars to reside here among you who will teach and preach to you what has been said about our presence here.

The fourth part details the advantages of submission.

If you will recognize the king and queen as you are obliged to do, you will be rewarded. We, in the name of the king, will treat you with all our love and charity. You can retain your wives and children, your lands in complete freedom without any entailments so that you may freely do with them what you wish just as you have done in the past. We shall not force you to become Christians unless you yourself when informed of the truth, should wish to convert to our holy Catholic faith as almost all the inhabitants of the other islands have already done. In addition, their majesties will bestow on you many privileges, exemptions, and other favors.

The Punishments for Refusal

The final section of the *Requerimiento* is very explicit about what will happen to the indigenous populations that refuse to submit:

If you do not receive and serve the king and queen, or if you maliciously delay in doing so, I am giving you a solemn warning that with the help of God, we will bring to bear against you all the might of our forces, and we will wage war against you in every place we can using any means at our disposal. We will place upon you the yoke of obedience to the church and their majesties, and we will enslave you, along with your wives and children, selling and disposing of them as their majesties will determine. We will confiscate your possessions and cause you every kind of harm and misfortune that we can, just as is done to vassals who neither obey nor want to give allegiance to their master by resisting and speaking against him. We affirm that the deaths and losses resulting from our actions will be your fault and not the fault of their majesties nor of these noblemen who have come with us. We ask that the notary here present give signed testimony that we have spoken the words of this document to you. We also ask that those present be witnesses to what we have communicated.

There is a resemblance between this section of the *Requerimiento* and biblical passages about the Jewish rejection of their covenant, such as Deuteronomy 20:10–16. This biblical passage has been used by advocates of the "submit or fight and be conquered" position within the Jewish, Christian, and Islamic traditions.

The document reflected the conquistadors' application of the royal worldview. When Las Casas read it, he did not know whether to laugh or cry (Las Casas 1986: 216). Given that the document was probably either poorly translated or read in Spanish, given that the authorities cited were unknown to the Maya, given the sophistry in the distinction between acknowledging the superiority of a religion and converting, and given the very length of the document, reading it was a meaningless exercise. It is questionable whether many captains carried out the order to make this proclamation (Poole 1992: 81).

Divine Assistance During the Conquest

The *Requerimiento* itself states that the devastation and enslavement of the indigenous populations was to be carried out "with God's help." The religious practices of Cortés' group before they engaged in armed combat show that they considered their activities to be divinely assisted. The Spaniards would attend mass in which they commended themselves to God, Jesus Christ, and the Blessed Virgin (Díaz 1928: 97, 104, 488). Attending daily mass appears to have been the routine even if no battle was expected. If there was no time for a mass, a simple prayer was recited. Before the attack on Mexico City, Díaz reports that "[we] commended ourselves to God, Our Lady his blessed Mother, . . . to put courage into our hearts to think that as our Lord Jesus Christ had vouchsafed us protection through past dangers, he would likewise guard us from the power of the Mexicans" (Díaz 1928: 267). Then the Spaniards would draw up their ranks for the attack. The armed band consisted of cavalry, crossbowmen, musketeers, and swordsmen arranged in various formations depending on the circumstances of the battle. They were led by a standard bearer carrying a large banner displaying a cross (Díaz 1928: 104, 185, 186, 194). Since it took all the standard bearer's strength to hold the banner, four guards were assigned to protect him. The Tlaxcalans or other Indian allies were used in an unknown manner in the battle formations. Then the army marched forward, urged on by Cortés' cry of "Santiago," which was also on the banners (Díaz 1928: 186). To this his men replied, "May good fortune attend our advance, for in God lies true strength."

Whenever the Spaniards were in trouble during a battle, Cortés or one of the captains rallied the forces by shouting "Santiago and at them" (Díaz 1928: 98, 188, 428, 480). (The Santiago cry has been mythologized into the actual appearance of Santiago. Valle (1946: 19–20) lists fourteen occasions in Latin America during which Santiago is said to have appeared in person to save a Spanish group.)[2] Díaz describes the various battles fought by the Spaniards, and on page after page he uses phrases such as "with God's help," "it pleased God to . . . ," "Jesus Christ spared our lives," and so on, to account for Spanish escapes or victories. Cortés' letters to the king constantly use the same phrases (Cortés 1986: 22, 36, 63, 77, 135, passim). The conquistadors considered themselves to be on a divinely inspired mission in which their God and saints would help them.

During Cortés' march to Mexico City, some incidents concerning baptism further illustrate some popular perceptions of Christianity held by the conquistadors. With one exception, all the baptisms noted by Díaz (1928: 112, 165, 226) were of Indian women given to the Spaniards. Before accepting them, the Spaniards would baptize them. The basis of this practice was a sixteenth-century Spanish belief that to have extramarital relations with an infidel women was a greater sin than to do so with a baptized Christian, probably a reflection of the Reconquista mentality (Borges 1960: 496). In Yucatán after the conquest, there was a disproportionate number of female baptisms for the same reason (Remesal 1964: 354). This practice shows the seriousness with which conquistadors were guided by religious considerations, be they orthodox or unorthodox.

The Mindset of Individual Spaniards

As previously pointed out, a cultural worldview seldom dominates all levels of any individual psyche. Nor is a culture a cookie cutter automatically turning out like-minded people. Individual Spaniards had various motivations involving multiple logics for undertaking the conquests. The desire for power and greed for material wealth were present along with the conversion and civilizing motive. The priority given to or vacillations between these competing logics were later to produce conflicting groups among the Spaniards themselves. Toward the end of his memoirs, the conquistador Bernal Díaz del Castillo summed up both the cultural and individual logics in referring to "the many good, noble deeds that we have performed for God, His Majesty, and all of Christendom . . . to serve God and Your Majesty, and to bring light to those who were in darkness, and also to acquire the riches that all men usually seek" (Díaz 1968: 366). Here Díaz is repeating the themes of an earlier exhortation by Cortés to some Spaniards thinking of deserting: "he begged them to leave behind them their resentment . . . and he promised to make them rich and to give them office, as they came to seek a livelihood, and were in a country where they could do service to God, and His Majesty and enrich themselves" (Díaz 1928: 401).

The Spaniards had not yet faced the latent contradiction in these statements. The situation is reminiscent of the situation facing the American colonists in their aspirations for freedom and independence and their simultaneous refusal to face the problem of slavery and its indispensable economic role in all sectors of the new republic.

Prior to Combat: Cultural Logics of the Maya

This section examines some of the pertinent cultural logics embedded in the discussion of the traditional Mayan worldview presented in chapter 5.

Divine-Human Activity

In the Mayan worldview, existence is the presence and continual renewal of the cosmic force in every aspect of the universe. As a corollary, "If we had an English word that fully expressed the Mayan sense of narrative time, it would have to embrace the duality of the divine and human" (D. Tedlock 1996: 59). Vogt (1976: 19) expresses the concept in this way: "The most important interaction in the universe is not between persons, nor between persons and objects, but among the innate souls of persons and material objects."

Application to Warfare

By the cultural logic just described, warfare for the Maya was a divine-human activity. And since each Mayan group had its own tribal god, war was a clash of tribal gods as well as of men. An example is provided in *The Annals of the Cakchikels*. The Kaqchikel were suffering a severe famine. Their hated enemies, the K'iche', decided to attack them in their weakened condition. The K'iche' advanced on the Kaqchikel capital, Iximché.

> At once they [the K'iche'] rushed out from the city of Gumarcaah to annihilate all the [Kaqchikel] Lords. They carried their god Tohil. The warriors came from all directions; it was impossible to count the people. . . . The tribes came, having covered themselves with feathers when they gathered, and armed themselves with their bows, their shields, and their weapons, their iridescent green feathers, and shining garlands, and with their metal crowns and with precious stones. . . . When the sun rose on the horizon . . . the war cries broke out and the banners were unfurled; the great flutes, the drums, and the shells resounded. . . . The Quiches [K'iche'] . . . advanced rapidly . . . followed by the kings Tepepul and

Iztayul, who accompanied the god. . . . The clash was truly terrible. The shouts rang out, the war cries, the sound of flutes, the beating of drums and the shells, while the warriors performed their feats of magic. Soon the Quiches were defeated. . . . As a result they were conquered and made prisoner, and the kings Tepepul and Iztayul surrendered and delivered up their god. (Recinos and Goetz 1953: 102–3)

The physical form of the god carried by the K'iche' kings is not stated. It may have been a sculptured image or a deerskin bundle (Christenson 2001: 169) or a banner embodying the god (Freidel, Schele, and Parker 1993: 294–96, 314–15). The surrender of Tohil, the god of the principal K'iche' lineage and therefore the protecting god of the whole group, proved the Kaqchikel god to be stronger.

Freidel's analysis of warfare based on the Popol Vuh and archaeological data echoes the Kaqchikel account. The Maya had mediators—their shamans, including shamanic kings—between the gods and themselves to maintain and renew the vital force in all things.

The function of the king was to intercede with the gods and the ancestors in order to sustain the balance of the world. Properly used, this power preserved cosmos and country. Improperly used . . . it became empty strength and a danger to all. . . . Decisive battles were fought on the supernatural plane—where the key combatants would all be attempting to train their destructive power on the enemy by means of their powerful talismans and ecstatic visions. Military defeat was a consequence of a king's spiritual failure to hold the covenant and alliance of the gods against the rival supplication and magic of the king across the field. (Freidel, Schele, and Parker 1995: 213, 316)

Hill, in his study of the Kaqchikel, reached much the same conclusion.

Through the use of the indigenous writing before the conquest, leaders of preeminent chinamitales traced their descent back to the legendary founders of their groups. This was done not only to legitimize their authority but also to establish themselves as possessors of the same supernatural powers those ancestors had. The concept of the ruler as a semidivine "man-god," possessing some "divine fire" (and, hence, supernatural abilities such as the power to transform or project his uxla [divine force] into another shape), is a widespread Mesoamerican belief. . . . By using their powers on behalf of the group (especially in warfare), the rulers were nearly as much responsible for its success as the patronal god. And this power was so great that it did not end or dissipate with the man-god's death. The natub [another type of divine force] in particular could be preserved by keeping it in an image or receptacle of some form, and it could continue to afford protection to the group. (Hill 1992: 92)

Hill's description fits the description of the grandesa by the Kaqchikel shaman Apolinario in chapter 5.

In Yucatán in the first part of the sixteenth century, two Mayan descent groups, the Itzá and Xiu, were locked in a power struggle. At one point the Itzá defeated the Xiu. The outcome is depicted as a victory of Itzá gods over those of the Xiu (Edmonson 1986: 45–54).

Confirmation: Mexica and Tlaxcalan Perceptions of Warfare

Some information about the perception of war among Nahuatl-speaking groups can be gleaned from the description of the Spanish retreat from Mexico City that culminated in the battle of Otumba. Here the Spanish force, with considerable help from Tlaxcalans, was able to escape annihilation by defeating larger Nahua forces.

> All gave many thanks to God for having escaped from such a great multitude of people, for there had never been seen or found throughout the Indies such a great number of warriors together in any battle that was fought, for there was present there the flower of Mexico and Texcoco, and of all the towns around the lake, and others in the neighborhood, and the people of Otumba and Tepetexcoco and Saltocan who all came in the belief that this time not a trace of us would be left. (Díaz 1928: 430)

This passage poses a problem: how were the Spaniards and Tlaxcalans able to overcome such a large massed force with their smaller numbers? One would expect them simply to be overwhelmed by oncoming waves of Nahua warriors no matter how well they fought.

Some clues may be given in Díaz's description of the battle. Cortés gave orders that "the cuts and thrusts that we gave should be aimed at distinguished chieftains, for all of them bore great golden plumes and rich arms and devices." Was this an order simply to destroy the command structure of the enemy thereby causing disorganization in the ranks and allowing the Spaniards to gain the upper hand? Or was there something about the Nahua chiefs or their banners that the Nahua saw as essential to the battle, so that without them they lost their ability to fight? Díaz describes the battle:

> They killed and wounded a great number of our soldiers, but it pleased God that Cortés and the Captains . . . reached the place where the Captain General of the Mexicans was marching with his banner displayed, and with rich golden armor and great gold and silver plumes. When

Cortés saw him with many other Mexican chieftains all wearing great plumes, he said to our Captains: "Now, Señores, let us break through them and leave none of them unwounded". . . . Cortés struck his horse against the Mexican Captain, which made him drop his banner, and the rest of our Captains succeeded in breaking through the squadron which consisted of many Indians following the Captain who carried the banner, who nevertheless had not fallen at the shock Cortés had given him, and it was Juan de Salamanca . . . who gave him a lance thrust and took from him the rich plume that he wore and afterwards gave it to Cortés, saying that as it was he who first met him and made him lower his banner and deprived his followers of the courage to fight, that the plume belonged to Cortés. . . . It pleased Our Lord that when that Captain who carried the Mexican banner was dead . . . their attack slackened . . . we followed up our victory killing and wounding. (Díaz 1928: 428–29)

Freidel sees more in this passage than the simple destruction of the command structure and subsequent disorganization in the ranks. He finds evidence in Mayan archaeological materials that taking the enemy standard was the equivalent of defeating the enemy god. Using this evidence to interpret the battle of Otumba, Freidel sees the Nahua as perceiving the standard itself as a "source of supernatural miracles," "an embodiment of a potent spiritual being whose presence and performance was critical to their success" (Freidel, Schele, and Parker 1993: 294–95). This implies that Cortés had learned about the Nahua belief and that this was his motivation for the order he gave at the start of the battle. Note that Cortés took care to protect his own standard bearer by surrounding him with four mounted guards. This interpretation finds some confirmation in the Mayan perception of the cosmic force in all beings noted in chapter 5. Battle standards or the chiefs themselves embody the vital force as the power of warriors for their troops. Once they had been struck down, the battle was considered finished.

The Spanish-Mayan Battles: How They Were Interpreted

In Guatemala there is documentation giving both Spanish and Mayan versions of the first major engagement of Alvarado's force against a large force assembled by the K'iche' rulers.

Spanish View of the Encounter

Alvarado wrote to Cortés, giving a very factual account of the battle with the K'iche' in the Quetzaltenango area:

We saw many warriors approaching and we allowed them to approach as they came over very wide plains and we defeated them. . . . We continued the pursuit for a full league [about three miles] and they brought us to a mountain and there they faced us, and I put myself in flight with some of my horsemen to draw the Indians to the plains, and they followed us, until reaching the horses' tails. And after I rallied with the horsemen, I turned on them, and here a very severe pursuit and punishment was made. In this affair one of the four chiefs of the city of Utatlan was killed, who was the Captain General of all this country. (Kelly 1932: 137)

But in keeping with the Spanish perception of war, Alvarado later noted divine assistance. "And in truth their evil plan would have come to pass but that God our Lord did not see good that these infidels should be victorious over us." Toward the end of the letter Alvarado makes the following request: "we are in the wildest country and people one has ever seen, and so that our Lord may give us victory I supplicate Your Grace to ordain that a procession be held in your city of all the priests and friars so that our Lord may help us. We are so far from help that if He does not help us, nobody can" (Kelly 1932: 140).

Mayan View of the Encounters

The Mayan accounts read very differently (Carmack 1973: 301–3; Bricker 1981: 38–42). Montezuma had warned the K'iche' as early as 1512 about the presence of the Spaniards. The K'iche' documents indicate more skirmishes and battles than Alvarado's account describes. It took Alvarado three months to subdue Zapotitlán and the nearby area before he ascended to the highlands. He was temporarily stymied again on the approaches to Quetzaltenango by stone barricades, pits, and ditches (Recinos 1957: 37). The K'iche' documents describe the battle with the Spaniards. There was

an Indian captain who became an eagle, with three thousand Indians to fight with the Spaniards. At midnight the Indians went and the captain of the Indians who had transformed himself into an eagle became anxious to kill the Adelantado Tunadiu [Alvarado], and he could not kill him because a very fair maiden defended him; they were anxious to enter, but as soon as they saw this maiden they fell to the earth and they could not get up from the ground, and then came many footless birds, and those birds surrounded this maiden, and the Indians wanted to kill the maiden and those footless birds defended her and blinded them. . . . Another Indian captain . . . went before the Spaniards as lightning wishing to kill the Adelantado, and as soon as he arrived he saw an exceedingly white dove above all the Spaniards, which was defending them, and which returned to repeat it again and it blinded him and he fell to the earth and could not get up. Three times this captain rushed against the Spaniards like lightning and each time his eyes were blinded and he fell to the earth. And since this captain saw they could not penetrate the Spaniards . . . [he] returned . . . [and] informed the chiefs . . . [about] the maiden with the footless birds and the dove which defended the Spaniards. (Bricker 1981: 39–40)

The qualities of the two K'iche' captains enumerated here and the logic of the narrative belong to beings of internal sky-earth. The K'iche' account sees the battle as a contest between the shamanic powers of the combatants who have the ability to turn themselves into their flying animal spirits or forces of nature to accomplish the goals of their rituals. Here these are an eagle and lightning. The K'iche' seem to attribute the same shamanic powers to the Spaniards whose defenders are described as "a very fair maiden," "footless birds," and an "exceedingly white dove." Chapter 12 will examine the identities of these Spanish gods protecting Alvarado and his force.

During another battle a few days later, one of the K'iche' captains, Tecum Umam, was killed by Alvarado.

And then Captain Tecum flew up, he came like an eagle full of real feathers, which were not artificial, he wore wings which also sprang from his body and he wore three crowns, one was of gold, another of pearls and another of diamonds and emeralds. That Captain Tecum came with the intention of killing Tunadiu [Alvarado] who came on horseback and he hit the horse instead of the Adelantado and he beheaded the horse with one lance . . . of shiny stone and this captain had placed a spell on it. And when he saw that it was not the Adelantado but the horse who had died, he returned to fly overhead, in order to come from there to kill the Adelantado. Then the Adelantado awaited him with his lance and he impaled this Captain Tecum with it. . . .

And as the rest of the Indians saw that the Spaniards had killed their captain, they fled, and immediately the Adelantado Don Pedro de Alvarado, seeing that the soldiers of this Captain Tecum were fleeing, said that they also should die, and immediately the Spanish soldiers pursued the Indians and caught up with them and killed every one of them. (Bricker 1981: 40)

The clash of the warriors may be seen as a clash of the vital forces embodied in the animal souls and shamanic powers of the combatants. Here again the animal soul is an eagle. At the battle of Otumba in Mexico, when the Nahua saw the fall of their preeminent vital force of war in the war captain's standard, they fled. Here it is the captain himself who falls. It appears that when the person or object containing the war power of the tribal god falls, the engagement is terminated as there is no hope of overcoming the power of the superior god, even with superior manpower. This interpretation is reinforced by the Mayan interpretation of the Spanish battle banners. They could not overcome the Spanish forces because of the power of the tribal god embodied in the maiden, footless birds, and white dove.

Results of the Encounters

The Spaniards' victory and Maya's defeat had long-term implications for both.

Outcome for the Spaniards

After the battle Alvarado returned to Quetzaltenango where he dispatched the caciques of the town to bring together their people who had fled to the mountains for fear of the Spaniards. Alvarado went on to conquer the K'iche' again at their capital, Utatlán; the Tz'utujil near Santiago Atitlán; and the Kaqchikel at Iximché when they rebelled after initially having assisted the Spaniards. He then proceeded to the south coast and El Salvador receiving allegiance of many towns by peaceful or forceful means. But the Maya did not meekly submit after their first encounters with the Spanish. Rebellions were reported in 1526 in the Quetzaltenango Valley; in 1529 at Xumay, Nebáj, Uspantán, Cuzcatán, and Chiquimula; and in 1534 when Alvarado left for Peru. Uprisings were continuous and lasted into the late 1530s (Carmack 1981: 307–9, 1995: 46; O'Flaherty 1979: 54–55; Kramer 1994: 27; Lovell 1985: 72). This was the beginning of the Spanish colonial empire in Central America that was to last for three hundred years and leave a deep imprint on the succeeding independent countries.

Consequences for the Maya

The repeated defeats of the Maya in the pacification period confirmed the outcomes of the first encounters. An acknowledgment of the superiority of the Spanish gods was implanted as a new dynamic within the Mayan worldview. By the cultural logics of their worldview, they would acknowledge and take advantage of this superiority by adopting the Spanish gods into the Mayan covenant. But at the time of conquest and during pacification, there was great confusion as to the identity of the Spanish gods.

Confirmation: Nahua View of the Consequences of Defeat

After the defeat of the Mexica, they and the Tlaxcalans considered the Spanish victories as a vindication of the superiority of the Spanish gods over their own gods. "The [Mexica] leaders and their advisors . . . receive Jesus Christ among their gods as one of them, and honor him just as the Spaniards do according to their ancient custom that whenever any foreign group settles down near an already established community, if it seems fitting, they consider the god of the recently arrived as one of their own. . . . In this way they were easily inclined to take as a god the god of the Spaniards, but without putting aside their own ancient gods" (Sahagún 1954: 382–83; also León-Portilla 1974: 15).

At one point prior to their defeat, the Mexica attempted to trap the Spaniards within Mexico City and cut them to pieces. The Spaniards barely escaped. Later the leader of the Tlaxcalans remarked to Cortés, "Do not think, Malinche [Cortés' translator], that it is a small thing you have done to escape with your lives from that impregnable city and its bridges, and I tell you that if we formerly looked upon you as very brave, we now think you much more valiant. . . . Much do you owe to your Gods who have brought you here and delivered you from such a multitude of warriors who were awaiting you at Otumba" (Díaz 1928: 432). Because they believed in the superiority of the Spanish gods, the Tlaxcalans were willing to give their allegiance to the Spanish king. "They [the Tlaxcalans] had thought to do the same [what the Mexica had done to the Tlaxcalans] against us [the Spaniards], but they could not do it although they had gathered against us three times with all their warriors, and we must be invincible, and when they found this out about our persons, they wished to become friends with us and the vassals of the great prince the Emperor Don Carlos, for they felt sure that in our company they and their women and children would be guarded and protected" (Díaz 1928: 213).

A short time later the Tlaxcalan cacique and his son expressed the desire to become Christians. The leader was baptized and received the Spanish name of Don Lorenzo Vargas (Díaz 1928: 450). The son was probably baptized as well, although this is not explicitly mentioned. Given both the Spanish and Indian interpretations of warfare, the Spanish victories were also theological statements.

Encomenderos and Their Religious Obligation

After the usually brief appearance in a Mayan community of a group of conquistadors seeking their submission, the next group of Spaniards to make their appearance were the encomenderos or their representatives seeking tribute and labor from the Mayan groups entrusted to them. As specified in this encomienda title given by Alvarado to Gonzalo de Ovalle, a veteran of the Mexican and Guatemalan marches, the encomendero assumed religious obligations toward the Maya.

I hereby entrust to you, Gonzalo de Ovalle, the province of Tianguiztheca Puyumatlan with its lord called Suchil, and the villages and peoples, so that you may use them in your estates and commerce, in accordance with the Ordinances of New Spain, and with the obligation that you instruct and indoctrinate the said peoples in matters pertaining to our Holy Catholic Faith, applying to this duty all possible diligence. Done in the city of Santiago [Iximché], the twenty-seventh day of October, 1524. (Kramer 1994: 249)

How the encomendero was to carry out his obligation to instruct the Indians was not specified. Given that he typically resided in a city and consequently was absent from the region of his encomienda, and that he lacked interest in education of any kind, the obligation was usually ignored. By 1537 it had become a legal fiction (Kramer 1994: 210), although there was an attempt to revive it in the first part of the seventeenth century.

A Peaceful Encounter in Yucatán

In spite of the key importance of the victories by arms, the first encounters of the Spanish with many Maya did not involve violence (see Restall 1998: 58–76). A Mayan document, *The Title of Acalan-Tixchel*, relates the entry of the Spaniards into this area of Yucatán. The first contact took place in 1525 or 1527 when Cortés passed through the area on his way to Honduras. He summoned the rulers of the area and gave them the gist of the *Requerimiento*. "I have come here to your lands, for I am sent by the lord of the earth, the emperor seated on his throne in Castile; he sends me to see the land and those who live in it, not for the purpose of wars. I ask only for the way to Ulua, to the land where gold and plumage and cacao come from, as I have heard" (Restall 1998: 63).

In Cortés' party were three Mexica prisoners, including their ruler, Cuauhtémoc. Cortés was wary about leaving them behind in Mexico City. Cuauhtémoc approached the Acalan ruler and repeatedly proposed that he murder Cortés and his band. The Acalan ruler refused and informed Cortés who put Cuauhtémoc in chains for three days, had him baptized, and then chopped off his head. Baptism in these circumstances is another indication of the Spanish view of religion at this time. Orthodox or unorthodox, it was taken seriously. (However, other sources say Cuauhtémoc was baptized prior to this event; see Restall 2003: 191.)

Francisco de Montejo received a license to conquer Yucatán. About 1530 his representatives came into the area, put the eldest son of the ruler in prison for two days, and demanded tribute. Thus began a routine of taking tribute goods to the Spaniards in Champoton and later to Campeche. The next Spaniards to arrive were the friars, whose entrance will be described in chapter 8.

Summary

At this point the analysis of cultural logics sheds some light on the anomaly. The Spaniards' initial defeats of the Maya showed the Maya that the Spanish gods were more powerful protectors than their own gods. Other Mayan groups, hearing about these defeats and understanding the superiority and political control of the Spaniards, came to the same conclusion. For these reasons, Mayan cultural logics mandated the adoption of the Spanish gods along with the covenant obligation to provide these gods with what they wanted. This adoption did not imply a rejection of their traditional gods, however. This is the first step in understanding the anomaly described in earlier chapters.

PART 4

Evangelization

The Spanish Attempt to Change the Mayan Worldview

Having seen the superior power of the Spanish gods revealed in battle, the Maya wanted to incorporate them into their own covenant so that these gods would be their protectors as well. To do this, the Maya needed to know who were the Spanish gods and what were their needs in order to provide for them under the terms of the covenant. For a generation or more during the period of conquest and pacification, the Spaniards made no attempt to communicate this information. The conquistadors usually made brief appearances in Mayan communities to obtain their submission to the king and make some mention of "Dios" as contained in the *Requerimiento*. As seen in the previous chapter, the encomenderos typically ignored their obligations.

Las Casas was instrumental in having the king and the Council of the Indies address the neglect of duty by the encomenderos through a decree issued in Madrid on January 9, 1540:

> To my governor of the province of Guatemala and the bishop, the reverend priest in Christ.
>
> I have been informed that in regard to the instruction of the Indians of that province in matters concerning our holy Catholic faith, there has been lacking the diligence necessary for their salvation and for fulfilling the obligations of those to whom they are entrusted. Therefore I command and charge you as your duty to give an order that in every community of Christians of that province, there be determined a set hour each day in which all the Indians, slaves as well as free ones, and Afro persons within the community, be gathered together to hear the *doctrina cristiana*; and that you appoint someone with the responsibility to teach it; and that you compel all the Spanish citizens to send their Indians and Afro persons to learn the *doctrina* without impeding them or occupying them in some other task. (Remesal 1964: 246)

The document continues with provisions that are to be made for those who live outside Christian communities. The king tells the bishop that it is his obligation to carry out the order and to inform him if anything necessary for this work is lacking.

In this way the king of Spain, guided by his medieval hierarchical view of the world, launched the evangelization of the Maya. The sixteenth century was the Age of Discovery, initiated by Portugal and Spain, followed by the French, English, Dutch, Belgians, and Germans. In most of these cases "discovery" was followed by colonization that subjugated the indigenous populations and attempted to convert them to the national religion of the colonizing country as a corollary of the fusion of church and kingdom (state). The result was a contradictory desire to bring the indigenous peoples Christianity and to control them for their land, labor, or taxes. Often this took place with the cooperation of indigenous elites who already had in place systems of forced labor. The exploration of the New World was not an encounter with "noble savages." While there were voices from within the various Christian denominations who cried out against the resulting injustices, the national religions became participants in one of the darker aspects of Western history.

The next four chapters examine the Spanish evangelization effort among the Maya and, within this effort, the work of the friars and secular priests. This examination is a selective treatment guided by the search to explain the role of Catholicism in Mayan religion. It deals with the theological worldview of the clergy and the strategy they employed to communicate it to the Maya. The friars themselves defined evangelization as primarily a process of verbal communication, and this is what will be examined. "Given the notion of the centrality of intellectual conviction and the comprehension of beliefs in matters religious, we doubt that a mere sequence of sounds could have any efficacy. But the friars knew those sounds could open the way to God's grace, and that sacramental grace could descend even on the ignorant" (Clendinnen 1987: 48). Successful or not from the friars' viewpoint, the conceptual content of evangelization and the manner in which it was carried out comprised the material presented to the Maya to answer their questions about the Spanish gods. It is an example of a directed change program instituted by one cultural group toward another group.

8

The Goals of Evangelization

The purpose of evangelization was to communicate Christianity in order to convert the Maya and, at the same time, make them loyal subjects of the king. Evangelization among the Maya lasted more than four hundred years and went through several phases that can be roughly defined by those primarily responsible for its implementation—the friars for more than two hundred years, then the secular clergy. Initially, the few secular (diocesan) priests in the New World worked only in Spanish parishes. Consequently, the orders of mendicant friars, mostly Franciscans and Dominicans in the Mayan areas, were called upon by the bishops to carry out the task of evangelizing the indigenous populations.

The Worldview of the Friars: A Brief History of Religious Orders

The friars' way of life was a result of historical evolution in the modes of Western religious life. The original ideal was exemplified by individuals who rejected the world as a place of sin, withdrew to an isolated region to seek their own spiritual perfection, and in so doing prayed for the spiritual welfare of the world they left behind. The solitary monks of the desert, the anchorites, were the prototypes of this lifestyle.

The Monastic Orders

Later, these monks decided that their way of life would be enhanced if they joined together in communities where they would take the three vows of poverty, chastity, and obedience and live a life of prayer and meditation. Their coming together as a monastic community was the original type of religious order for which Saint Benedict formulated the classical rule and commentary. The monastic day centered around chanting the Divine Office composed of passages from scripture, especially the Psalms, and other sacred songs and writings. It was divided into sections called "hours" because of the times of the day at which they were chanted. In a typical routine, the friars rose and chanted matins at 2 a.m., a practice followed by reading and meditation until lauds was recited at 5 a.m. Breakfast followed lauds (sometimes matins and lauds were combined). Prime, chanted around 6 a.m., was followed by a period of work or study. Terce came next at 9 a.m. followed by mass and then another work or study period. Sext was recited at noon followed by meditation and rest until none at 3 p.m. Dinner and another work or study period followed none. Vespers at 6 p.m. was followed by meditation; compline was recited at 7:30 p.m.; and the monks retired around 8:30 p.m. In this way the entire day was consecrated to God for the spiritual welfare of the monastic community and the world outside.

The Semimonastic Orders: The Friars

In the next evolutionary step, some religious thought that the monastic retreat was not well suited to spreading the word of the gospel. A new type of religious order evolved whose members left the monastery to preach and teach. The Franciscans and Dominicans (whose official title is the Order of Preachers) were founded during this phase. But their leaving the monastery was temporary. They always returned and still observed the monastic lifestyle, retaining their liturgical obligations but reducing the time spent on them (Knowles 1966: 58).[1] Prayers requesting God's assistance were considered necessary for the success of the friars' work outside the monastery. Saint Francis practiced and emphasized mystical contemplation for his friars (Moorman 1968: 14). The Constitution of the Dominicans reads

> Because we share in the mission of Apostles, we also follow their way of life as Saint Dominic conceived it: with one mind leading a common life, faithful to the evangelical counsels; fervent in the common celebration of the liturgy, especially the Eucharist and the Divine Office, and in prayer; committed to a life of study and constant in religious observance. All these practices contribute not only to the glory of God and our own sanctification, but are of direct assistance in the salvation of others, since they prepare and impel us to preach, they inform our preaching and are informed by it. These elements are all inter-connected; they modify and enliven one another and in their total harmony are the life of the order. In the fullest sense this is an apostolic life in which teaching and preaching ought to spring from the fullness of contemplation. (Ashley 1990: 16)

The European Model of the Friars

Because the friars originated in Europe, much of their activity outside the monastery was influenced by cultural conditions there. The local parish, with its church and secular priest as a teacher and minister of the sacraments, was the heart of the Catholic system. Supplementing the local priest, the friars would visit parishes as specialists in preaching the word of God. Their services were especially needed given the poor training of large numbers of the secular clergy at that time. "The situation of the people followed inevitably from that of their pastors. Spanish religion of the early sixteenth century was still in all essentials late medieval, with a heavy emphasis on local rituals and folk religion" (Kamen 1991: 180). This is the Christianity of popular devotions characteristic of the conquistadors described in chapter 7. In contrast, the preaching of the friars centered on Christ. They urged repentance and a reform of devotions. As visiting priests they would also hear confessions as some local parishioners were reluctant to confess to the local priest (Ximénez 1971b: 51; Christian 1981: 14–15). When finished preaching and hearing confessions, the friars retired to their monasteries to continue their liturgical routine.

The Missionary Experience of the Friars

The friars also had a history of missionary work. The medieval Franciscans followed the Crusaders, engaging Muslims in the Near East as well as in North Africa and Spain; they were also involved in embassies and work among the Mongols. During the Age of Discovery they followed the Portuguese, establishing monasteries at their trading posts in Africa and India, and they came to the Americas with Columbus on his later voyages (Moorman 1968: 226–39, 576–77). The early preaching of the Dominicans was directed against the Albigensian heresy (a Catharistic sect) as well as Islam and Judaism in Spain (Ashley 1990: 4, 30, 54). "The monastic tradition of the Middle Ages incorporated pilgrimage and the propagation of the faith among pagans as acts of piety and devotion—and of separation from the world. Life among the pagans or life in a convent cell both were forms of solitude and voluntary exile" (Oss 1986: 3).

The Monastic Routine in the New World

The Franciscans and Dominicans in the New World retained all the basic elements of the monastic discipline, including living in community and occupying a considerable amount of their time in contemplation and chanting the Divine Office. To provide the additional time required for preaching and teaching in a different culture, the Office was shortened (Remesal 1964: 448). Vazquez (1938: 294, 1940: 253) describes a typical twenty-four-hour day of a Franciscan friar in Guatemala: two hours for prayer and meditation, two hours for chanting the Office, one hour for the performance of penance, six hours for study, one or two hours for visiting and helping the sick, and additional hours for hearing confessions or studying about problems encountered in confessional work. This accounts for a minimum of thirteen hours and possibly up to sixteen hours of the friar's day.

This schedule with its ritual components was considered essential to the life of a friar, and it was diligently observed. During a brief stopover in Mérida on their way to Chiapas, the friars, because of their numbers, were put up in various houses of Spaniards. Every evening they would gather in the church to sing mass, chant vespers and compline, and recite the remaining hours. They did much the same upon their arrival in San Cristóbal. When they were able to move into their own quarters, they reverted to their traditional monastic routine (Remesal 1964: 353, 400). This was the cultural backdrop of the friars from which they sought to evangelize the Maya.

The Mercedarians

The Mercedarians were the third religious order to evangelize among the Maya in Guatemala. Although semimonastic, they were not friars in a technical sense. The spirituality of the friars emphasized poverty while the Mercedarians emphasized works of charity. They were founded in 1218 by St. Peter Nolasco and focused on raising funds to ransom captives from the Muslims (Borges 1992: 11–19; 25–34). They were guided by the Rule of Saint Augustine. Compared to the rules of other semimonastic groups, Saint Augustine gave more latitude for the adaptation of the monastic routine to the needs of ministry outside the monastery. This was shown by Mercedarians accompanying Columbus on his second voyage and by the chaplain Bartolomé de Olmedo, who accompanied Cortés in his conquest of Mexico from 1519 to 1521. After the conquest they initially worked in Spanish parishes, although a few were working among the Maya in the 1540s (Remesal 1964: 241).

The Mercedarians were not a missionary order. Spanish authorities did not consider evangelization of the Maya as work of the order until 1575, a change that was probably a result of the inadequate manpower of the Franciscans and Dominicans. Consequently, they were not financed by the king until then, and through the remainder of the colonial period only 46 Mercedarian priests were sent to Guatemala from Spain compared with 388 Franciscans and 231 Dominicans (see table 9.1). Since Mercedarian evangelization copied the goals and strategies of the Franciscans and Dominicans, they are usually included here whenever the term *friar* is used.

Sixteenth-Century Spanish Catholicism and the Primacy of Orthodoxy

At this period Christianity had an evolutionary history of sixteen hundred years behind it. Its theological expressions and interpretations had passed through several stages as summarized in Kung's (1999: end papers) paradigms, the first three of which are of concern here: (1) Early Christian, the Jewish phase, (2) Early Church, the Hellenic phase; and (3) Roman Catholic, the medieval phase. During these centuries there was a definite change in how Christianity presented itself, a shift from the Jewish worldview of early Christianity to a Hellenic theological expression with an emphasis on orthodoxy and later, a medieval view of a universal hierarchy of authority to enforce orthodoxy. To understand sixteenth-century Spanish Catholicism and what was presented to the Maya requires some knowledge of this evolution.

Christianity in the Early Church

Theologically, the shift from Jewish expression in most of the gospels took place through their narratives being explained in terms of the Hellenic worldview. This shift had its beginnings when early Christians were persecuted by both Jews and Gentiles. The Gentile persecutions "provoked early Christian theology. . . . The apologists, who all wrote in Greek, were the first Christian literary figures to present Christianity as credible to all interested parties by employing Hellenistic terms, views, and methods which could generally be understood. In so doing they showed themselves to be the first Christian theologians who sparked off in the catholic church an impetus toward Hellenization which is still tangible in the formulations of the faith" (Kung 2001: 24–25).[2]

The work of the apologists was followed by the Patristic period in which theologians applied categories of Greek philosophy to the biblical narrative.

This led to contentious theological disputes that were frequently entwined in power conflicts between rival sectors of the Roman Empire and their successors. In this period the correlated doctrines of the Trinity and Incarnation were formulated. "The Christian state religion was crowned by the dogma of the Trinity. Only now can this term be used, since the Second Ecumenical Council of Constantinople convened by Theodosius the Great in 381, defined the identity of substance of the Holy Spirit with the Father and the Son" (Kung 2001: 39). Although the dogmas of the Trinity and the Incarnation functioned within the framework of the Christian covenant, at times insistence on belief in these dogmas overshadowed other elements of the covenant logic.

Other important historical events influencing theological formulations were the threat of Gnosticism, Christianity being made the state religion, the development of the hierarchical church and the emergence of the papacy, divine-right kingships, efforts to hold the Roman Empire together, the split between Eastern and Western Christianity in 1054, and for Spanish Christianity, the centuries of Islamic rule.

All these conflicts and more resulted in sharply defined theological positions and an insistence on the orthodoxy of these positions, making orthodox belief the prime requisite for being a Christian. As a result of this paradigm shift, "one thing cannot be ignored from the beginning in this Hellenization of the gospel: now Christianity was understood less and less as existential discipleship of Jesus Christ and more—in an intellectual narrowing—as the acceptance of a revealed doctrine about God and Jesus Christ, the world and human beings" (Kung 1999: 134). Kung explains the intellectual narrowing that occurred in this shift from a Judaic to a Hellenic expression of Christianity.

> The negative effects of this Hellenization of Christian preaching were unmistakable. In accordance with its Hebraic origins the truth of Christianity was not to be seen, or theorized on; rather, it was to be done, practiced. . . . The Christian concept of truth was originally not contemplative and theoretical like the Greek concept, but operative and practical.
>
> But in Hellenistic Christianity the arguments turned less and less on the practical discipleship of Christ and more on the acceptance of a revealed teaching . . . [that] increasingly forced the Jesus of history into the background in favor of a doctrine and finally a church dogma of the Incarnate God. Whereas in Judaism from Jesus' time to the present day there have been arguments about the correct practice of the law, in Hellenized Christianity the arguments have been increasingly about the right, the orthodox, truth of faith. (Kung 2001: 26)

Sixteenth-Century Spanish Christianity

Beginning in the fifteenth century, two additional situations arose that increased the emphasis on orthodoxy within Spanish Christianity.

Spanish Unification

As discussed in chapter 6, with the unification of Spain under Isabella and Ferdinand, the Catholic faith became the foundation of Spanish cultural unity with a consequent insistence on orthodoxy. For this purpose the Inquisition was established in 1478, primarily to root out Jewish and Muslim converts who were still practicing their religion in secret. In 1492 unconverted Jews were expelled from the country and in 1502 the Muslims from Castile. The Spanish friars were caught up in this environment of orthodoxy in opposition to non-Christian religions. Therefore, in addition to the pressures for orthodoxy arising from a Hellenized Christianity, the friars in the New World had a strong additional pressure arising from the fact that they were Spaniards.

Reform of Popular Devotion Christianity

The previous chapter described the emergence of a Christianity centered on popular devotions to the saints that included a number of unorthodox practices. A reactionary reform movement was brewing. Some demanded radical reforms, which led to the Protestant Reformation and included the suppression of the saints. Others wanted reform but were unwilling to go the Protestant route. One of the leaders of this reform movement was Erasmus who condemned many devotional practices in his voluminous writings: "someone will begin to talk of the great superstition of certain people in worshipping and invoking the saints, and we too in our writings have frequently warned against it. Many ask from the saints what they would not dare to ask from an upright person, and they do not think that the saints will hear them unless they are won over by certain rituals, almost magical in nature. What they ask for from one saint they do not ask from another, as if particular functions are assigned to each one" (Erasmus 1998: 197–99). "Some ask the saints for a healthy mind as if they are not simply intercessors, but the source of such things" (Erasmus 1963: 99).

At times Erasmus excoriates such practices. "What superstition there is in many places when the relics of the saints are shown! In England the shoe of Saint Thomas, the former bishop of Canterbury, is offered to be kissed. This shoe perhaps belonged to a jester, and even if it is Thomas' what is sillier than to venerate a man's shoe? When they were showing the torn pieces of linen with which he is said to have wiped his nose and the little case that contained them was opened, I myself saw the abbot and all the others who were standing take up the posture of worship; they were filled with reverence, they fell to their knees and even raised their hands" (Erasmus 1998: 198).

Erasmus sees many practices of devotion for the saints as pagan in origin, and he warns against the magical use of fixed prayer formulas: "I have pointed out three prayer formulas, although nothing forbids us from revealing our feelings to God in whatever words we wish, especially when we pray alone. We must, however, ask in the name of Jesus and seek what does not conflict with the goal of eternal salvation and is not at odds with the Lord's prescription for us in his prayer. It was not safe for pagans to invoke Jupiter other than in the proper rites and words, and it is dangerous for someone not knowing the established formulas of speaking to speak before a king or a judge. Although God is above all others, he is not, however, fastidious in this kind of thing; he thinks well of everything he hears, he is not offended by solecisms, provided the mind is pure" (Erasmus 1998: 212).

The reform model of Erasmus wanted a return to the early church and a Pauline vision of Christianity with its Christocentric covenant. "So that we will not imitate the Jews in trying to ingratiate ourselves with God by means of certain rituals, as if there were some magic in ceremonies, he [Paul] teaches us that our works are pleasing to God only to the extent that they are consonant with charity and have originated in charity. 'Above all these things,' he [Paul] says, 'hold fast to love, which is the bond of perfection, and let the peace of Christ the Lord, in which you have been called members in one Body, triumph in your hearts'" (Erasmus 1963: 118).

In Spain the reform movement was initiated by Cardinal Cisneros and promulgated by Alfonso de Valdés (Bataillon 1966). The Franciscans and Dominicans were part of the movement. The friars saw their missionary work in the New World as an attempt to implement the ideal Christian community espoused by the reform (Rubial 1978). Some saw their work as part of the preaching of the gospel to the whole world, a sign of the end of the world and the second coming of Christ. Since many friars had been brought up with devotions to the saints, reform did not mean suppression as it did for the more radical reformers.

Doctrina: The Content of Evangelization

With this background shaping their worldview, the friars undertook the communication of Christianity to the Maya. In any contact situation only a portion of the donor culture is communicated (Foster 1960: 8). Following the Reconquista, the Spaniards wrote manuals summarizing Catholic doctrine for the instruction of Muslims and Jews. These summaries were called *doctrinas* in Spanish and were used as the basis for translations of catechetical materials into the Indian languages.[3] An examination of three examples shows the specific content that the evangelization effort was trying to communicate.

The Doctrina of Alonso de Molina

The manual of Alonso de Molina (1941, 1984) was typical and widely used by both Franciscans and secular priests (Ricard 1966: 101). Clendinnen (1987: 215) thinks it was the basis for Landa's translation into Yukatek. Around 1570 the Franciscans of the Mexican Province prepared a detailed report of their activities for the king. It included a copy of the shorter version of Molina's catechism in both Spanish and Nahuatl, with a note that it was the best catechism both linguistically and pedagogically and should be used as the basis for translations into other Indian languages (Anonymous 1941: 29). Molina was born in Spain but brought up in Mexico speaking both Spanish and Nahuatl. During his life Molina's primary effort was to translate Christian doctrine into the Nahuatl language for the benefit of his fellow Franciscans and for Nahuatl speakers (Moreno 1984: 9). Molina's catechism was published in two versions: an elaborated version of which there is no known surviving copy, and in 1546 the *Doctrina breve,* a shorter version for wide circulation (Duran 1984: 366–75).

Table 8.1 lists the contents of the *Doctrina.* It opens with a prologue stating that its contents were to be learned by all Indian children in order to save their souls and to know what to respond when questioned about Christianity. Learning in this context means memorization. The first five topics are prayer formulas. These prayers were considered the first thing every Christian should know. The creed is treated as a prayer, although it is a statement of orthodox belief rather than a prayer in the more usual sense of an honorific salutation or petition. The fourteen articles of faith describe the attributes of God and summarize the biblical Jesus story. This section is the core explanation of Christian belief. For the most part the remaining topics are an ascetical-psychological model that serves as a basis for the practice of a Christian life. Molina simply lists most of the topics by name with a brief descriptive phrase. This apparently served as a basis for quick memorization. The topics were probably explained in the longer version that has been lost. In brief, the catechism contains several prayers and in a popular and pedagogical form, the highlights of Catholic dogmatic, moral, and ascetical theology.

The Doctrina of Bishop Marroquín

Although Alvarado brought Francisco Marroquín to Guatemala to minister to Spaniards, the future bishop quickly took an interest in the Mayan population and began learning Kaqchikel. Probably using Molina's doctrina as a model, Marroquín composed one for his diocese with the assistance of the Franciscan Juan de Torres and the Dominican Pedro Betanzos, both of whom had

Table 8.1. Contents of Doctrinas by Molina, Marroquín, and Córdoba

Molina	Marroquín	Córdoba
Prologue	Prologue	—
Sign of the cross	Sign of the Cross	Sign of the Cross
Creed	Our Father	—
Our Father	Hail Mary	—
Hail Mary	Creed	—
Hail, Holy Queen	Hail, Holy Queen	—
14 Articles of Faith	14 Articles of Faith	14 Articles of Faith
10 Commandments of God	10 Commandments of God	—
5 Commandments of Church	5 Commandments of Church	—
7 Sacraments	7 Sacraments	7 Sacraments
9 Venial Sins	9 Venial Sins	—
7 Mortal (Capital) Sins	Mortal Sin	—
Virtues opposed to Capital Sins	4 Things that Pardon Mortal Sins	—
3 Theological Virtues	7 Mortal (Capital) Sins	—
4 Cardinal Virtues	7 Virtues opposed to Mortal Sins	—
7 Corporal Works of Mercy	Enemies of our Souls	—
7 Spiritual Works of Mercy	7 Corporal Works of Mercy	7 Corporal Works of Mercy
7 Gifts of the Holy Spirit	7 Spiritual Works of Mercy	7 Spiritual Works of Mercy
5 Senses	General confession	—
3 Powers of the Soul	How a Christian should hear mass	—
3 Enemies of the Soul	What must be done on entering a church	—
8 Beatitudes	—	—
4 Qualities of Glorified Body	Blessing before and after meals	—
Obligation of Godparents	Declaration of Faith	—
Formula for General Confession	Act of Contrition	—
13 Questions before Baptism	"Alabado" hymn	—
Exhortation to Newly Baptized	—	—
Blessing before and after	—	Blessing before and after
Meals (Latin)	—	Meals (Latin)
Colophon	—	Short History of the World

Sources: Molina 1941, 1984; Marroquín 1905; Córdoba 1970.

worked in Mexico. It may have been originally written in K'iche', although the only surviving copy, printed in 1556, is in Kaqchikel (Medina 1905). Table 8.1 compares its sections with those of Molina's doctrina. The main bodies of the two doctrinas are almost identical with only a slight shift in order. In the final section Marroquín dropped most of the moral-ascetical model for living and substituted an extended section on what the Maya should do and what prayers should be said upon entering church and attending mass.

The Doctrina of Pedro de Córdoba

By way of contrast, the manual of Pedro de Córdoba (1970) is much shorter but highlights the core of the friars' message. It was probably the first doctrina produced in the New World, written shortly after 1510 in Santo Domingo. Pedro de Córdoba worked with Indians in Hispaniola, quickly became a defender of their rights, clashed with Spanish authorities over his denunciations of slavery, and encouraged Las Casas to join the Dominican order. In 1544 this manual was one of the first books to be printed in the New World. The topics it covers are also listed in table 8.1. The colophon by the second bishop of Mexico City, Domingo Betanzos, states, "The Bishop requests and implores the holy fathers to be diligent in the instruction and conversion of the Indians. And, above all, to preach and make them understand this short and plain doctrine, since they well know the Indians' capacity for learning and their greater need for this than for other sermons that may be preached to them. This doctrine [doctrina] will serve better for beginners . . . because of the style and manner that it bears toward the Indians, and it will be of great profit to them, and will suit best their capacity" (Córdoba 1970: 135–36).

Pedro de Córdoba attempted to adapt his explanations to the indigenous mentality as the Spaniards perceived it. The booklet was probably primarily intended for use by the friars themselves, giving them a template and suggestions for the content of their preaching oriented toward the immediate goal of conversion with further instruction considered a later task. It lacks the emphasis on confession and the ascetical psychology of Molina's work. In Hispaniola and Cuba the friars probably heard few indigenous confessions due to the language barrier and lack of opportunity for instruction.

The opening paragraph of the manual explains the presence of the friars among the Indians and shows an effort at adaptation absent in the other doctrinas:

My dearly beloved brothers: I want you to know and to understand that we love you dearly and through this love that we have for you, we have suffered great hardships in coming from distant lands and crossing wide seas. And we have subjected ourselves to many risks of death, in order to come to see you and to tell you about the great and marvelous secrets that God has revealed to us. We have come so that we may tell this to you, and so that we may inform you of the wonders that God has given us and of the great joys and pleasures that will be given us in Heaven. These joys and delights are of such quality that as soon as you learn about them and understand them, you will prize them more than all the gold and silver and precious stones, and even more than all the wealth there is in the world. We beg you, therefore, to remain very attentive to our words and to try diligently to understand them, because they are the words of God. He has commanded us to tell you all of this because He wants to make you His children so that He can give you the very great wealth, pleasures and delights that you have never seen or heard until now. (Córdoba 1970: 53–54)

The Essence of the Message: The Fourteen Articles

The three manuals contain the fourteen articles of faith that were the common denominator of all the doctrinas. A comparison of these doctrinas with those of the Dominicans in New Spain, of Bishop Zumárraga, and of Pedro de Feria, shows their presentation of the articles to be almost identical (Borges 1960: 309–10). The doctrina of Pedro de Córdoba opens with a brief introduction that contains the heart of the message the friars were attempting to convey (see figure 8.1).

> First, please know that for God to love you dearly, and for Him to carry your souls and bodies to heaven, and for Him to lift you up to the place of His palace and large house, so that you may enjoy the great blessings and pleasures, it is first necessary for you to know God, and to know who God is, and what He is like. You must learn and believe fourteen things that we call the fourteen Articles of Faith. Anyone who wants to be a good Christian must learn and believe these Articles of Faith firmly, without any doubt whatsoever. (Córdoba 1970: 57)

Figure 8.1. The bishop of San Cristóbal preaching in Zinacantán.

He summarizes the contents of the articles:

[There are] seven Articles of Faith that pertain to the divinity of God.
. . . With the first we know and confess that there is one God and not
many gods. With the other three we know and confess that God is in
three persons: Father, Son and Holy Spirit. With the other three we know
the powers that belong only to God. You should remember that He is the
Creator who created all things from nothing. He is the pardoner of our
sins. He alone is the one who can forgive our sins. And He is receiver of
the dead and the rewarder and glorifier of the good.

There are seven other Articles, or acknowledgments of Faith, that pertain to the humanity of our Lord and Savior Jesus Christ . . . that is to God
in the form of man.

In the first we learn that the Son of God became the Son of Holy Mary,
and that He took on human form in her womb, and became man, not
through the aid of any male, but through the power of God and Mary
who remained a virgin.

In the second we learn that she bore Him miraculously, because Mary
remained a virgin.

In the third we learn that the Son of God, in the form of man, died in
order to free us from the power of the devil and of Hell and to carry us
with Him to heaven.

In the fourth we learn that He descended into Hell with His soul, and
He removed Adam and Eve, our first parents, and all the other saints who
were there awaiting His holy arrival.

In the fifth we learn that on the third day He arose from the dead.

In the sixth we learn that in the form of man He ascended into heaven
forty days after He arose from the dead.

In the seventh we learn that He is to come to judge the quick [living]
and dead at the end of the world, and He will give eternal punishment to
the evil and eternal glory to the good. (84, 98)

This is an explanation of Jesus within the Hellenized framework of the
Trinity and Incarnation. The fourteen articles define Christianity, and their
communication to the Maya was the ideal goal of the evangelization effort in
Guatemala, Chiapas, and Yucatán. Later, they will serve the methodological
purpose of analyzing whether the friars were able to accomplish their goal of
conversion.

The Saints

The content of the doctrinas was influenced by the European Catholic reform
movement. They were Christocentric with practically no mention of the saints

or devotions to them. The Virgin is an exception, but in Catholic orthodoxy she is a sacred being superior to the saints but less than a goddess. In spite of their omission in the doctrinas, however, the saints were part of the friars' message. The colophon at the end of Molina's catechism gives instructions about the way services were to be conducted on Sundays and Holy Days of Obligation. In discussing preaching it advises,

> one of the things that the Indians of New Spain will greatly benefit from in confirming themselves in the law of Christ and in making themselves new men capable of many spiritual goods which they are lacking at present would be to interpret in their language the life of Christ our Redeemer and the lives of his saints. For this reason a book with this material should be printed and a copy kept in every town. From it should be read the life of each of the saints on their feast day. This will serve as a sermon when there is no friar present. In order that [the Indians] know and reject the vanity and misery of the world and follow the true path of their salvation, we know that one of the things that always moves human hearts is to read and understand from one's earliest years the life of Jesus Christ and the lives of his saints. In order that this kind of reading have such great value, the first thing to do is to translate [from Latin into Spanish] the "Flos Sanctorum" [Noble Lives of the Saints]. (1941: 60)

In this way the saints entered into the preaching of the friars. Examples from the lives of the saints were preached in Zinacantán (Remesal 1966: 40). Among the K'iche', "It happened in this kingdom [Utatlán] that a little after being conquered [they heard] the lives of Christ and Our Lady, John the Baptist, and Saint Peter and others, which the friars taught them." Saint Paul is mentioned later in the same passage (Ximénez 1929: 57).

Summary

The primary goal of the friars was the conversion of the Maya to Christianity. The content of conversion was the fourteen articles contained in all the doctrinas. In the friars' eyes this knowledge would enable the salvation of the Indians' souls and thereby prevent the damnation of hell to which they were presently headed because of their worship of idols under the influence of Satan. The monotheism of Christianity required the Maya to renounce the pantheistic basis of their covenant and its rituals. For the friars, there could be no compromise on this issue. An additional goal of conversion was to make the Maya loyal subjects of the king as Christianity was to be the basis of the cultural unity of the Spanish Empire.

9

The Strategy for Communicating the Doctrina

Once the goals of evangelization had been established, the bishops and friars had to decide how to implement them.

The Infrastructure of the New World Church

Prior to carrying out its mission, the church had to organize its infrastructure in the New World. The initial step was the creation of dioceses with the recruitment of manpower as the first priority of their bishops.

Guatemala

The following account of Guatemala is drawn from Sáenz de Santa María (1964) and O'Flaherty (1979: 59–62, 105–17, 150–66). In 1530 a secular priest,

Francisco Marroquín, arrived in Almolonga, then the site of the Guatemalan capital. The previous year he had arrived in Mexico with the Franciscan Zumárraga, the first bishop of that city, as his vicar general (an ecclesiastical term for an aide-de-camp and second in command). Zumárraga quickly ran into difficulties with the king's officials, making Marroquín's situation difficult. Alvarado, whom Marroquín had known in Spain, invited him to come to Guatemala as a preacher for the Spanish citizens of the capital, many of whom were encomenderos. At that time there were only two priests in the city, Juan Godinez, a chaplain in Alvarado's expedition, and another priest who soon left for El Salvador. Marroquín became interested in the Maya and started to learn the Kaqchikel language. In 1537 Guatemala was made a diocese that included El Salvador, Honduras, Yucatán, and Chiapas. Marroquín was appointed its bishop. It was a suffragan diocese subject to the archbishop of Mexico City as were Puebla, Oaxaca, and later Chiapas and Yucatán (including the Petén) when they were made independent dioceses. Verapaz was made an independent diocese in the latter part of the sixteenth century but was reincorporated into the Guatemalan diocese in 1608.

The immediate problem was manpower. Marroquín continually implored Spain for help to carry out his mandate. He requested that fifty religious priests be sent and told the king that even five hundred priests would not be enough. He also sought financial support for the priests, buildings, ritual materials, and adornments for the churches. Shortly before 1540 the Franciscans were in residence in the capital and Quetzaltenango, from which they visited several nearby towns. In 1541 the Dominicans entered Verapaz. At the same time Franciscans were active in Santiago Atitlán and Dominicans in Tecpán.

Chiapas

In 1539 Chiapas was made a separate diocese from Guatemala and evangelization assigned to the Dominicans (Aubry 1988; Gosner 1992: 28–68). The first two appointed bishops never arrived due to the resignation of one and the death of the other. In 1543 the Dominican Bartolomé de las Casas was named bishop, but he did not arrive until late 1545. In the same year the Dominicans took up residence in Zinacantán before moving to Ciudad Real (San Cristóbal) in 1547. From there, they developed a network of residences to carry out evangelization.

Yucatán

Evangelization in Yucatán was entrusted solely to the Franciscans (Farriss 1984: 24). From 1535 to 1537 they were in Champoton, but had to leave because of warfare in the still-unpacified region. They re-entered the area after 1542. From Champoton the Franciscans evangelized Acalan beginning in 1550. Some caciques still resisted the Spaniards and, aided by the Mayan priests, led an uprising over much of the peninsula in 1546–47. Following its suppression, the Franciscans continued their work. In 1549 they held their first chapter meeting, and in 1561 there was sufficient manpower to erect a Franciscan province (a defined area of administration). In the same year Yucatán was made an independent diocese with the Franciscan Francisco de Toral as its first bishop.

Friars from Spain

In response to the urgent requests of Marroquín, Las Casas, and others, the Dominicans and Franciscans began sending personnel to the Mayan region. Table 9.1 shows the number of friars sent from Spain by the king during the colonial period. Almost eleven hundred friars were sent to the Mayan regions to bring about their conversion, about 72 percent were Franciscans, 21 percent were Dominicans, and 7 percent Mercedarians.

In the early years of the dioceses Spain was the principal source of personnel, although a few friars with previous experience were sent from Mexico where the orders had been active for almost twenty years. Later the entrance of creoles into the orders would supplement the Spaniards and diminish the numbers sent from Spain. Strong support for Yucatán did not come until the seventeenth century. The Mayan regions competed for missionaries with all the other regions of the New World, influencing when, to where, and how many Spanish missionaries were dispatched. Mexico and Peru received a total of 35.7 percent of all the friars sent by the king (Oss 1986: 7), probably due to both their larger Indian populations and Spanish populations drawn by their mineral resources. The low priority given to Guatemala-Chiapas and Yucatán is indicated by the fact that they received only 6.4 percent and 2.9 percent respectively of all missionaries sent from Spain by the king.

Table 9.1 does not include all types of friars, only friar-priests. *Friar* refers to a man who has taken the three traditional vows of poverty, chastity, and obedience in an order whose members emphasize poverty, that is, mendicants. There were three classes of friars: friar-priests, friar-brothers, and friar-seminarians. Friar-brothers were not ordained as priests and usually performed manual work or artisan tasks to provide logistical support for the friar-priests. During the colonial period the Franciscans sent seventeen brothers to Guatemala and twelve to Yucatán; the Dominicans sent nine to Guatemala-Chiapas. Friar-seminarians were men in the process of studying to be priests and took the three vows on a temporary basis for this period. The Franciscans sent thirty-seven seminarians to Guatemala and eleven to Yucatán; the Dominicans sent forty-six to Guatemala-Chiapas; and the Mercedarians sent four to Guatemala. A fourth group sent from Spain were lay helpers. These were laymen who worked for the orders, either as volunteers or for wages, but were not members

Table 9.1. Number of Friar-Priests Sent from Spain by the King, 1530–1800

Year	Guatemala-Chiapas[b]			Yucatán	Friars[a]	Total
	OFM	OP	MR	OFM	per Year	Friars
1530–39	20				20	20
1540–49	12				12	32
1550–59		7		16	23	55
1560–69	1	70		16	87	142
1570–79	46	28	12		86	228
1580–89	64		24		88	316
1590–99	65	30	13		108	424
1600–09	40	20		13	73	497
1610–19	35		17	24	76	573
1620–29				12	12	585
1630–39				58	58	643
1640–49				20	20	663
1650–59	6			40	46	709
1660–69	6	19			25	734
1670–79	10	16		12	38	772
1680–89	40	26	4	22	92	864
1690–99				30	30	894
1700–09		15		19	34	928
1710–19	6			12	18	946
1720–39					0	946
1740–49	11			19	30	976
1750–59	10			19	29	1,005
1760–79					0	1,005
1780–89	16			20	36	1,041
1790–99				30	30	1,071
Total	388	231	70	382		1,071
	36.2%	21.6%	6.5%	35.7%		100%

Source: Borges 1977: 477–535.
Notes: OFM: Franciscans; OP: Dominicans; MR: Mercedarians
a. Although the numbers in the table show the bulk of the Spanish departures, they are deficient in two respects. They overstate the number dispatched because they do not distinguish multiple crossings by the same individuals. On the other hand, they understate the departures by not including those sent directly and financed by the Orders themselves. I have removed those listed as dying en route.
b. The figures for Guatemala and Chiapas are combined in this table because in Borges 1977 there are only two entries for Chiapas, all Dominicans. All other Dominicans are listed with Guatemala as their destination. Although Guatemala and Chiapas were separate dioceses, all the Dominicans belonged to the same province under the jurisdiction of the Dominican provincial, and consequently, the friars were easily moved between the two dioceses.

of the orders. The Franciscans sent twenty-five laymen to Guatemala and four to Yucatán.

Towns as Instruments for Accessing, Civilizing, and Converting the Maya

With the establishment of the dioceses, the entrusting of evangelization to the orders of friars, and the translation of the doctrinas completed, the next step was a strategy for contacting and instructing the Maya. Evangelization among the Maya began around 1540 in Guatemala, 1545 in Chiapas, and 1550 in Yucatán, approximately twenty or more years later than in central Mexico. Consequently, these regions drew upon the Mexican experience and the models formulated there (Poole 1992: 26). Guatemala, Chiapas, and Yucatán were considered backwaters compared to central Mexico. The major towns were few, silver and gold were scarce, and therefore fewer Spanish settlers were attracted to these regions.

A basic premise of Spanish thinking about civilization in general and religion in particular was the importance of towns. The Spaniards thought they first had to civilize the indigenous peoples by congregating them into towns, and only with this as a foundation could they hope to Christianize them (Borges 1960: 203–44).

> [The Spaniards] invested settlement patterns with a moral and symbolic significance that had at least as much to do with their own need to establish boundaries as it did with the need to supervise Indian behavior. . . . Settlement formed a part of a dyadic code, in which the world was divided into two opposing parts, town and forest. The town represented Christianity, civilization and indeed all that was human life, in contrast with the forest, where wild beasts lurked and man risked being overwhelmed morally as well as physically by the untamed forces of nature. . . . Armed with the general cultural bias in favor of town life, reinforced by the not wholly fanciful conviction that once the Indians were outside the town limits they could and would do as they chose, the friars maintained consistently throughout their ministry in Yucatan that Christianity could prevail only if the Indians were all gathered together under the watchful eye of their pastors. (Farriss 1986: 160–61)

This was also the view in Guatemala. In 1548 Bishop Marroquín wrote the king: "One of the three principal and necessary things for the good of the Indians is to bring them together because without this there can be no civilized living; for this reason Your Highness has sent me two cédulas [royal decrees] so that the religious and I might bring this about. Since this is a matter of the greatest importance, let Your Majesty order that a judge or two give it their heartfelt attention so that we may give them as much of civilized life as they can absorb" (O'Flaherty 1979: 200).

Towns were needed for other reasons. Most Maya were corn farmers living in or near their cornfields. Many of the inhabitants of the pre-Columbian towns had fled at the approach of the Spaniards. This created the logistical problem of contacting them for instruction in the doctrina and administration of the sacraments. The encomenderos had a similar problem with regard to management of Mayan labor and the collection of tribute. Therefore, to civilize and gain access to the Maya, Spanish authorities decreed that they were to be gathered into towns. This task was given to the friars who with the assistance of the Mayan elites engaged in concentrating the Mayan populations. Descent groups from several settlements were frequently congregated into different sections of a single town called *parcialidades* (wards).

Types of Towns

Instead of attempting to increase contact with the Maya by placing a priest in as many towns as possible, the friars followed a pattern that was dictated by the necessities of their semimonastic communal life. Because the friars perceived the prayers and rituals of the monastic routine as necessary for seeking God's help to bring about the conversion of the Maya, maintaining this lifestyle was a high priority. In the larger towns called *residencias* they built living quarters (monasteries) usually for two to four friars. This was the communal residence with an adjoining church where the Divine Office was chanted daily. With at least one friar constantly present in these towns, the friars could implement more of their idealized plan (discussed later).

From these towns of residencia (or cabeceras de doctrina) the friars would travel to outlying towns or villages (*visitas*) to implement as much of their plan as feasible. The ideal was to be present every Sunday to preach, teach, and administer the sacraments, returning to the monastery the same or the following day to resume the routine of communal life.

As the number of friars increased, some would take up permanent residence in visitas, making them residencias. This would allow the friars to enter more distant towns or increase their trips to other visita towns. This pattern can be seen in Momostenango (Carmack 1995: 54–55). Around 1540 Franciscan friars based in Quetzaltenango visited the area. In 1542 the friars with the help of the local cacique congregated the people into the present town. Sometime before 1550 a church was constructed. In 1587 three Franciscans took up permanent residence in Momostenango, changing it from a visita to a residencia, and from there visited the towns of Santa Maria Chiquimula and San Bartolo Aguas Calientes.

The Churches and Their Patron Saints

In both types of towns the friars gradually organized resources and labor for building churches. The friars preferred simplicity in their churches, which meant minimal ornamentation—"in theory carving was banned and even moldings were frowned upon. . . . The lavish church is as rare in sixteenth century Mexico as the simple one of comparable size in Spain" (McAndrew 1965: 175). The first churches were small, with flat rather than vaulted roofs. In central Mexico, "The nave was long, high and plain. Ordinarily its walls were uninterruptedly flat. . . . Often the surfaces were enlivened with didactic black-and-white paintings in imitation of European models" (McAndrew 1965: 137). At that time the Spanish were more interested in painting than sculpture, a preference reinforced by the high cost of sculpture relative to painting.

The interiors of the churches were furnished with the typical Catholic altar above which was a statue or picture of the saint designated as the town's patron and whose name was added to the existing Mayan name for the town itself. Again Momostenango provides an example (Carmack 1995: 53–58). Santiago became the town's patron. Sometime before 1550 the first church was built. This means that mass kits with their picture of Santiago (to be discussed in chapter 12) were used for five to ten years prior to construction of a church. In 1587 the Spanish established the town governance (cabildo) and divided the town into four wards whose populations were drawn from preconquest descent groups (Cook 2000: 193; Hill and Monaghan 1987: 43–62). A patron saint and corresponding festival ritual was assigned to each of these wards: Santiago, Santa Isabel, Santa Ana, and Santa Catarina.

Initially, the friars took a guarded attitude toward sculpted human figures. "In the [Nahua] cities of the most advanced cultures there had been large workshops devoted to making sculpture. Inasmuch as their repertory was entirely religious, the Spaniards looked upon the native sculptors as heathen idol-makers" (McAndrew 1965: 195). It is not known whether any images were shipped to the Mayan region from Mexico City where artisans carved some images for the cathedral. In 1598–99 some images were sent from Spain to Guatemala to be used as the main pieces above altars: an image of St. Francis to the Franciscan monastery in Santiago de Guatemala and an additional one to be used in processions; images of St. John the Baptist to Comalapa and Alotenango; and a Santiago image to Santiago Atitlán (Vazquez 1938: 315). King Charles V sent an image of the Virgin to Antigua (Vazquez 1940: 67).

A ward could honor its patron saint in numerous ways. The more common arrangement seems to have been to build a small shrine or chapel in the ward itself where an image of the saint was placed and cared for. As the population increased, these shrines were expanded and became churches. Another arrangement was for the ward to buy an image of its patron and place it in the town church where a cofradía from the ward cared for it. In central Mexico some wards built chapels for their patrons on the perimeter of the large plaza in front of the church (McAndrew 1965: 280). This appears to have been the case in Santiago Atitlán in Guatemala.

Liturgy and Teaching the Doctrina

The colophon added to the 1557 edition of Molina's manual designates that all or only part of the doctrina should be taught according to the mental capacity and social status of the individual being instructed (Molina 1941: 54). Children and nonliterate adults were to be taught only "what any faithful Christian should know, the ordinary doctrina." This included all the topics from the sign of the cross to the seven capital sins and the formula for a general confession (see table 8.1). A concession was made for elderly or mentally slow people. They were required to know only the sign of the cross, the Our Father, the Hail Mary, and the fourteen articles of faith. Before anyone received the sacraments of baptism, confirmation, confession, the Eucharist, or matrimony, the friar was first to quiz them to make sure they could repeat the required doctrina for their respective group. All those who knew how to read—that is, those who had attended the monastery schools—had to know all the topics of the doctrina (Anonymous 1941: 55).

Below are schedules for the liturgy and doctrina sessions of Franciscan towns in 1648 and 1689 (Vazquez 1944: 343, with additional information from his other account on pages 34–37 enclosed in curly brackets). While differing slightly, the accounts are in basic agreement, and each adds some information not included in the others. As described in chapter 5, prior to the arrival of the Spaniards, the Maya had classes of religious instruction to prepare the youth for their later roles in the community. Children were divided by social standing, elite versus commoners. The friars used the same division in their schedules of instruction (Anonymous 1941: 55–65; Vazquez 1944: 34–37, 343).

Towns of Residencia

Since the friars were in residence in these towns, there was a daily liturgy as well as a doctrina session.

Every Weekday

The daily order in these towns included doctrina lessons for sons of commoners and for all daughters, both commoners and elite. (The education of the sons of the elite is discussed later.)

> Every day without fail the church bell would ring for mass, and the community mass would be sung or said. The cofradía officials and the "texeles" [female cofradía members] attend and hold lighted wax candles from the entrance prayer of the canon of the mass until the Communion of the priest. The organ is played even though the mass is not sung. Other prayers are said according to the number of priests in residence [probably the third canonical hour of the Divine Office].
>
> Every day at two o'clock in the afternoon the bell is rung to assemble in the church all the young girls of the town six years and older until [they are] married. For about two hours they recite all the doctrina and the prayers in answer to questions. Two old Indian principales called fiscales conduct the lesson. Immediately afterward, the priest . . . rewards those who excel with candy, bread, or a pinch of tobacco, which the Indians generally like. At four o'clock every day vespers are sung. At sunset the young boys of the town {after returning from the cornfields} gather in front of the church and recite the doctrina and prayers {as far as the Hail Mary} as the girls had done in the afternoon. {At both sessions the friar in charge of doctrina is present to see to it that there is no error in pronunciation, that all attend who are on the church roll, and that the recitation is done with restraint and devotion.}
>
> After evening supper those who work in the priest's house and the sacristy ascend the bell tower to toll the De Profundis prayer for deceased souls and to sing the whole doctrina. It is wonderful to hear them because many have fine voices. In the silence of the evening from the height of the bell tower, it sounds very nice. . . . This group is on duty in weekly shifts and in this way, they do not forget the religious education they have received. (Vazquez 1944: 34–37, 343)

Daily an elderly man in each ward of the town would gather the children and march them to the church to attend mass. There they would be divided into small groups and instructed in the doctrina. Afterwards they would be returned home where the commoners would work with their parents for the remainder of the day.

The towns of residencia constructed stations of the cross that the faithful walked every Friday during Lent carrying an image of Christ. On returning from the last station, they chanted the rosary (Vazquez 1944: 37).

Sundays and Feast Days

On these days all the adults, both commoners and elite, as well as their children, were involved.

> On feast days the third hour of the Office and the mass are always sung. The tower bells are rung at intervals, which gives the whole town time to get to the church, no matter how large the town may be. {A sermon was usually preached in the Mayan language of the town.} When the mass is finished, the doors of the church are shut and all the prayers learned in the doctrina are recited, including the Our Father, the articles of faith, and the teaching about death, judgment, heaven, and hell. This is done by responding to questions about the doctrina (taught in the Mayan language), beginning with the teacher in the choir loft and proceeding through everyone in the church, first the men and then the women. Usually the priest in charge of the doctrina attends, seated in the larger side chapel. (Vazquez 1944: 34–37, 343)

The account accompanying Molina's work has a slightly different order.

> On Sundays and Holy Days of Obligation, this is the procedure to be followed: at dawn the Indians are to be gathered in the patio of the church and kept separate according to the wards from which their officials have the duty to collect each one of them. These officials are to take the roll . . . and when finished, they are to be seated to hear the sermon. But before the sermon, they are to recite out loud the doctrina two or three times. Then a friar should preach to them in their own language. After the sermon, the friar sings the mass. Following the mass at about nine o'clock, they are to return to their houses. (Anonymous 1941: 58–59)

Towns of Visita

The bulk of the Mayan population lived either in visitas or the far-flung areas theoretically served by them. Ideally, every week the friar would leave the monastery for a visita on Saturday evening or Sunday morning to preach, celebrate the mass, baptize, hear confessions, and quiz the children about the doctrina learned the previous week. Upon completion of these tasks, the friar returned to the monastery. As will be seen later, some towns were visited once a month, others once a year, and still others only once every several years (see figures 9.1 and 9.2).

Figure 9.1. The chapel in the village of Apas, Zinacantán. A priest seldom visits this village.

Figure 9.2. The chapel in the hamlet of Salinas, Zinacantán. No priest ever comes to this chapel.

Every Weekday

Since no friars were in residence in the visitas, there was no liturgy during the week, only the doctrina lesson. The daily routine here included the sons of commoners and all daughters, both common and elite. "Even though there is no priest present, all come for the instruction in the towns of visita just as in the towns of residencia, because they know that every week at least they will be examined. And so they come, even though they are only with the teacher of the doctrina, the fiscal. In this way both the boys and girls know they cannot be married by the church without being examined" (Vazquez 1944: 343). The weekly examination would be conducted by the priest during his Sunday visit.

Sundays and Feast Days When a Priest Visited

On these days all adults, commoners and elite, with their children attended services and instruction.

> In villages where there are no resident priests, almost the same routine [as in towns of residencia] is followed. A priest travels to these towns the day before the fiesta if it is a league [about three miles] or more distant from the town of residence. If it is closer, he goes at dawn on Sunday. ... It is rare that an Indian town does not have mass on Sundays and feast days of obligation. {A sermon is preached if the priest is qualified in the Mayan language.} If some are sick, the sacrament is administered if it is necessary. He baptizes the infants who have been born recently so that an infant seldom reaches eight days before it is baptized. The doctrina is recited after mass in the same manner as in the town of residencia. If the priest arrives on Saturday or is detained by the celebration of a festival, he examines and assists at the doctrina instruction of the boys and girls at the appropriate hours. (Vazquez 1944: 34–37, 343)

Enforcement of Religious Instruction

These descriptions present the Franciscan view of a liturgical utopia and wildly exaggerate the acceptance and cooperation of the Maya. The reports from the Mercedarian doctrinas note the difficulties of persuading the Maya to attend Sunday masses and doctrina sessions (Ruz et al. 2002 I: 426, 447, 452). In an agricultural community, the time requirement alone was a great burden. Chapter 6 described the Spanish use of force with regard to the *Requerimiento*. This applied not only to the conquest itself, but also to evangelization. The friars saw the broad task of civilizing the Maya as part of their mission. Since frequently they were the only Spaniards in direct contact with the Indians, they assumed powers normally belonging to civil authority. Following Mendieta's thesis of mitigated force, the friars imposed physical punishment for failure to attend doctrina lessons and the liturgy. After taking the roll and noting the absentees, the friars would order the fiscal to

> give those who fail to be present when they should be six lashes on top of their clothing. When anyone fails to be present for their share of community work in the church, even if it is a slight matter, they should receive some lashes. This includes those whose duty it is to gather the work crews. Punishment is done in matters temporal or spiritual for no other reason than to save and control them [the Indians], because they are like children and to control them, they must be treated in the same way as schoolteachers treat their young students. When they fail to know the lesson or misbehave, they are to be punished with six lashes. (Anonymous 1941: 58–59)

In Verapaz the following punishments were used for failure to attend the doctrina lessons. For the first offense the individual was to stand in the stocks for three hours; for the second offense, six hours; and for the third offense, the head was to be put in the stocks for three hours and the person could be whipped if the town authorities so decreed (Tovilla 1960: 130). These punishments are slightly different from those listed in the Franciscan document, probably because Verapaz was a Dominican region. Later, enforcement became one of the duties of Mayan civil officials instead of church personnel (Ruz et al. 2002 I: 426, 447, 452). These punishments show the friars' estimation of the Maya as childlike. Ximénez excoriates his fellow friars for these practices (Ximénez 1965: 719). Spaniards were also punished for failure to attend Sunday mass, but the punishment consisted of fines rather than standing in the stocks or whippings (Remesal 1964: 102, 389).

Schools for Sons of the Elite

To carry out their plan of instruction, the friars needed the help of Mayan doctrina teachers. Despite the large decrease in the indigenous population in the sixteenth century, there were too many people needing instruction for the friars to manage alone, even had they been fluent in a Mayan language. The many friars lacking fluency in a Mayan language also required translators. The Mayan assistants who performed these tasks were the fiscales and those who worked under them. To train these assistants, in several residencias the friars established a school adjacent to the church or monastery. In Yucatán there were schools in Mérida, Campeche, Mani, Conkal, and Izamal. In 1539 the Franciscans and Dominicans initiated schools in Guatemala, one of which was in

Santiago Atitlán (Anonymous 1941: 57–58; Landa 1941: 73; Remesal 1964: 392; Vazquez 1937: 177, 1938: 294; Borges 1960: 293, 393–418; Chamberlain 1966: 319–20). Probably, there were additional ones not noted in the sources. In keeping with the pre-Columbian practice of training the elite to assume positions of community service, the sons of the elite were trained in these monastery schools.

The purpose of the monastery schools was to prepare not only fiscales, but also the civil leaders and schoolteachers of the next generation. Beside becoming teachers of the doctrina, some graduates would assist in performing church rituals, especially the daily singing of the Divine Office. Other skills taught included serving mass, caring for the altar cloths, singing, and playing musical instruments. This select group was also taught to read and write in Spanish. Some students were taught ordinary tasks such as gardening or answering the monastery door.

During the period of instruction, the sons of the elite boarded at the monastery schools where they followed a monastic routine prescribed by the friars. In Yucatán the boys arose in the early morning hours to chant a section of the Divine Office. They would retire briefly, then rise again to attend mass and recite the doctrina in unison. This was followed by breakfast and then morning and afternoon classes. At the end of the day, the doctrina was recited again, followed by vespers singing and then supper.

The monastery schools in Yucatán are estimated to have educated more than a thousand boys in this manner (Borges 1960: 410). In Guatemala "some children had more devotion for their teachers than for their biological fathers" (Vazquez 1937: 96–97, 236). These children would denounce their parents and relatives to the friars if they were performing rituals for the traditional gods. Some of the elite resisted the friars taking over the education of their sons and without the friars' knowledge substituted slaves or commoners in their place.

The Mayan Elite (Caciques)

The friars and Spanish civil officials were few in number compared with the Maya, even after the decline of the Mayan population. To carry out the conquest and conversion program, they established a system of indirect rule (Remesal 1964: 127). The traditional Mayan elite were retained in their preconquest roles as community leaders, both civil and religious.

Although the unarmed friars [in Guatemala] were hardly in a position to impose themselves and their beliefs with force, the veiled threat of Spanish arms hovering in the distance surely provided them with a persuasive advantage. Missionaries aimed their proselytizing efforts at the Indian nobles, or *caciques*. Although direct evidence is lacking, most caciques surely understood that sooner or later they would have to reach an accommodation with the Spanish if they were to conserve their communities intact. . . . The Indian leader, in the case of a successful conversion, brought his people with him, and lent his personal power to the cause of the church. . . . The initial conversion to Christianity as practiced by Guatemala's friar-missionaries thus depended as much on shrewd human calculation—tying the fate of the cacique to the cause of religious colonization, and by extension, to the acceptance of Spanish rule—as on Christian doctrine. (Oss 1986: 16–17)

In Yucatán, "Insofar as colonial rule impinged on the Maya world, it did so through the Maya elite, who mediated almost every form of contact between Spaniards and the Maya masses. Their attitudes and motives were therefore crucial in determining the effect on the Maya of the many pressures, direct and indirect, exerted by the colonial regime. . . . Once the military conquest was complete, all the Maya leaders cooperated with the new rulers. They had no other choice if they wished to remain in power" (Farriss 1984: 96).

The cacique was not an authoritarian ruler, but worked as a consensus builder among the heads of the various kin groups in his area. "Each town had its own cacique who was its ruler, but he did not have absolute power. By himself he could not execute any matter except that commanded by the district leaders. First, he had to summon the heads of the descent groups. Only after discussing the matter with them and reaching an agreement, could it be executed. These heads of descent groups collected from each household its share of the tribute. . . . If someone was involved in a dispute or accused of a crime, the head of his descent group was summoned to act as his defender so that no injustice was done to him" (Ximénez 1929: 104).

The Cargo/Cofradía System: Assisting and Financing the Rituals

As waves of epidemic diseases swept the Mayan regions, the populations needing the services of the friars drastically declined along with the numbers available to help with the construction of churches and maintenance of the monasteries. "Consequently the friars began to ask His Majesty for lands or pastures . . . and filled them with mares and cows, which multiplying with time served the community greatly. . . . These measures . . . did not yield sufficient income to maintain the friars in their day-to-day activities or to provide them with working capital. Beginning in 1559 . . . they organized *mayordomos* and *cofradías* in indigenous communities throughout the region. So successful did this system prove to be in augmenting clerical stipends that within a century virtually all Indian men served the greater part of their lives in such organizations. . . . And yet the popularity which *cofradías* enjoyed among Dominican missionaries cannot be attributed exclusively to their utility in collecting alms and fees. On the contrary, these institutions . . . also lent themselves quite readily to Dominican theological purposes. . . . *Cofradías* and ceremonial functions proved to be particularly useful by extolling and glorifying such mysteries (e.g., the Eucharist, the Virginity of Mary), they lent themselves ideally to the Dominican struggle against New World heterodoxy" (Wasserstrom 1983a: 27–28). The cofradía members' ritual duties were to be present at the daily celebration of the mass where they held lighted candles from the beginning of the canon to the priest's Communion, to carry images and banners of the saints in processions, to escort the priest when he carried the Eucharist to the homes of the sick, and to help to bury the dead (Vazquez 1944: 344).

Chapters 2 and 3 discussed the Zinacanteco cargo structure and rituals. In other Mayan communities these organizations had variant structures that evolved over time. In some, the head of the cofradía provided the necessary funds for rituals; in others, all the members of the cofradía contributed; or additionally they collected funds from the entire community with the cooperation of the civil authorities. There were also variations in the relationship of cofradía positions to civil positions within the community structure.

Summary

This chapter has outlined the friars' strategy for transmitting the doctrina to the Maya in order to convert them to Christianity. The dispersed Maya were gathered together in towns that became centers of liturgy and instruction to varying degrees depending on the frequency of the friars' presence. Monastery schools were founded to train the sons of the elite in Spanish ways as preparation for future service as church assistants, civil officials, and schoolteachers. Cargo or cofradía organizations were founded to participate in and finance the introduced rituals.

Problems Facing the Friars

This chapter describes some of the major problems the friars encountered in attempting to implement their plan of evangelization. This background will help in understanding how the Maya perceived Christianity, the subject of part 5.

It is important to realize what the friars were attempting to accomplish. Their main goal was to introduce the sixteenth-century Spanish reform model of Hellenized Christianity. Chapter 8 treated the manuals containing its pedagogical expression. The friars were to teach this material to the Maya so that they understood it, assented to it by converting, and used it as a guide for their lives. This was a particularly difficult task because by the terms of Christian theology, the Maya were required to renounce their traditional gods and rituals. From the Mayan point of view this renunciation of the Mayan covenant was a severe threat to their very survival.

To bring about true conversions required the presence of a teacher-motivator with communication skills equal to the difficulty of the task. The question is, Did the Spanish clergy have the manpower and ability to accomplish this? They had to face a series of problems that progressively diminished the likelihood of success: if they had contact with a Mayan group at all, was the contact only sporadic or frequent enough for communication under ordinary circumstances; if frequent, was the contact intense enough to overcome the difficulties posed by the cross-cultural situation, and if so, did this lead to permanent conversion? In short, the problems were logistics, communication, and attitude.

Logistics: Magnitude of the Problem

The first and continuing problem was the relative sizes of the populations involved, the number of Maya compared with the number of friars.

Size of the Mayan Populations

The Spaniards at the time of the conquest encountered numerous Mayan groups. The main period of conquest and pacification lasted from 1524 to 1550 in the various regions, although some areas of the Yucatán and the Petén were not reached until the late seventeenth and early eighteenth centuries. Before the arrival of the Spaniards the Mayan population was already in decline due to disease, droughts, and locust invasions. The Spaniards brought Old World communicable diseases with them that spread among the previously unexposed populations taking a heavy toll. The problems of drought and disease continued in the three regions during the period of evangelization with varying degrees of intensity and duration.

Historical demography has attempted to estimate the size of the precontact Mayan populations, but given the problems of the sources the figures in table 10.1 can only be rough approximations. (There are gaps in the table because of the fragmentary nature of the data available.) The 1550 Mayan population is estimated at around 800,000. This is probably a conservative estimate because it does not include Maya in the Petén and in large sectors of Yucatán outside of Spanish control at that time. This writer would speculate that the friars in their initial evangelization efforts were attempting to reach at least a million Maya. Later this number was substantially reduced by high mortality. Lovell and Lutz (1995: 79) estimate that the population low point and recovery took place in the seventeenth century. Using the lowest population figure cited for each region in the seventeenth century yields an estimate of around 400,000 Maya at that time. But given the problems of underenumeration in areas reached by cen-

Table 10.1. Rough Estimates of Mayan Population, 1520–1940

Year	Guatemala	Yucatán	Chiapas	Total
ca. 1520	2,000,000		275,000	
1525		800,000		
1550	427,850	236,283	125,100	789,233
1575	236,540			
1586		155,000		
1595	133,280			
1609		176,320		
1611			85,000	
1625	128,000			
1643		209,188		
1650			70,000	
1684	242,020			
1700		130,000	72,000	
1710	236,208	182,500		
1736		127,000		
1750			65,000	
1765		194,300		
1770	220,500			
1778	248,500			
1780		175,287		
1794		254,000		
1800			53,000	
1804	292,000			
1809		291,096		
1821	383,000[a]	390,000	58,000	831,000
1830	445,000[a]			
1840	525,700			
1850	592,700	200,000		
1860	665,775			
1870	756,000			
1880	844,384			
1893	1,005,767			
1914	1,462,721[a]			
1921	1,343,283			
1940	1,560,000			

Sources: Guatemala and Chiapas, Lovell and Lutz 1994: 136 and 1995: 7; Yucatán, Farriss 1984: 59 and Restall 1997: 174.

a. The author derived this figure by interpolation and averaging from sources.

suses and of areas not under effective Spanish control, a very speculative guess might be 500,000 to 600,000.

The Number of Friars

As table 9.1 indicates, in the colonial period more than a thousand friars were dispatched from Spain to convert the Maya. The Franciscans worked in Yucatán and part of Guatemala. Originally, the Dominicans alone staffed Chiapas as well as a wide expanse of northern Guatemala. Later the Mercedarians undertook evangelization in some areas of Guatemala originally contacted by Dominicans who withdrew due to manpower shortages. Around 1600 there were about 424 friars available for building the infrastructure of their doctrinas and contacting Mayan groups. Assuming a Mayan population of one million, the manpower ratio would have been one friar for every 2,358 Maya, or 472 households, assuming five persons to a household.

Logistics: Contacting the Maya

The previous chapter described the friars' strategy of congregating the scattered Maya into newly founded towns where evangelization would take place even though the friars themselves did not reside in many of these towns. As the number of friars gradually increased, residences would be established in some of the visita towns allowing expansion of contact to additional towns or more frequent visits to the already contacted towns. Information collected by Oss (n.d.) helps map the expansion.[1]

Guatemala and Chiapas

The Franciscans initiated evangelization around 1540 in Guatemala; the Dominicans around 1543 in Guatemala and 1545 in Chiapas, a generation or more after the initial conquest and pacification. Roughly thirty-two friars had been sent from Spain up to that time (table 9.1). A 1556 report to the king by a judge of the Audiencia describes the situation in Guatemala, which is representative of the situation that prevailed in the early years in Chiapas and Yucatán:

> [the friars] although they do all they can, they cannot reach all the pueblos which are in their charge because there are so many and because of their size. There is a lack of doctrine in the pueblos because the religious cannot get around to all of them. They might be eight or fifteen days or a month in a pueblo and in this time they say Mass, baptize and preach and then they go to another. Then four months pass or eight or sometimes a year before the Indians hear Mass or preaching and there is no one to baptize them. There are many pueblos of five hundred houses and

more which are most of the year without Mass and without anyone to watch over their spiritual state, and being young in the faith, they forget what has been taught them . . . except for [in] four or five pueblos, the people in the town never go to confession and in all the diocese there are not a thousand Indians, men and women, who go to confession. There are more than sixty thousand Indians who do not go to confession . . . [in] three pueblos which are three leagues from the city and there was such a multitude of sins among them and so few who knew the prayers of the Church and people twenty years old and older who had not been baptized and in order to receive baptism, they had to be instructed, so that one would have to be there a year and a half and still not finish. (O'Flaherty 1979: 185)

This letter may have been responsible for the increased number of friars sent from Spain beginning in 1560. Of all friars sent from Spain to Guatemala-Chiapas in three hundred years of colonial experience, 73 percent arrived between 1560 and 1620.

Prior to 1541 representatives of the three orders passed through the Guatemalan capital Santiago de Almolonga and probably had small residences there. In 1541 Almolonga (Ciudad Vieja) was destroyed by gigantic mudslides, and the capital moved to Santiago de Guatemala (Antigua). There, each order was given land on which to build a monastery that became their headquarters and from which they developed their networks of evangelization.

Franciscans

Table 10.2 shows the growth of Franciscan doctrinas (a town of residencia with its towns of visita) in the colonial period. The Franciscans followed a strategy of concentration within a small area with a relatively dense population. Using the monastery in Santiago as the eastern anchor, another one in Quetzaltenango as the western anchor, and Sololá and Santiago Atitlán in the center lying north and south of Lake Atitlán, by 1689 the Franciscans had created twenty-four doctrinas. A journey from Santiago west through the highlands to Totonicapán and Quetzaltenango, then south toward the coast, and then east along the piedmont back to Antigua approximates the boundaries of their efforts. Within this region there were no unpopulated areas (Vazquez 1944: 351). It appears that the Franciscans contacted all the Mayan groups in the region.

The town of Sololá provides an example of Franciscan expansion (table 10.3). It was originally visited by Dominicans in 1542, but the Franciscans established a residence there in 1547. As the Franciscans congregated towns on the northern side of Lake Atitlán, as well as being responsible for three towns on the southern piedmont, contacts with the Maya increased. Later, one town

Table 10.2. Number of Franciscan Doctrinas in Guatemala, 1540–1700

Year	Doctrinas
1540	0
1550	8
1600	11
1650	17
1700	24

Source: Oss 2003:30.

Table 10.3. Examples of Franciscan Expansion in Guatemala, 1541–1821

Residencias	Their Visitas	Dates as Visitas	Dates as Residencias	Dates as Visitas
Sololá	S. Jorge Laguna	1580–1806		
1557–1821	S. Cruz Laguna	1580–1806		
	S. Lucia Utatlán	1580–1806		
	S. Marcos Laguna	1584–1738[c]		
	S. Jose Chicaya	1680–1806		
	Patulul	1572–1586	1586–1821	
	S. Tomás Chicichin[a]	1586–1673[c]		
	Pochuta[a]	1572–1586		1586–1763
	S. Juan Bautista			1632–1821
	S. Bárbara Costilla			1753–1821
	Panajachel	1580–1641	1641–1821	
	S. Andrés Semetabaj	1580–1641		1641–1806
	S. Antonio Palapó	1580–1641		1641–1806
	S. Catarina Palapó	1580–1641		1641–1806
	Concepción	1580–1641		1641–1806
Santiago Atitlán	S. Lucas Tolimán	1579–1821		
1541–1821	S. Tomás Chicichin[a]	1673–1716		
	S. Francisco Costilla[a]	1579–1586	1587–1716	
	S. Andrés Costilla[a]	1586–1587[b]		1600–1716
	S. Bárbara Costilla	1586–1587[b]		1600–1716
	S. Pedro Laguna	1590–1643	1643–1821	
	S. Juan Laguna	1590–1643		1643–1821
	S. Pablo Laguna	1590–1643		1643–1815
	S. Clara Laguna	1590–1643		1643–1818
	S. María Visitación	1590–1643		1643–1821
	S. Marcos Laguna			1738–1821

Source: Oss n.d.
Notes: Towns in **bold** are residencias, either from their foundation or beginning at a later date.
a. No longer in existence.
b. Visitas of San Bartolomé de la Costilla from 1587 to 1600.
c. Transferred to Santiago Atitlán.

in each of these sectors, Patulul and Panajachel, became residencias, increasing Franciscans' contact with their respective visitas as well as with the remaining visitas of Sololá.

Another example is Santiago Atitlán (table 10.3) where the Franciscans took up residence in 1541 and from there expanded their evangelization efforts by founding six towns around the southern and western sides of Lake Atitlán. In 1587 three towns on the south coast were spun off from Atitlán with San Francisco Costilla becoming a residencia and the other two its visitas. In 1643 the towns on the west side of the lake were spun off under a residencia established in San Pedro Laguna. Due to changing international demand for cacao from this area and consequent population shifts, two of these towns were later abandoned and the third was made a visita of Patulul.

The Dominicans

To the north of the Franciscan area, the Dominicans established residences in the present departments of Guatemala and Baja Verapaz, and in the southern portions of Alta Verapaz and K'iche'. Like the Franciscans, the Dominicans began by building monasteries in certain key towns and then proceeded to visit other congregated towns in the surrounding area. In addition to Santiago de Guatemala, Dominican monasteries were located in Cobán in 1543 as the eastern anchor of their efforts, in Ciudad Real (San Cristóbal de las Casas) in Chiapas in 1547 as the western anchor, and in 1553 in Sacapulas as the midpoint. It appears that the Dominicans originally hoped to fill in the wide expanse between Cobán and Ciudad Real with Dominican doctrinas. Table 10.4 shows the friars' expansion from Cobán. The Dominicans had a system of priories with

Table 10.4. Example of Dominican Expansion in Northern Verapaz, 1543–1821

Residencia	Visitas	Dates as Visitas	Dates as Residencias	Dates as Visitas
Cobán	**Cahabón**	1543–1638	1638–1809	
1543–1821	Lanquín	1544–1809		1809–1821
	S. Cristóbal Verapaz	1544–1638	1638–1821	
	Santa Cruz Verapaz	1544–1638		1638–1821
	Carchá	1544–1638	1638–1821	
	Chamelco	1544–1638		1638–1821
	Tatic	1545–1638	1638–1821	
	Tanahú	1544–1638		1638–1821
	Tucurú	1544–1638		1638–1821

Source: Oss n.d.

Note: Towns in **bold** are residencias, either from their foundation or beginning at a later date.

smaller jurisdictions canonically subject to them. It is not clear in the documents Oss cites whether some of these dependencies were towns of residencias or simply visitas from the priories. Table 10.4 assumes visita status.

The Dominicans had fewer friars and a much larger territory than the Franciscans. They established additional doctrinas in Santa Cruz del K'iche', Rabinal in Baja Verapaz, Amatitlán and Mixco in the department of Guatemala, and three Pipil towns in the department of Escuintla. In 1616 the monastery in Santiago de Guatemala had twenty dependencies served by eleven friar- priests and three friar-brothers. Cobán had nine or ten dependencies with six friar-priests and one friar-brother. Sacapulas had eleven dependencies with eight friar-priests. Later, the Dominicans attempted to extend their doctrinas northward into Chol-speaking areas in northern Alta Verapaz, northern K'iche', and southern Petén. They established eight visitas there among the Manché Chols, but withdrew due to warfare (Jones 1998: 112). The Petén was later penetrated by Franciscans from Yucatán.

Las Casas became the bishop of Chiapas in 1545, and in the same year the first Dominicans took up residence in Zinacantán. Two years later they moved to Ciudad Real (San Cristóbal de las Casas). From there they gradually built up a network of doctrinas. They established monasteries among the Maya in Chiapa de los Indios, Copanaguastla in 1555, Comitán in 1579, and two among the Zoques in the western part of the region (Wasserstrom 1983a: 24). In the northern Chiapas piedmont the Franciscans opened a residence in Hueitiupán around 1589 (Oss 2003: 30; Laughlin 2003: 6–10).

In 1616 the monastery in Ciudad Real had twenty dependencies, Chiapa had six, Copanaguastla had ten, Comitán had nine, and Ocosingo had eight. The Dominicans gradually expanded into the central highlands from Ciudad Real on the south and Ocosingo on the north. By 1712 they were in Chamula with eight visitas; Huistán with two visitas; Cancuc, Guaquitepec, with one visita; Bachajón with one visita; and in Oxchuc and Yajalón with none. The Franciscans later moved their residence from Hueitiupán to Simojovel with Hueitiupán remaining as one of its four visitas. Secular priests were in Tila and Tumbalá (Wasserstrom 1983a: 53).

Therefore it is probable that the Dominicans made contact with many of the Mayan groups within the areas of their doctrinas. While the Franciscans were pushing southward into the Petén from Yucatán, the Dominicans from Chiapas joined those from Guatemala in going north and attempting to contact and evangelize Chol-speaking groups.

The Mercedarians

At the time of the first congregation of Mayan towns, Dominicans were congregating a number of towns in Huehuetenango—probably from a residence in Jacaltenango (Remesal 1964: 243–44). After the Dominicans found that they were too few in number to cover the wide expanse of territory embraced by their province, they withdrew from Huehuetenango and the Mercedarians took their place. The bishop added San Marcos and the western part of Quetzaltenango to their region.

Table 10.5 shows the Mercedarian expansion in Huehuetenango from their original residences in the towns of Huehuetenango and Jacaltenango. Two of the visita towns under Huehuetenango, Santa Ana Malacatán and Chiantla, later became residencias. The travel distance from Chiantla to its outlying visitas was shortened by transferring four towns to Jacaltenango in 1632. Travel in the area northwest of Jacaltenango was lessened by establishing a residencia in Soloma in 1673. This is the same pattern of expansion used by the Franciscans and Dominicans. Mercedarian residences were also located in Cuilco and San Juan Ostuncalco (not shown in table 10.5).

Therefore it appears that the Mercedarians made contact with most of the Mayan groups in their doctrinas. Like the Dominicans, the Mercedarians in the seventeenth century went north and attempted to reach uncontacted Chol groups, but they do not appear to have established a continuing presence among them (Jones 1998: 112, 132, 243, 376, passim).

Yucatán

The Yukatek Mayan population was spread over a very large area. The population figures in table 10.1 are only for regions under Spanish control. To escape the Spaniards many Mayan groups had fled to eastern Yucatán and south to the Petén, theoretically a part of the Yucatán diocese (see map in Fernández 1990: 114).

There were only four Franciscans in the colony in 1545. From 1550 to 1569, thirty-two more Franciscans were sent from Spain, the only ones sent to the Yucatán in the sixteenth century (table 9.1). By 1580 there were thirty-eight friars working in twenty-four doctrinas (table 10.6) There were secular priests in Bacalar and Peto. The doctrinas and parishes on the fringe on the Spanish controlled territory, Campeche in the west, Chancenote in the east, Bacalar in the southeast, Peto in the south, had much larger areas to administer than those within the Spanish controlled area (table 10.6). These large fringe areas and the number of vistas within the controlled area compared with the number of available friars and secular priests indicate how seldom the priests appeared in the visitas.

The Franciscan provincial, Diego de Landa, initiated an inquisition against Mayan idolatry that was opposed by the bishop of Yucatán, the encomenderos, and some friars. As a result the dissenting friars left Yucatán and went to other mission areas (González 1978: 104–8, 124–27). This internal dispute among the

Table 10.5. Examples of Mercedarian Expansion in Huehuetenango, 1572–1821

Residencias	Visitas	Dates as Visitas	Dates as Residencias	Dates as Visitas
Huehuetenango	S. Lorenzo	1586–1821		
1572–1821	Petatón[a]	1586–1602		
	S. Juan Atitán[b]	1632–1821		
	S. Pedro Necta[b]	1632–1821		
	Santiago Chimaltenango[b]	1632–1821		
	S. Isabel	1632–1821		
	S. Ana Malacatán	1632–1673	1673–1821	
	S. Gaspar Ixchil[b]	1632–1673		1673–1821
	S. Bárbara	1602–1673		1673–1821
	Ixtahuacán[a]	1632–1673		1673–1821
	Colotenango[b]	1632–1673		1673–1821
	Chiantla	1586–1602	1602–1821	
	Aguacatán	1548–1632		1632–1821
	S. Sebastián Huehuetenango	1632–1821		1602–1632
	S. Martín Cuchumatán[a]	1586–1602[c]		1632–1821
	Todos Santos[a][b]	1586–1602[c]		1632–1821
	Soloma[a]			1602–1632
	S. Sebastián Coatán[a]			1602–1632
	S. Eulalia[a]			1602–1632
	S. Mateo Ixtatán[a]			1602–1632
	S. Juan Ixcoy[a]			1602–1632
Jacaltenango	Concepción Jacaltenango	1632–1821		
1574–1821	S. Andrés Huista	1673–1821		
	S. Antonio Huista	1673–1821		
	S. Marcos Huista	1673–1821		
	S. Ana Huista	1602–1821		
	Petatón[a]	1602–1821		
	S. Martín Cuchumatán[a]	1602–1632		
	Todos Santos[a]	1602–1632		
	Soloma[a]	1632–1673	1673–1821	
	S. Sebastián Coatán[a]	1632–1673		1673–1821
	S. Eulalia[a]	1632–1673		1673–1821
	S. Mateo Ixtatán[a]	1632–1673		1673–1821
	S. Juan Ixcoy[a]	1632–1873		1673–1821

Source: Oss n.d.

Notes: Towns in **bold** are residencias, either from their foundation or beginning at a later date.

a. Visita transferred from Huehuetenango to Jacaltenango, hence listed twice.

b. Originally a visita of Cuilco.

c. From 1602 to 1632, S. Martín Cuchumatán and Todos Santos were visitas of Jacaltenango.

Table 10.6. Franciscan Expansion in Yucatán

Residencias	No. of Visitas	Radial Area of Responsibility	Religious Group[b]
Campeche	12	90	F
Calkini	14	15	F
Xequelchekan	5	15	F
Cical	25	15	F
Valladolid	8	21	F
Tinum	6	18	F
Tizimin	23	21	F
Chancenote	9	60	F
Cozumel	4	6	F and S
Ichmul	8	15	F
Bacalar	24	40	S
Mérida	14	15	F
Hunacamá	4	9	F
Conkal	7	6	F
Tixcocob	6	6	F
Ticul	8	6	F
Cincontum	9	9	F
Tecanto	8	6	F
Izamal	16	9	F
Hocabá	9	12	F
Homún	6	12	F
Oxkutzcab	5	9	F
Tekax	3	9	F
Sotuta	10	5	F
Peto	7	36	S

Source: Fernández 1990: 80, 82.
a. Distances have been converted from leagues to miles based on estimate of three miles to a league.
b. F indicates Franciscan priets; S indicates secular priests.

Franciscans was probably the reason why friars did not come from Spain on any regular basis until the seventeenth century (see table 9.1).

During the seventeenth century the Spanish civil authorities and the Franciscans kept pushing east and south from western Yucatán, attempting to bring the Mayan groups in these areas under Spanish authority (Fernández 1990: 100–101). An important impetus was the attempt to open a road connecting Yucatán with Guatemala through southern Yucatán, the Petén, and northern Verapaz from Mérida to Cobán. This effort lasted for almost a century (Jones 1998). The finale of the contact effort came with the Spanish defeat of the Itzá in 1697. The fall of the Itzá was followed by a period of evangelization among them and the groups they had dominated. This period was marked by devastating disease along with congregations and rebellions (Jones 1998: 387–421). It is probable that the Franciscans and secular priests contacted most Mayan groups in western Yucatán, but in southern Yucatán and the Petén the contact was superficial.

In summary, it appears that by the early eighteenth century the friars and some secular priests had made at least nominal contact with the majority of the Mayan groups in the three regions. This contact was accomplished in spite of a shortage of manpower. From a logistical standpoint it represented a Herculean effort.

Logistics: Where Did the Populations Live?

As described in the previous chapter, to overcome the logistical problems posed by the scattered settlement pattern of the Maya, the strategy of the crown and the friars was to congregate them into towns to facilitate access to them.

Impact of Congregation

The friars founded new towns but were unable to sustain their hope of permanently congregating the Maya. Waves of epidemic disease continually swept over Mayan areas, greatly reducing the size of the population (Lovell 1985: 84–85; MacLeod 1973: 98–100; Farriss 1984: 61–62; Wasserstrom 1983a: 72). To escape the contagion, many Maya fled the congregated towns for the safety of the forest or the scattered hamlets from which they came (see figure 10.1). Some fled the towns to escape the encomenderos' excessive demands for tribute and labor (Carmack 1981: 311). Others simply wanted to remain on the land their descent group had inherited from their ancestors. Two Dominicans involved in the congregation of Sacapulas noted, "This part of the sierra, being so rugged and broken, caused us to encounter settlements of only eight, six and four houses tucked and hidden away in gullies and ravines where, until our arrival, no other Spaniard had penetrated. . . . Among all these Indians there is not one who wishes to leave behind the hut passed on to him by his fathers, nor to abandon a pestilential ravine or desert some inaccessible craggy rocks, because that is where the bones of his forefathers rest" (Lovell and Swezey 1990: 36). The years between 1575 and 1578 saw many Indians near Santiago de Guatemala "'move out, in hiding, from one place to another' rather than pay not just their own tribute but also that part owed by deceased relatives. Around this same time we have several reports that mention the virtual disintegration of congregation in parts of Verapaz, where parcialidades and entire families leave to live idolatrously in the mountains. Two sizable pueblos—Santa Catalina and Zulben—had been abandoned almost completely by 1579, only five years after the Bishop of Verapaz himself had supervised the process of congregation. At

Figure 10.1. To the right is the mountain trail (barely visible) leading to the hamlet of Salinas and its chapel, pictured in figure 9.2. This is typical of the conditions of many small Mayan settlements tucked away in the mountains of Guatemala and Chiapas or the flatlands of Yucatán.

Cahabón [see table 10.4], Indians allegedly gave up civilized life to join unconquered Lacandón and Chol-Manché tribes in pre-Christian barbarism on the other side of the frontier" (Lovell and Swezey 1990: 37).

While many of the towns survived with reduced numbers, the flight from them resulted in more Maya living in small settlements distant from the towns of residencia and visita. Ximénez described the difficulties of ministering to small settlements scattered in the ravines of the mountainous terrain. He cited this dispersed settlement pattern as the reason that many Maya were a rustic people, were shy and fainthearted, and had an aversion for and distrust of Spaniards including the friars and anything they said (Ximénez 1965: 18).

In Yucatán the congregation strategy also ended in failure.

The program was a forced nucleation dictated by criteria and motives wholly external to Indian society. The point is not whether congregation was good or bad but whether it would last. It did not. The Spaniards imposed a degree of territorial integration without a corresponding degree of social cohesion to support it. Therefore the territorial integration could not be maintained and a slow process of fragmentation began. . . . Indians were moving out into the bush, recreating hamlet clusters, which eventually became recognized under the label of *ranchos* as settlements administratively dependent on but physically separate from the original town. (Farriss 1984: 206–7)

The dispersal was underway as early as the 1580s when there was easy access to milpa land. Some dispersals were carried out with either the assistance or tacit approval of Spanish authorities (Restall 1997: 39). Epidemics were probably also an important factor. The friars saw the flight from the towns as a return to idolatry although it was more likely a continuation of the Mayan rituals that had never been suppressed (Remesal 1966: 180).

Spanish Demand for Labor

As the Spanish population of the colony grew, some colonists founded haciendas to produce market crops and mills to process cane sugar. Others started small settlements in wilderness lands by the ocean where they mined salt. Workers were needed for these undertakings. This created more flight from the towns as Maya went to live and work in these scattered communities. A large floating population of Mayan workers was created. Seeking seasonal labor, they went from one hacienda or mill to another throughout the year losing their roots in any one place (Cortés y Larraz 1958 II: 210, 222, 227 passim).

Summary of the Situation in the Guatemala

In 1768–70 the newly arrived archbishop of Guatemala, Pedro Cortés y Larraz, made an inspection tour of the eighty-nine parishes in Guatemala and thirty-four in El Salvador. With a doctorate in theology and fresh from parish work in Spain, he was appalled by the conditions in his diocese. With the Spanish perception of town life as civilizing, he lamented the moral state of those who lived in the mountains, those on the haciendas and at the sugar mills, and those who were perennially floating from place to place. He complained that they were living without the mass, without the doctrina, and without the sacraments, doing whatever they pleased, and that their one goal was to flee the authority of the church and the king (Cortés y Larraz 1958 II: 200, passim). In the towns the archbishop was horrified at the *zarabandas* of the cofradías, the drunken music and dancing that took place during the nights of the festivals. He forbade the practice of taking images from the churches to the cofradía houses during the festivals and contemplated doing away with what had become a heretical cult of the saints (Cortés y Larraz 1958 II: 251, 227–28, 259–60).

The archbishop estimated that at least 50 percent of the population in his diocese lived in areas not served by either residencias or visitas (Cortés y Larraz 1958 II: 200, 213, 224, 269). This dispersal of the population weakened the strategy of congregation and implies that the majority of the Mayan population lived scattered in the countryside theoretically served by the towns but at some distance from them and consequently seldom visited.

Logistics: Quality of Contact

Even if nominal contact was made with Mayan groups, this alone does not necessarily mean the doctrina was being communicated effectively. Given the conditions they faced, were the friars able to spend a sufficient amount of time with the inhabitants to instruct them about the doctrina?

A Norm of Adequacy

Trying to evaluate the quality of the friars' contact with the Maya raises the problem of setting a criterion to indicate such a presence. Frequency of contact would be an indicator but these data are lacking. A rough proxy is the ratio of the number of households in a doctrina or parish per priest assigned to the area (Oss 1986: 62–64). The parish is the heart of the Catholic structure. Parishes in Europe, where the system was developed, provide long historical experience of its logistical requirements. To reflect this experience, ratios for some Spanish and other European parishes can be used as norms for estimating the adequacy of the friars' presence for communicating the doctrina. Marroquín, in a letter to the crown, says "in the kingdoms of Spain where everybody is a Christian and . . . the Church is enlightened by the Holy Spirit, the distinction exists of having one parish for a hundred or two hundred *vecinos*" (O'Flaherty 1979: 158–59). A vecino means a head of a household, a married adult taxpayer or Indian tributary (Roys, Scholes, and Adams 1940: 14; Sanders 1992: 95). Marroquín's ratios are confirmed in table 10.7 section A that reflects European experience from the eleventh to the sixteenth centuries. It shows a range of 43 to 150 households per priest with a mean of 82. All these ratios presuppose a similar cultural background for both priest and parishioners. When the cultural and religious backgrounds of priest and parishioners are greatly dissimilar, as they were between the Maya and the Spanish, the ratios logically should be lower to reflect the increased time needed to overcome these differences. Marroquín's lower estimate of one hundred will be used here as a rough criterion even though this does not fully compensate for the additional time required to accommodate cultural differences. In the New World, the Council of the Indies set a normative ratio of four hundred tributaries (an approximation

Table 10.7. Indicator of Intensity of Contact: Ratios of Households to Priest (Friar)

A. European Experience

England, c. 1086 (Domesday Book)	43:1
Valencia, parish in Spain, late 1200s	150:1
Paris, 1328	82:1
Kingdom of Castilla, 1591	43:1
Andalucía, rural Spain, 1591	91:1

B. Guatemala

Order	1572–74 Priests[a]	1753–54 Households[b]	Ratio Range	Priests	Households[c]	Ratio Range
Franciscan	17–23	10,273	447–604	28	28,017–14,009	500–334:1
Dominican	27–35	13,364	382–495	33	34,957–17,479	530–353:1
Mercedarian	19–13	5,500	432–550	6	5,364–2,682	447–289:1
Average			420–550			492–325:1

C. Chiapas about 1611

Doctrina	Dependence	Friars	Population[d]	Ratio Range[f]
Ciudad Real	20	11	36,911	839:1–671:1
Ocosingo	8	6		(included above)
Chiapa	6	8	11,958	374:1–300:1
Copanaguastla	10	4	8,267	517:1–331:1
Comitán	9	5	12,665	633:1–507:1
Total/Avg.	53	34	69,801	591:1–452:1

D. Yucatán, 1586

Doctrina	Visitas	Friars	Population[e]	Ratio Range[f]
Hocabá	9	3	3,464	287:1–231:1
Homún	5	2	2,584	323:1–258:1
Mani	8	5	7,591	380:1–304:1
Tikanto	7	2	4,664	583:1–466:1
Tixchel	4	1	685	171:1–137:1
Total/Avg.	33	13	18,987	349:1–279:1

Source: For Europe, Oss 1986: 62; for Guatemala, Oss 1986: 62–64; for Chiapas, Remesal 1966: 486–87; for Yucatán, Borges 1960: 533.

a. The range is due to the ambiguity of the sources, which sometimes give the number of friars present in the country without distinguishing between those working in the doctrinas and the administrative personnel at the monastery headquarters in Santiago de Guatemala. In light of this fact, I favor the lower number of friars working in the doctrinas and the higher ratios for the 1572–74 period.

b. Numbers of tributaries

c. Numbers of communicants; Oss does not define this term or give the Spanish word he translated as communicants. Probably, it means a person old enough to distinguish right from wrong and therefore capable of making a valid confession in preparation for receiving the other sacraments. Vazquez (1944: 64) uses the phrase "de confesión," by which he means the population nine years of age and older. The range of ratios depends on the assumptions about the number of communicants in a Mayan household. Oss used two and three.

d. 1616

e. 1611

f. The lower end of the range is calculated by assuming four persons per household, the upper end by assuming five persons per household.

of the number of households) per priest in a doctrina. Given the difficulties facing the friars, this high ratio appears to be another example of the inability of Spanish authorities to recognize the realities of the New World.

Priest-to-Maya Ratios in the Three Mayan Regions

Table 10.7 sections B, C, and D show the ratios for some sectors and towns in Guatemala, Chiapas, and Yucatán. Overall in the three regions, the ratios for individual doctrinas range from 137 for Tixchel, a small doctrina in Yucatán, to 839 for Ciudad Real (San Cristóbal) in Chiapas. For each region, depending on the specific assumptions about household size and number of active friars, the average ratios for Guatemala range from 420 to 550 in 1572–74 and 325 to 492 in 1753–54; for Chiapas they range from 452 to 591 in about 1611; and in Yucatán from 279 to 349 in 1586. Regardless of the assumptions made, the roughness of the index, and the use of a biased norm that does not fully take into account the need to overcome cultural differences, all the ratios are extremely high by European standards. They indicate the inadequate quality of contact for meeting the desired objective.

A more detailed view is given in table 10.8, a 1689 listing of each Franciscan doctrina in Guatemala with its ratio of friars to households. There are ratios above 300 to 1 in either four or one doctrinas depending on the assumed household size; ratios between 200 and 299 to 1 in seven or five doctrinas; and ratios between 100 and 199 to 1 in nine or twelve doctrinas. Three doctrinas on the south coast approximate the European norm. These were plantation areas with shifting market centers and fluctuating labor demands to which the friars probably had not adjusted. Later, one of these doctrinas went out of existence. Again regardless of the assumption used or the roughness of the index, these ratios indicate a serious manpower shortage all through the colonial period, even in the most concentrated area of the evangelization effort.

The same picture emerges from the other regions. In Chiapas in the eighteenth century some highland pueblos were visited only five or six times a year. "There were also complaints that even when priests visited the pueblos they often refused to be inconvenienced to go out to the milpas [small outlying settlements] to attend the sick or to give the last rites. Direct contact between priests and most Indian men and women must have been limited and infrequent" (Gosner 1992: 57). In Yucatán "the friars and the Spanish in general lacked the manpower to force more than formal compliance with the norms they introduced. Their superior coercive power proved an effective deterrent to organized resistance or open defiance; it was no proof against the immense inertia of the Maya's passive, perhaps at times uncomprehending, resistance to changing their ways" (Farriss 1984: 93).

Table 10.8. Populations and Structural Characteristics of Franciscan Guatemalan Doctrinas, 1689

Doctrina	Patron Saint	Population[a,b] Residencia	Visita	Total	Ladinos	Visitas	Friars	Cofradías	Households[c]	Ratio Range[c]
1 Almolonga	N. Señora Limpia	1,429	3,614	5,043	257	7	3	16	1,261–1,009	420–336
2 Juan Obispo	Juan	3,286	1,194	4,480	0	7	5	24	1,120–896	224–179
3 Itzapa	Andrés	571	1,286	1,857	46	1	4	7	464–371	116–93
4 Patzicía	Santiago	2,857	0	2,857	134	0	3	5	714–571	238–190
5 Acatenango	Antonio	714	1,394	2,108	36	2	3	8	527–422	176–141
6 Comolapa	Juan	3,714	500	4,214	0	1	3	8	1,054–843	351–281
7 Tecpán	Francisco	2,714	471	3,185	29	1	4	8	796–637	199–159
8 Patzún	Bernardino	2,286	0	2,286	43	0	3	5	572–457	191–152
9 Panajachel	Francisco	1,143	1,381	2,524	26	4	4	12	631–505	158–126
10 Sololá	Asunción	2,357	2,643	5,000	0	5	5	18	1,250–1,000	250–200
11 Laguna	Pedro	621	1,774	2,395	0	4	3	11	599–479	200–160
12 Atitlán	Santiago	2,714	993	3,707	0	2	4	13	927–741	232–185
13 Totonicapán	Miguel	2,900	2,046	4,946	17	2	4	10	1,237–989	309–247
14 Totonicapá	Cristóbal	2,900	1,221	4,121	34	2	3	14	1,030–824	343–275
15 Quetzaltenango	Espíritu Santo	3,571	1,889	5,460	214	5	6	22	1,365–1,092	228–182
16 Momostenango	Santiago	857	736	1,593	17	2	3	9	398–319	133–106
17 Samayac	Limpia Concepción	1,243	1,150	2,393	26	2	5	12	598–479	120–96
18 Xocopilas	Pablo	2,571	0	2,571	0	0	2	5	643–514	322–257
19 Suchitepequez	Bartolomé	114	657	771	0	3	3	7	193–154	64–51
20 Costilla[d]	Francisco	563	253	816	0	2	3	12	204–163	68–54
21 Patulul	Magdalena	1,714	1,171	2,885	0	3	4	12	721–577	180–144
22 Cotzumaluapa	Santiago	171	914	1,085	57	6	3	22	271–217	90–72
23 Siquinalá	Catarina	486	950	1,436	3	3	3	7	359–287	120–96
24 Alotenango	Juan	2,571	311	2,882	0	3	3	6	721–576	240–192
Total/Avg. ratio		44,067	26,548	70,615	939	67	86	273	17,655–14,122	205–164
Antigua	Santiago	727	0	727	1428		37			

Source: Vazquez 1944: 34–67; also in Ruz et al. 2002 I: 465–98. Antigua ladinos estimated from Lutz 1994: 106. (Mayan population was highly acculturated.)

a. Vazquez uses the number of "communicants" to enumerate the populations served by the doctrinas. These are people eligible to receive Communion and defined by Vazquez (1944: 64) as nine years of age or older. Thus, the percentage of the population under nine years of age is needed to determine the size of the total population. The following table shows the percentage of the population under ten years of age for some typical Mayan communities and countries with large rural populations. The average for the populations corrected for underenumeration is 29.7 percent and 34.9 percent with this correction. Because data broken down by year of age are lacking, these percentages are based on five-year age classifications. To offset the inclusion of nine-year-olds in the percentages, I have used an estimate of 30 percent. MacLeod (1973: 131) and Zamora (1983: 301) used 20 percent without giving their rationale.

Table 10.8.1. Percent of Rural Populations under 10 Years of Age

Year	Place	Size of Population	% under 10 Years	Source
1755	S. Juan Obispo	478	26.4	Lutz 1995:77
1813	Seven Lake Towns	4909	32.2	Early 1982:129
ca. 1940	12 National Censuses[1]	146,537,313	29.6	United Nations 1950: 1049–1167
1950	Rural Guatemala	2,094,410	34.9	Early 1982:54, corrected data
1964	Rural Guatemala	2,846,286	35.5	Early 1982:55, " "
1973	Rural Guatemala	3,882,030	34.9	Early 1982:55, " "
1964	Santiago Atitlán	10,462	34.4	Early 1970a:169, " "
	Average		32.6	
	Average of uncorrected		29.4	
	Average of corrected		34.9	

1. Egypt 1937, Moslem Algeria 1936, Angola 1940, Moslem Tunisia 1940, Guatemala 1940, Mexico 1940, Brazil 1940, Peru 1940, Venezuela 1941, Philippines 1939, Thailand 1937, Turkey 1935.

b. "Population" means people under the administration of these respective towns, not the population of the towns themselves. People outside the towns, however many or few they may be, are counted as being administered to by the residencia or visita. This can be seen in cases such as Patzicía and Patzún. These are large municipios located in a very mountainous area where there evidently was no logical place for a visita. Consequently, the whole municipio is listed under the town of residencia. This fact and the probability that there was a higher percentage of underenumeration in the visitas are the reasons why the total for towns of residencia is greater than that for the visitas.

c. For the number of households and the ratio columns, the lower end of the range represents an assumption of an average of four people per household, the upper end an assumption of five people per household.

d. No longer in existence.

Therefore, the indigenous population was far too large and the number of friars far too small to teach the doctrina in European circumstances, much less in the Mayan situation. It is clear that there was a problem of quality instruction.

A Case History, Santiago Chimaltenango

The Mercedarian residencia of Huehuetenango and its visita of Santiago Chimaltenango provide an example of the problem of quality time (see Watanabe 1992: 42–53). Pedro Alvarado gave Chimaltenango as an encomienda to Juan de Espinar around 1530. At that time the town and its surrounding area consisted of five hundred houses, suggesting a population of about 2,500. In a dispute between encomenderos, the town was burned but was reconstituted shortly afterward, though with a reduced population. Dominicans entered the area and apparently made Chimaltenango a center for congregating people from the surrounding countryside. The Dominicans did not remain and Chimaltenango became a visita of the Mercedarians in Cuilco from 1570 to 1632 (Oss n.d.). In 1632 it became a visita from Huehuetenango until at least 1821 (table 10.5) and probably until the 1950s, when a Maryknoll priest took up residence there. In 1649 it had two hundred tributaries suggesting a population of around one thousand.

From 1633 to 1673 Huehuetenango had nine visitas, after 1673 there were five (table 10.5). An inspection of the baptismal records shows that the Mercedarians visited Santiago Chimaltenango an average of nine times a year between 1633 and 1766, with a low of five visits in 1728 and a high of sixteen in 1749 (Watanabe 1992: 50). The other visitas were probably visited with similar frequencies. This sporadic contact was insufficient for instruction about Christianity. Secular priests replaced the friars in the 1760s, and in 1770 there were 110 families with a population of 451 in the doctrina. There were Mayan instructors who taught the doctrina to the girls in the afternoon and the boys in the evening. But the discouraged pastor noted,

> About a year ago I seized an old Indian woman kneeling with a smoking clay censer on an artificial mound on a small hill, and there were several eggs broken open with much chicken blood on the ground. . . . And having her seized by those who accompanied me, I asked her why she was burning incense in the mountains, and she replied that she was asking God for her health and that all the people went there to do likewise. . . . I have gone to that place again and found the same thing, and once I asked an Indian what motive or purpose they had in doing that, and he answered that such was the method that they used to ask for the death of their enemies.

Regarding the respect that Indians have for the Holy Sacraments, I say that in my judgement they have little or none. I infer this from the tedium and repugnance with which they receive them. The experience of nine years, in which I have worked so hard to meet my yearly duties, has taught me this. [Their indifference] can also be attributed to the fact that the Indians positively do not desire salvation nor fear damnation. (Watanabe 1992: 51–52)

The Maya covenant was clearly still alive and well in this visita town after two hundred years of evangelization efforts. This example appears representative of many towns of visita.

The Problem of the Monastic Routine

Until now the analysis has assumed that the friars were available full time to concentrate on the conversion of the Maya. But chapter 8 described the considerable amount of time the friars spent on monastic rituals. The first bishops in the Mayan regions were either Franciscans or Dominicans with one exception, the secular priest Marroquín in Guatemala. His life had no structured ritual schedule. The Office was read privately at any time of the day. Marroquín thought that the lifestyle of the secular priest was better suited for the work of Mayan conversion. While Marroquín appreciated the work of the friars, he thought that the requirements of their monastic routine interfered with their developing a personal relationship with individual Maya. In Marroquín's view of the Christian life, theological belief was less important for teaching the Christian message than the good example of a priest's life and his personal contact with his parishioners. Marroquín notes in one of his letters: "A good cleric [secular priest] does more than four friars because he is not tied down to ceremonies and I do not take it too much account that they do not know the language. I prefer a little bit of good example to much wordiness. Language boundaries change quickly, it is more important that clerics be good. The need which we have here makes us conceal and put up with those who are not (good) because of the abundant harvest" (O'Flaherty 1979: 176–77). The last sentence is a reference to the fact that some Mercedarians had been expelled from his diocese for misconduct. Marroquín further explains his position in a report to the king:

Your Majesty will think that he has discharged his duty with the four friars that have been sent, but do not believe it. I repeat what I said that although there were many more, even innumerable religious, they cannot discharge the royal conscience because these people need, by reason of their numbers and their lack of so much, to be taken into personal account and be known by their own parish priest. If in the kingdoms of Spain where everybody is a Christian and . . . the Church is enlightened by the Holy Spirit, the distinction exists of having one parish for one hundred or two hundred vecinos—a parish priest who teaches them and administers the sacraments and takes account of all and says daily Mass and helps them in their sickness and strengthens them in the hour of their death and buries them when they die and a thousand other ceremonies; (you can imagine) how much a necessity these things are for people here. The essential and the accidental cannot be done by the religious, because for each religious there are ten thousand Indians and he does not know them, nor can he know them, nor does his habit give any reasonable hope of what these people need being done. In the whole year the greater part of a pueblo does not hear twenty Masses, the sick cannot be visited nor the dead buried; if this were lacking from a few pueblos of the kingdoms there for a year or two, truly the charity and devotion of many good, traditional Christians would grow cold. What will happen to these poor people who yesterday were born and do not yet have deep roots (in the faith) and honor? (O'Flaherty 1979: 158–59)

The bishop of Guatemala was obviously highly skeptical about the effectiveness of the evangelization strategy being used by almost all the priests working in his diocese as well as by those in Chiapas and Yucatán.

The scarcity of friars, the demands of their semimonastic way of life, and the consequent strategy of most towns being towns of visita prevented the development of the personal bond between the friars and the people that was required for the task at hand. The friars' physical presence was limited to an occasional performance of ritual in the many towns of visita whose broad ecclesiastical boundaries contained the majority of the population, although many Maya did not actually live in or even visit these towns.

The Problem of Excessive Transfers

Another impediment to a friar getting to know a parish well was frequent transfers from one doctrina to another. One of the cardinal principles of the religious life was detachment from earthly things in order to attain union with God. To prevent a friar from becoming too attached to the people or town in which he worked, the Dominicans beginning in 1566 circulated the friars every three or four years from one doctrina to another (Oss 1986: 25, 171, 178). The Franciscans also followed this principle, as can be seen from the numerous moves of individual friars detailed in the four volumes of Vazquez's Crónica.

Communication Problems

The shortages of friars with respect to the size and location of the Mayan population as well as the time limitations of the available friars greatly hindered teaching the Christian doctrine. But even where the physical presence of the friars was frequent enough and the Mayan groups of manageable size, communication obstacles prevented understanding passing from teacher to student. These problems were related to language, the use of Mayan substitutes, and the method of teaching.

Language

Even in communities where friars lived or visited frequently, the Mayan languages were a barrier to their communication with the catechumens. There are several aspects to the language question: What was to be the language used for teaching, Spanish or the local Mayan language? If a Mayan language, how many friars were capable of preaching and teaching in it?

There was an internal debate among the Spaniards about the appropriate language of instruction. The king and the royal officials held that the Maya should be taught in Spanish (O'Flaherty 1979: 186–87). The crown was not hostile to the Indian languages, but "believed that none of them were sufficiently rich and supple to allow them to be used for explaining the mysteries of the Christian faith" (Ricard 1966: 51). Also, the crown associated the ceremonies of the Indians with their language, and thought that if they got rid of one, the other would disappear as well. In order to teach the doctrina in Spanish, the crown wanted the friars to teach the Spanish language to the Maya before beginning religious instruction. Many friars thought the order impractical (O'Flaherty 1979: 204, n. 64). The Franciscan provincial in Guatemala rejected the order. "A *cedula* of Your Majesty came here to the effect that we should teach the Indians Spanish. This is a very difficult thing to do especially as we are not enough to teach them the Our Father, Hail Mary, Credo and Salve Regina, for the fewness of our numbers and the largeness of theirs. Even less can we teach them Spanish and more so that they do not give themselves to it, nor do they desire to speak it, and some [who] do learn it, they corrupt it so that it is unintelligible" (O'Flaherty 1979: 176). As seen in chapter 8 the manuals of the friars and accompanying documents all recommended teaching in the Indian languages.

Another language problem was the use of Latin. Some friars required the recitation of doctrina prayers in Latin as a prerequisite to receiving baptism. Ximénez raged at the practice, saying that the Latin words were mispronounced and the practice was completely useless for communicating the meaning of the sacrament. He saw it as promoting the Mayan interpretation of baptism as a ritual by which a person acknowledged allegiance to the king and became a Spanish citizen (Ximénez 1965: 713–14).

But the more important linguistic question was the friars' ability to communicate in the Mayan languages. In the historical accounts some priests are noted as speaking a Mayan language fluently. The Mayan languages, with their structure and concepts based on the Mayan worldview, differ greatly from European languages and worldviews. This makes it very difficult for Europeans to master them. Some friars were excellent linguists and spoke the Indian languages fluently. But in the writer's experience in Mayan areas, I have heard fluency attributed to a number of priests and anthropologists whose level of skill was sufficient for day-to-day practical purposes, but not for engaging in the use of metaphor, word play, and philosophical or theological discourse. Scholes found a 1579 Mexican manuscript confirming this view. "In this land [Mexico] the languages spoken by the natives are many and very different from one another; and most of these so unintelligible and poorly articulated that it is extremely difficult to understand them sufficiently to be able to discuss in them the mysteries of our holy religion; and for this reason, among many ministers, those who know how and can explain to them in a fitting manner the meaning of the gospel are very rare" (Landa 1941: 69–70, n. 313).

Molina, in the introduction to his *Confesionario mayor* wrote that he composed the manual so that the friars "might know the proper words as they are understood by the people as these words must be used in asking questions and understanding responses in the administration of the sacrament of penance." He further says that the friars "must know the true and literal meaning of a word and the people's way of speaking (which many do not) even though they speak the language and are learned" (Moreno 1984: 12).

To some extent the friars recognized their difficulties. A 1582 document from Yucatán notes that of the forty-two Franciscan priests ministering to the Maya, nineteen (45 percent) were capable of preaching and hearing confessions in Yukatek Maya, nine (22 percent) could hear confessions only, and fourteen (33 percent) could do neither (Montalvo 1938: 77–79). The criteria on which these assessments were made are not given. For some, preaching may have meant reciting a memorized text. Hearing confessions may have consisted of the friar memorizing a list of sins and the Mayan penitent, having memorized the same list, parroting back those pertinent to his or her case. Neither of these situations required much fluency in the language.

Literal translation is often impossible between languages that are based on radically different worldviews. When their concepts do not completely overlap, or in some cases do not overlap at all, an attempt should be made to transpose meaning between the two worldviews. This always involves loss of some intelligibility. This was the heart of the language problem and what Molina was writing about. Burkhart has described these problems with regard to translating Spanish moral terms into Nahuatl, a language with some similarity to the Mayan languages. As an example of partial overlap of concepts, there was no word or concept in Nahuatl that exactly expressed the Christian concept of sin. The Nahuatl term the friars used as a noun literally means something damaged. Its verb form means to go bad, become corrupt, spoil, or injure oneself. "These terms have quite a broad range of meaning. . . . Any sort of error or misdeed could be labeled *tlatlacolli* from conscious moral transgression to judicially defined crimes to accidental or unintentional damage" (Burkhart 1989: 28). The term could be applied to a weaver who tangled her yarn or to a feather worker who ruined the feathers. Burkhart concludes,

> Christianity as presented at the dialogical frontier did not constitute a coherent, internally consistent system, but, rather, a hodgepodge of concepts—shreds of Christian orthodoxy and patches of Nahuatl meaning. Not only was the whole religion confused, but its presentation varied from friar to friar and even from one sermon to the next. The concept of *tlatlacolli* did not fit with the concept of individual moral responsibility. The friars' talk of filth, penance and peripheral dangers resembled indigenous discourse while their talk of love and salvation did not, and since the former concepts were interpreted in ways consistent with indigenous thought, the latter concepts could make little sense in relation to them. Christian purification reiterated too neatly their Nahua cognates to be perceived as linked to a wholly different kind of reality. The differences between the two world views were not consistently stated and stressed in terms that would have made them clear to the Nahuas. (1989: 187)

A similar problem arose with regard to the word to be used for God, an issue that was long debated among the friars (Ximénez 1965: 715; Vazquez 1938: 127).

In summary, among the friars who could speak the Mayan languages at all, probably few spoke them fluently (O'Flaherty 1979: 172). But regardless of their degree of fluency, all ran into the problem of trying to convey concepts partially or completely different from those in the Mayan worldview.

The Quality of the Substitutes for the Friars

Mayan communities were obliged to maintain the church and to provide the priests with the goods and services for meeting their physical needs, for performing Catholic ritual, and for teaching the doctrina. Depending on the size of the town, this obligation could require the full-time services of one, several, or many local people. The local person in charge of these functions was the fiscal. When the priest was present in a community, the fiscal assisted in all ritual activity as well as translating sermons for those priests who needed help. The fiscal or an assistant also taught the doctrina whether the priest was present or not (Farriss 1984: 304–5, 335; O'Flaherty 1979: 188). When present, the friar in charge of instruction attended the doctrina sessions to make sure that the sessions were being conducted properly, but he did not teach the doctrina himself.

The friars operated schools in some towns of residencia where they instructed the future fiscales and teachers (Vazquez 1944: 66). But how many attended these schools and how well the fiscales performed their function of transmitting the intended message of the friars is open to question. Given the logistics of training them and the previously described difficulty of translation between Spanish and the Mayan languages, there were bound to be problems. In the seldom-visited villages, "Such catechism as the children learned was taught by the fiscal who was ordinarily no less ignorant and confused than his pupils" (Farriss 1984: 213). In Yucatán some doctrina teachers used their positions to disseminate the Katun prophecies (Jones 1989: 274).

Method of Teaching

As a result of their ethnocentrism, the friars viewed the Maya as children. They did not realize that a firmly embedded cultural structure was already in Mayan minds, much less understand anything about it. They assumed they were dealing with young minds who could absorb the doctrina by rote memory (O'Flaherty 1979: 170; Farriss 1984: 305). When questioned as to what they had learned, the Maya were only required to parrot the drilled material. The doctrina in its entirety would be very difficult to memorize, even for persons in a nonliterate culture who were accustomed to extensive memorization. As a result, learning the doctrina was frequently reduced to memorizing the opening five or six prayers in Molina's manual (see table 8.1). For his part the friar needed only to memorize the prayers in the Mayan language so that he could examine the students. When the fiscal substituted for the friar, he used the same method. This made instruction easier for him as he did not have to understand the content of his drill.

The Friars' Attitudes

The previously described problems are based on the assumption that evangelization consisted of the friars communicating a set of orthodox ideas to be learned by the Maya. The friars assumed that once the Maya understood their message, they would automatically accept it. But an impediment to this acceptance was the attitude with which some friars approached their task. As Spaniards utterly convinced of their divine mandate, some assumed a haughty manner, looking down upon and demeaning the "uncivilized" Maya. Ximénez, himself a friar, lashed out against these men in a biting chapter. He said that three things were necessary for the conversion of the Maya. The first was to treat them as people and not as beasts. Therefore, they were to be taught all the doctrina and baptized with all the solemnity the church requires. Ximénez appears to be reacting to the practice of quick baptism after the memorization of a few phrases of the prayers. The second was to treat the people with love, charity, and openness, rather than using stocks, detention cells, and whippings as punishment for nonattendance at mass and doctrina sessions. Ximénez saw these methods as characteristic of the law of Mohammed, not the law of Jesus. The third was for friars to give an example in their own lives of what they were teaching, especially honesty and poverty. In this chapter, Ximénez attributes the failure of evangelization to the friars themselves, although at other times he also places blame on the lack of support by Spanish officials (1965: 713–21).

Discouragement among the Friars

The Maya, encouraged by their ruling elites, reluctantly and evasively submitted to baptism, attendance at mass, and the doctrina sessions. The first friars were pleased and thought that the Maya were being converted. León-Portilla (1974) has shown that in New Spain the first generation of friars were euphoric over their apparent successes among the indigenous populations.

But as the friars matured in their experiences, they began to understand that the effort of evangelization was not succeeding as they had hoped. The euphoria gave way to discouragement. They realized the Maya had not understood the orthodox doctrina; were still worshipping their own gods, either openly or in secret; and in the great majority of cases had not really converted. In Yucatán, Landa and the friars were horrified at the continuing worship of the Mayan gods and, as related in chapter 4, conducted an inquisition resulting in the torture and death of numerous Maya (Clendinnen 1987: 72–92).

But such efforts were futile and the majority of the Maya simply continued their accustomed way of seeking survival by the terms of the Mayan covenant: "by the late colonial period, [there was] a conviction ranging from resignation to despair that vigilance was largely futile, since the Indians would do and think as they chose regardless of their pastors' effort" (Farriss 1984: 96). Disillusioned, some friars lost their zeal for and focus on evangelization. In Chiapas and Guatemala, "a series of profound changes . . . occurred within the Dominican Order itself. . . . Whereas in 1545 the friars had arrived in Chiapas as true mendicants, determined to share the poverty of their native followers, by 1590 they had acquired a substantial number of cattle ranches, sugar ingenios and other valuable properties. In fact as the century drew to a close, they regularly devoted so much of their time to such matters that in 1589 they were ordered to sell their holdings in both Chiapas and Guatemala—an order which did not inhibit in the slightest degree their growing appetite for land. . . . Dominican monasteries which even as late as 1572 'owned in the province not one handsbreath of land,' were by 1580 deeply involved in the area's expanding agricultural economy" (Wasserstrom 1983a: 26–27, see also 35–37, 40–42). Originally, these enterprises were intended to support the Dominican monasteries, but in the climate of discouragement, some friars focused on the more tangible and attainable goals of amassing wealth (Aubry 1988: 9, 11).

In summary, the problems that existed from the beginnings of evangelization became entrenched early in the seventeenth century and remained for the entire colonial period. In most areas the role of the friars was reduced to an infrequent ritual presence while the teaching role was passed to the fiscal who became a drill instructor of the doctrina. This situation maintained the social distance between the friars and the Maya that Marroquín had lamented.

Continuation of a Case History—Acalan

Chapter 7 closed with the story of the Spaniards' peaceful entry into Acalan and the arrival of the encomenderos. It continues here with the arrival of three Franciscan friars as described in *The Title of Acalan Tixchel* (Restall 1998: 65–76). "These padres came at a time when they [the Maya] had not yet destroyed and finished with listening to the words of their [own] priests. The Castilian men came with the padres to conquer the land; they came to bring the true god and his word. They taught the people that already our gods were destroyed and the day had already come when their worship would be ended; 'You will never again see them worshipped, and he who does worship them lives a life of deceit; anyone who does worship them will be really punished. For they have had their time. Therefore nobody shall deceive the people, for that time has now passed'" (Restall 1998: 65). Notice that the document reveals how the transition between the traditional gods and the god of the Spaniards is interpreted by Mayan metaphysics as the ending of one cycle and the beginning of another.

Sometime later the ruler was dying. He assembled the district leaders and addressed them: "As my life is ending, I entreat you to serve the one god. I have seen and heard the word of the priests; it will not be destroyed or ended. The truth and goodness of their statements is becoming realized. Therefore you should seek and bring the teaching padres to preach to you and teach you" (66). His successor sent a delegation to Campeche to request a visit by the friars, "so that you will come and explain to our ears and teach us the word of god *Dios*, for we have already heard news that men are being baptized by you padres. We wish this too and thus we have come to seek you" (66).

The friar who received them replied, "My sons it gives me much pleasure that you wish to take your souls out of the hands of the devils and that you wish to hear and understand the word of God, for such a duty and burden is mine and that of us padres" (66). The friar was unable to come but promised to send another as soon as he could arrange it.

A friar arrived in 1550 and began to evangelize in Acalan, more than twenty-three years after the visit of Cortés and twenty years after first contact with the encomendero. The friar immediately summoned the Mayan authorities and as the first order of business, attacked their idols:

> My sons, I am aware that in order to seek me and bring me to you, you went a long way, a journey of ten to fifteen days. I am pleased to be with you, although I have endured the miseries of the road and the canoe. First of all I must tell you that you cannot worship two lords, two fathers, only one father is to be loved. I have come to tell you, to explain, that the one single God is three in one person—God the Father, God the Son, God the Holy Spirit—who created the invisible heaven. . . . I wish you all to come and show me your devils. (67)

The Acalans brought some idols to the friar, who proceeded to burn them.

The question of the idols did not immediately go away. "The devils which had been buried in secret places by the people . . . were sought out in all the *cahob* [districts] of the jurisdiction. The guardians of the devils went to fetch them to be burned, for those men who kept them were imprisoned and beaten before the eyes of all the people. In this way the idols disappeared. Some willingly caused them to disappear; other caused them to disappear out of fear" (67).

The Doctrina and Baptism

Then the friar "began to teach them to recite and sing the Paternoster [Our Father], the Ave Maria [Hail Mary], the Credo [Creed], and the articles of faith. Then they were given their names [were baptized]. . . . "And thus they became Christians" (67). Chapter 8 described the content of the doctrina. In this instance, it had been shortened to some of the prayers and the articles of faith.

Why did the people of Acalan submit to the previous Spanish demands for tribute and to the requirements for baptism? "conversion was for the Mayas, as with all Mesoamerican peoples, an assumed consequence of conquest. Because military victory and political dominance were evidence of spiritual strength, the acceptance of a new system of rituals was a logical, political decision" (Restall 1998: 149). They were accepting the stronger gods of the Spaniards by the same cultural logic as the Guatemalan Maya. The difference here was that it was accomplished without force, an "insinuated conquest" to use Restall's phrase.

There were also many political advantages for the Maya who accepted baptism. They were able to expand their area of rule and incorporate other Mayan groups.

Congregation

The friar did not remain among the Acalans, but later two other friars appeared; one to baptize and administer the sacraments, the other to organize and encourage the people to move from inland locations and congregate in Tixchel nearer the coast. Through this area passed the trails connecting Acalan with the coastal Yukatek towns of Champoton and Campeche in one direction and with Tabasco and the rest of Mexico in the other. The rationale for this relocation was that the inland towns were "a long way for the padres to come and so they seldom administered the sacraments to them, and because [Tixchel] was just a league from where the padres came through from Mexico, those of St. Francis, St. Augustine, St. Dominic, and the [secular] clergy, who spoke of the word of God, and because the Castilian men, the Spaniards, often passed through that way, and also because they would be near the governor and principal magistrate sent by our lord the king in order to administer justice to the subject people" (68–69). The congregation began in 1557 but was not completed until 1560. Initially, some resisted or were not allowed to move by their encomendero. Sometime before 1586 the Franciscans established a residencia in Tixchel with four dependent communities.

Later some groups fled Tixchel because of famine but returned at the urging of the cacique who was also the Spanish-appointed governor of Acalan. Another group fled to escape abuse by their encomendero and founded the community of Zapotitlán. "Tixchel was given a great deal of work because of these people—because of the commission which don Pablo Paxbolon, our governor, held from the governor who was serving in the city of Mérida, by dint of which he made us clear the road and open the difficult rapids of the Acalan river where the padre passed, and carry him in a chair where he could not pass. This was so the unconverted who were in Zapotitlán might become Christians, as we have said, and in order to carry ornaments from our church, such as chalice, missal, chasuble, frontal [altar cloth], adornment for the mass and also the images. And our sons went to teach them the Christian doctrine" (70).

Refugees and the Maya Conquistador

At this time the Spaniards were attempting to extend their control of Yucatán. Some Mayan groups who fled the Spanish advance found refuge on the frontiers of Acalan. In 1574 the cacique of Acalan encouraged a refugee group to settle in Acalan and acknowledge the king and the church with these words:

"Lords, I do not come to wage war nor did I come to seize you. I come only to preach to you the word of God and that which his Majesty orders me to tell you, in order that we may love one another and have the same will in our hearts, so that we may love God and enjoy the justice of his Majesty—which is the good life. It is for this reason that I come. And if we bring weapons, it is to secure ourselves against whatever might happen to us, for we do not know what people we may encounter" (72). The cacique brought a delegation from this group to Tixchel to meet the friar who taught them "the four prayers and the articles, commandments and what [the] Holy Mother Church ordains, and having learned it, the padre baptized them." From the church in Tixchel they carried back ornaments and images for the church in the new community. The same pattern was repeated to settle several other refugee groups.

At the end of 1602 the Franciscan friars were ordered to leave Tixchel and hand the parish over to a priest of the secular clergy who arrived early in 1603. This is an early example of the secularization of Mayan parishes that will be discussed in the following chapter.

Conclusion

Although the friars appear to have made some contact with most Mayan groups, or at least the elites of these groups, they faced a series of problems that blocked their evangelization efforts. Where they did make contact, in many instances the problems of insufficient manpower, of the distance and time of travel to the scattered Maya, and of the time required to practice their monastic routine, all hindered the frequency and quality of their contact with groups of manageable size. For those towns where these difficulties were overcome, there remained the problems of language barriers and incompatible worldviews, incompetent fiscales, teaching by rote memorization, and the demeaning attitude of some friars. This funnel of problems progressively diminished the probability that the content of the Christian covenant would be accurately communicated to the Maya. The Dominican friar Ximénez who lived in Guatemala for more than forty years, seventeen of them in K'iche' towns of residencia, and who knew the Maya better than any of the other colonial chroniclers, came to the same conclusion (Ximénez 1965: 713). He echoes the conclusion of Sahagún in Mexico. (The evangelization effort can be viewed as an immense project of applied anthropology intended to change the worldview of the Maya. The appendix looks at the program from this perspective.)

The Secular Clergy

A new phase of the evangelization effort began with the replacement of the friars by the secular clergy. A few of these transfers took place in the seventeenth century, but most were enacted in the latter part of the eighteenth century.

The Situation Inherited from the Friars: The Separation of the Teacher Role from that of the Ritual Specialist

As discussed in chapter 10, there were many more towns of visita than residencia in spite of occasional attempts to recongregate the Mayan populations. The majority of the Mayan population lived in or surrounding the visitas. At most a friar make a weekly visit to these towns, more often visiting only a few times or once a year and not infrequently only once every several years. The friar celebrated the mass and performed baptisms, all in Latin. Hindered by their lack of fluency in a Mayan language, most friars relegated the religious instruction to the fiscales who became drill sergeants inculcating the doctrina by rote memory. In this context, many Maya came to view the priest exclusively as a ritual functionary who performed masses and baptisms in a symbolic code that was foreign to them. This situation created a wedge, splitting the priest's role as ritual performer from that of teacher. This role splitting began at the very beginning of evangelization as the logical outcome of the problems associated with the bicultural situation.

The friars apparently did not fully realize the implications of sloughing off their teaching role. In a Catholic culture the celebration of the mass, with its symbolic code, had a partly pedagogical function and was intended to increase morality. The friars' complacency with a mechanical ritual function was aided by their view that the monastic routine and the administration of the sacraments were of far greater importance than their other roles. In Catholic theology the sacramental rituals, especially the mass, were seen as conferring divine grace simply by their performance. This is the theological thesis known as *ex opere operato* that was enshrined in the decrees of the Council of Trent (Denzinger 1955: 63, no. 851): "If anyone shall say that by the said sacraments of the New Law, grace is not conferred from the work which has been worked [*ex opere operato*], but that faith alone in the divine promise suffices to obtain grace: let him be anathema."[1] A narrow but frequent interpretation of this position was that the mere presence of the priest celebrating the mass would call down God's grace on the Maya to help bring about their conversion and salvation. As seen in chapter 6, making ritual an end in itself has been a frequent problem of biblically based covenants.

Secularization

Catholic policy for mission areas was to have the missionary orders be the first clerical groups to enter them, evangelize the population, build up local parishes and a secular clergy, then turn over the parishes to the bishops and the secular clergy. For this reason the king originally entrusted the task of evangelization to the friars. They were subject to their own provincials and were not under the immediate jurisdiction of a bishop except that he had authority to allow or disallow their presence as functioning clerics in his diocese. Most of the early bishops were friars, with the exception of Bishop Marroquín, but secular clerics were appointed as bishops as soon as it was feasible.

As more secular clergy became bishops, they began demanding that the friars hand over the doctrinas as soon as there were enough secular clergy to staff them. The friars, however, did not want to give up their doctrinas. This problem created long-standing tensions between the bishops and the religious orders, with the Audiencia frequently playing the role of referee. This ongoing dispute began early in the colonial period but did not reach a climax until the latter part of the eighteenth century. In the case of Acalan described in the pre-

Table 11.1. Secularization in Guatemala: Number and Percentage of Towns Administered by Friars and Secular Clergy, 1550–1820

Year	Towns with Secular Clergy	Towns with Friars	Percentage with Friars
1555	1	83	99
1600	98	216	69
1650	130	236	65
1700	150	225	60
1750	160	236	60
1776	350	69	16
1820	380	43	10

Source: Oss 1986: 135. Numbers estimated from a graph.

vious chapter, the Franciscans were required to hand over the parish as early as 1604.

By 1737 the Franciscans still retained control of about half of the Mayan parishes in Yucatán, twenty-nine out of sixty. By 1766 they held twenty of these parishes, containing 36 percent of the Mayan population, and retained them until independence from Spain in the next century (Farriss 1984: 90). In Guatemala an order for secularization was issued in 1583 but never carried out. The friars administered to 99 percent of the Mayan towns in 1550 (table 11.1). When Guatemala was raised to the rank of an archdiocese in 1743, the archbishop intensified his efforts at secularization. With the intervention of the Audiencia in favor of the archbishop, the abrupt change came between 1750 and 1776, when the percentage of towns administered by friars declined to 16 percent, then to 10 percent by the end of the colonial period. The majority of parishes were transferred by 1770, although the process continued until 1815 (Oss 1986: 137–39). In Chiapas efforts to secularize the parishes began in 1584 initiating a long, drawn-out battle between the Dominicans and various bishops, encomenderos, and Spanish officials. It did not end until 1771 when almost all the parishes were secularized (Wasserstrom 1983a: 51–59; Gosner 1992: 58–60). The impetus toward secularization was not exclusively a regional phenomenon. It was encouraged by the Spanish Bourbon monarchy. In Europe the same trend of weakening the orders existed and culminated with the suppression of the Jesuits.

The Subculture of the Secular Clergy

The secular clergy did not live the communal life of the friar with its intense focus on spirituality and chanting the Divine Office; they were not bound by formal vows of poverty, chastity, and obedience, although they made promises of chastity and obedience to their bishops. Ideally they lived in the parish assigned to them by the bishop. If several priests were assigned to a parish, they shared a residence but there was no monastic routine. The Divine Office was recited privately, not chanted, at any convenient time. As Bishop Marroquín argued, the secular priest's function was to be among the people so that he would be personally known to them and readily available to serve their spiritual needs, especially by his example and his administration of the sacraments at the important moments of transition in the human life cycle. Marroquín considered these characteristics of the secular clergy as better suited for carrying out the task of evangelization than the monastic lifestyle.

The secular priest lived and worked more independently than did the friar. "A secular priest was free—and indeed expected—to promote and advance his own career by competing for honours and appointments with his fellows. In contrast to the monastic ideal of submission and obedience within the community, the secular mentality was more aggressive and individualistic. It stressed success, reflected in promotions from a lowly clerical station through a series of more lucrative benefices" (Oss 1986: 172). Most priests would start out working as a coadjutor priest to a beneficed priest whose position was financed by an endowment. The coadjutors changed parishes frequently in search of a better-paying position or one that would be more advantageous for advancement to a benefice position. The secular clergy did not embrace poverty as a virtue in itself. They could own and manage in their own name tangible and intangible property acquired by inheritance, private investments, or parish stipends. These characteristics created a more independent and individualistic lifestyle than that of the friar. In theory, the priests' acquisition and management of their personal finances was to be subordinate to their priestly duties, but in the absence of supervision, there was opportunity for abuse.

In spite of the differences between the secular priests and the friars, the secular clergy continued evangelization among the Maya with much the same structure as under the friars. As the secular clergy took over the doctrinas, the expected result would be that they would be subdivided into parishes with a secular priest living in each of the former towns of visita. But the secular priest who took over a doctrina did not wish to give up the endowed income (benefices) and the large number of Maya that were attached to the visitas. Thus, instead of subdividing the doctrinas, the benefice priests retained them and employed coadjutor priests at lower salaries to attend to the former towns of visita with the result that many remained without resident priests and were seldom visited (Oss 1986: 65).

The Creolization of the Secular Clergy

As time passed the clergy, both friars and secular priests, was composed of fewer Spaniards and more creoles. Ximénez (1973: 1) notes that as of the centennial of the Dominican Province in Guatemala in 1651, there had never been a creole provincial. As a remedy to the discrimination by the *peninsulares* (friars born in Spain) against creoles, the pope ordered that administrative posts in the religious orders were to be rotated (*alternativa*) between peninsulares and creoles so that neither group could dominate. In 1781 80 percent of the Franciscans were creoles, and in 1800 60 percent of the Dominicans were (Oss 1986: 159).

But the great majority of creole priests were secular clergy. The creoles had been socialized in the colonial culture and carried into the priesthood many of the characteristics of that background. Religion in creole culture, as in Spain, was a cultural religion, a single religious tradition, most frequently the folk or "little tradition," that was almost universally accepted from childhood. This tradition was not questioned but simply taken for granted and for many it operated at a subconscious level.

Training for the priesthood did not alter the "little tradition" outlook of many of the clergy. A report to the crown on the condition of the clergy noted "in 1678 Ciudad Real had its own seminary. Only sixteen of the forty-eight were judged functionally literate, and only twelve of them knew the native languages. . . . The failures were blamed in part on neglect for letters in the curriculum of the seminary, but the commission also attributed the seculars' lack of intellectual sophistication to the cultural environment in the homes of Ciudad Real's Spanish families, where the children grew up speaking a mix of Nahuatl and Castilian learned from Indian servants from the city's barrios" (Gosner 1992: 59).

The creole priests thought that by administering the sacraments they were doing their duty (*ex opere operato*) and either took for granted that the people understood the basics of Catholic orthodoxy or complained about their ignorance. The Maya considered themselves Catholics, and the creoles assumed they basically were. A typical example of the creole mentality was the secular priest who visited Zinacantán for the festivals. Rus describes what this writer also experienced in conversations with this priest: "In the 1960s, when anthropologists working in Zinacantán . . . began publishing detailed accounts of animal-soul companions, native seers who solved health complaints by divining their spiritual causes, and rituals on mountaintops and at cave entrances, San Cristóbal's new bishop, Samuel Ruiz, asked the parish priest—a man who spoke some Tzotzil and had lived in Zinacantán off and on since his youth [on a small ranch of a ladino relative]—what he knew of such things. The priest emphatically denied they existed. At most, he claimed the anthropologist may have picked up some vague notion of them from the oldest, most ignorant people. Ten days later, however, he retracted his words, having discovered on direct questioning that . . . [the fiscales], men with whom he had worked closely for many years, in fact, had a private, or maybe better, 'hidden' ceremonial life of which he had known nothing" (Rus 2002: 1024).[2]

Lack of Instruction in and Concern for Orthodoxy

The creole priests retained the situation they had inherited from the friars—that of functioning as ritual specialists and making little or no effort at teaching. Because the secular clergy were largely indifferent to Mayan religious practices, the insistence on orthodoxy gave way to toleration. This was a sharp reversal from the days of book burnings and idol smashings in the early colonial period. The creoles grew up personally knowing Maya. Some were nursed and taken care of by Mayan nannies in their childhood (Ximénez 1971b: 94). Although a few priests spoke a Mayan language as their first language, the language problem escalated with secularization. The secular clergy were more intent on Hispanicizing the Maya and wished to do it by eliminating any use of the Mayan languages (Oss 1986: 144, 170). This put more distance between the clergy and the Maya.

The secular clergy knew the Maya had some religious customs different from theirs, but they saw no harm in these. A Yukatek bishop observed about his clergy, "Since they suck no other milk but that of Indian women, they are very partial to the local rites" (Farriss 1984: 342). Farriss aptly labels these priests as "Mayanized clergy." Cortés y Larraz (1958 II: 270) concluded that the cultural background of the creole priests allowed them to take for granted and excuse the concubinage, robberies, murders, incest, and the lack of Christian moral values in the parishes on the part of both Spaniards and Indians. The archbishop was perplexed about how to solve the problem.

Problems of the Secular Clergy

A number of difficulties thwarted Marroquín's hope for a secular clergy immersed in their communities.

Recruitment

From the very beginning there were problems with the quality of recruits. Footloose priests came from Spain and other European countries. They were allowed to negotiate their salaries with parishes and casually moved on when not satisfied. They were "unemployed and perhaps unqualified members of the peninsula's spiritual proletariat . . . [who] crossed the Atlantic in hopes of improving their lot . . . poor idiots and ignorant . . . understanding that within their dioceses in Spain they would not achieve any office or ecclesiastical benefice." Some were wanted for crimes in Spain (Oss 1986: 13, 42).

Another problem was corrupt bishops including Marroquín's successor,

Bernardino de Villapando. Due to the manpower shortage, he would accept any priest that came along regardless of character, training, or past history (Oss 1986: 42–43). He exercised no supervision over them, allowing them to do what they wanted in exchange for flattery and tolerance of his opulent lifestyle.

Economic Abuse

The recruitment problems led to problems of economic abuse. The crown had exempted the Maya from the obligation of paying tithes in order to facilitate evangelization. "The removal of the tithe as a source of parish income had pushed the clergy to develop other sources of income outside the boundaries of central control and supervision. This took away in advance a tool that colonial authorities in the capital could have employed to influence local priests, whether regular or secular. Instead, parish fees and contributions came to outstrip tributes and tithes in value, and they represented the richest tax base rural Guatemala had to offer. The clergy administered these revenues autonomously" (Oss 1986: 155). For some priests this lack of supervision led to a lifestyle marked by a large number of servants, fine clothing, and travel by sedan chair carried by servants when they visited outlying parts of the parish (Oss 1986: 156–57). Some secular priests came to view their parishes simply as benefices, were seldom present in them, and occupied their time in managing plantations, raising cattle, or other business activities. No sooner did some pastors take over a parish than they proceeded to take land away from the Maya for a plantation of indigo dyestuffs, cattle, cacao, or sugar, or sometimes all of these (Ximénez 1971b: 51). As a result, there were many complaints from the Indians that they were forced to work on these plantations by priests who paid no attention to the king's law against such practices and who neglected their religious ministry. In Yucatán, "the detailed diocesan records of the late colonial period, even discounting general fulminations from bishops about the laxity of the local clergy, lead to the unavoidable conclusion that the vast majority of the secular clergy had come to view an Indian parish as a lucrative but tedious sinecure, which was left in the hands of the *maestros cantores* [fiscales] even when the curate was technically in residence" (Farriss 1984: 336).

Another abuse arose because of the priest's position as an intermediary between the Mayan communities and Spanish townspeople demanding goods and services from the Maya. This led to the priest performing and sometimes abusing the functions of a mercantile trader or a labor contractor (Oss 1986: 44–45). Some secular priests were relatives or close friends of members of the encomendero class. Bishops would be pressured to appoint these priests to parishes within certain encomienda areas. Such priests would then be put in charge of collecting the tribute for the encomendero.

Whatever the priest's personal situation, he typically simply appeared at the Mayan festivals to celebrate the mass and perform baptisms in a very mechanical fashion. The increase of creole priests more than compensated for the loss of those sent from Spain. But relative to the task at hand, many Mayan areas continued to have only incidental contact between the priest and individual parishioners. The dream of Marroquín was never realized. In spite of this state of affairs, the Maya still insisted on the services of the Catholic priest and his rituals. Recall that during the Quisteil uprising of 1761 (see chapter 4) a major complaint was neglect of the visita towns.

Evangelization in the New Republics

The nineteenth century saw the colonies gain their independence from Spain followed by a period of internal struggles to control the new republics.

Independence from Spain

The clergy was divided on the question of independence. In Guatemala the religious orders—who as a result of secularization were mostly concentrated in the schools, hospitals, convents, and monasteries in the capital—were against it. They were influenced by the peninsulares as well as the threat to their considerable landholdings and other assets. The secular clergy, largely creole and usually stationed in the rural parishes, were highly sympathetic to independence.

Independence from Spain came in 1821 and brought a new philosophy of government and economics to the former colonies under the label of "liberalism." Inspired by the philosophy of the French Enlightenment, liberalism gave importance to social and economic progress. These goals placed an emphasis on the individual rather than the group, and the use of reason rather than blind acceptance of tradition. The new governments refused to recognize the privileged position of the Catholic Church, which led to confrontations. In 1829 the archbishop of Guatemala and most members of the religious orders were expelled from the country. This was followed by government seizure of silver ornaments and jewels from the churches, and of other ecclesiastical assets to finance its modernization programs. In 1839 there was a conservative reaction against the liberal reforms that brought to power Rafael Carrera and Vicente Cerna. Carrera invited back the expelled religious and cooperated with the higher clergy, although always on his own terms. During this period "almost one third of the territory of Guatemala was in the hands of the Church and the upper class. Commerce was insignificant, communication almost unknown" (Holleran 1949: 146).

Although the liberal-conservative battles were taking place at the national level and primarily in Guatemala City, they reached into the Mayan communities and some Maya were important components of various armies. But the worldview of the Mayan population in the countryside continued essentially unchanged. During the war with El Salvador in 1906, four shamans were hired to perform rituals for a Momostenango military unit, with each soldier contributing two to four reales for their services (Carmack 1995: 188).

The Dismantling of the Church Infrastructure

In 1871 the liberals regained power under the leadership of García Granados and Justo Rufino Barrios. They undertook a determined effort to remove the influence of the church. They expelled all the religious orders and nationalized all their properties, including furnishings, investments, or anything else of value. The former schools, hospitals, monasteries, and convents were converted into public buildings for various civil and community functions. Although the secular clergy were not directly affected, all seminaries were closed creating a recruiting problem (Holleran 1949: 166–81).

These policies remained in effect until the overthrow of the Arbenz government in 1954. The conservative government put into power by the United States in that year allowed the religious and foreign clergy to enter the country. Protestant missionaries were invited to begin their programs of evangelization. These events began a period of change that is beyond the scope of this work.

Near Extinction of the Clergy in the Mayan Areas

The church had extremely serious manpower problems under the policies of the liberal governments. After the expulsion of the religious orders in 1872, there were only 119 secular priests left in the country. Most of them were foreigners located in Guatemala City, resulting in an acute shortage of clergy in the Mayan areas: "The province of Quezaltenango, with over 1,000,000 inhabitants has only thirty priests. The parish of Huehuetenango, with 176,000 souls, has only two priests" (Holleran 1949: 236). In the nearby Mayan town of Santiago Chimaltenango, "Until the fiesta of Corpus Christi in 1937 a priest had not visited Chimaltenango in over two years. The Padre at Huehuetenango has more than twenty *municipios* under his care" (Wagley 1949: 50). In the overall picture,

> Guatemala with its population of over three million has only one hundred twenty Roman Catholic priests, about one priest to every 30,000 faithful.
> . . . The priests are very poor, and although well-meaning and sincere, they are obviously ill-equipped to deal with the problems at hand, the exigencies of the time. They have been brought up in an old world tradition. They are, without exception, courteous and willing to talk all day

about the tragedy of the situation, and the plight of the people, but seem to be without the semblance of an idea to do anything to remedy matters. (Holleran 1949: 235–36)

Much the same thing was happening in Mexico. The impact can be seen in the contrast of the manpower situation in the San Cristóbal diocese between the late colonial period in 1778 and 1963. In 1778 there were sixty-six secular priests, sixty-six Dominicans, fifteen Franciscans, and eight Mercedarians in the area (Laughlin 2003: 82). In 1963 when the diocese was still trying to recover from the anticlerical policies of the 1930s and 1940s, there were only thirty-eight secular priests and several Jesuits. One secular priest was responsible for 75,000 people in Zinacantán, Chamula, Mitontic, Pantelhó, Chenalhó, and El Bosque (Early 1965).

The Maya continued their practice of the Mayan covenant little affected by any evangelization:

To much of what the official church says the Indian is apparently indifferent. This is in part due to the fact that there is such a dearth of priests; many villages see a clergyman only once a year and they have become accustomed to carrying on their own projects, independent of any supervision. Yet, even in villages in which priests are in residence, the Indians pay little attention to formal ceremonials [of the priest]. It seems absolutely necessary for each Indian to be doing something or saying something that makes him a personal participant in religious acts. I have attended countless services where Mass was in process of being celebrated, only to have the Indians going and coming constantly, lighting their candles, scattering their flower petals on the floor, visiting the saints' statues, murmuring prayers for their families, their crops, their animals, etc., oblivious of the sermon and the ritual. And yet the Indians are anxious for the padre to come down the aisle and bless each one of them and sprinkle holy water on petals and candles. (Holleran 1949: 232–33)

Holleran's experience echoes the description of the festivals in Zinacantán in chapter 3. This author, in his experiences in Mayan areas in the 1960s, believes the account accurately represents conditions that existed in many Mayan parishes. The main outlines of the situation began in the early colonial period and have persisted and been strengthened by the continuing problems described in this and the previous chapter. The Catholic Church was devastated by the liberal reforms and was in worse condition in the mid-twentieth century than in the early colonial period. In areas where a priest was seldom seen, the local Mayan communities assumed complete jurisdiction over the churches with their saints and fully integrated them into their worldview making them Mayan churches and images.

A Case History

In 1932 Oliver LaFarge made a community survey of Santa Eulalia, a Kanjobal-speaking Mayan community in the upper reaches of the Cuchumatán Mountains in the department of Huehuetenango, Guatemala. During the period from 1602 to 1632 it was a Mercedarian visita from Chiantla; from 1632 to 1673, a visita from Jacaltenango; and from 1673 to the 1930s, a visita from Soloma (table 10.5). LaFarge's commentary describes the typical situation of Mayan parishes and Catholic priests in the first half of the twentieth century following the liberal reforms. The priests were

> presented with an impossible task. . . . The cure [parish] of Soloma embraces San Juan Ixcoy, San Rafael Independencia, San Mateo Ixtatán, Santa Eulalia, Quetzal and Barrillas, with a population of not less than twenty thousand Indians, speaking two distinct languages, and two thousand ladinos. Even the most energetic priest would find it difficult to give adequate service to all these villages in that exceedingly difficult and mountainous country, where the precipitous downward and upward pitch of the ridges renders travel extremely difficult, fatiguing and seldom permits one to ride at a trot.
>
> In actual practice it must be stated that the priests of backcountry sections show little desire to do more than carry out the formal requirements of their liturgy. The best of them—I generalize from experience in Mexico and Guatemala—are good and devout men, anxious to maintain interest among their congregations and willing to undergo hardships. But even these men habitually wink at such non-Christian practices as come under their observation and make no attempt to investigate or deal with the completely distorted and even blasphemous [to LaFarge] religious beliefs which lie behind the Indians' Catholic observances. In this there is more than a little of the general caste attitude, which regards the Indians as somehow subhuman.
>
> . . . The most earnest pastor has to fight against the inertia of custom. When the priest at Soloma visited us, the Indians were agonized because we had not given them warning so that the church bells might be rung while he rode through town and the appropriate gifts gathered and brought. Established custom expects the priest to travel with a large retinue furnished without charge by the town from which he comes and to be entertained lavishly where he arrives. At Jacaltenango in 1932, there

was a most remarkable man, the Padre Ybisate. This priest had completely broken through the traditions, visiting his missions without warning or fanfare, and demanding no more for himself, either there or in the home village, than was necessary to maintain life. He was an unfailing source of astonishment to the Indians, who were beginning vaguely to feel that he was admirable, not merely foolish.

. . . Save where an exceptional pastor has brought his office back to life, it may be said for these Indians that they require him only for baptism and the Fiesta. (LaFarge 1947: 79–81)

Summary

The last two chapters have described the many problems Catholic clergy encountered in their efforts to evangelize the Maya. In spite of these problems, during the period of evangelization the Maya developed a strong devotion to the saints, the mass, and baptism, as demonstrated in chapters 2 to 4. They continued to go to considerable effort to obtain the services of the non-Mayan Catholic priest for their festivals. This continued Mayan insistence in the face of all the problems encountered and caused by the priests constitutes the anomaly presented in chapter 1. The insistence was based on the meanings the Maya attached to the Catholic ritual elements. The question at this point is: What were these meanings?

PART 5

The Mayan Perception
of Spanish Christianity

Chapter 7 demonstrated that to the Mayan mind, their defeats by the Spaniards showed the victors' gods were superior. Consequently, they wanted to adopt these gods into the Mayan covenant. There was a lapse of a generation or more between the conquest and the initiation of evangelization. During that period the Maya were left to their own resources to figure out who were the Spanish gods. Later, when the friars and the secular clergy began to carry out their plan of evangelization, the problems described in chapters 10 and 11 resulted in the Maya receiving a confused if not unintelligible message.

In spite of all the problems, the evangelization effort did have an impact on the Maya as shown in part 2. Part 5 now investigates this impact: how the structure of the evangelization effort was interpreted by the Maya and how the saints, mass, baptism, and Catholic priest were incorporated into the Mayan ritual matrix. "The initial Maya reaction to Christianity was thus not a question of ready conversion or spiritual resistance, but a question of the degree to which the potency of the new religion could be appropriated for Maya purposes. As many aspects of that religion as possible were soon localized in terms of meaning, participation and supervision. Actively and opportunistically, the Maya wove Christian symbols, rituals and organizational practices into the complex fabric of political, social and economic life in the *cah* [local municipal community]" (Restall 1997: 165).

The Necessity of the Saints
in the Mayan Worldview

The Mayan perception of the Catholic saints was conditioned by the situation of the postconquest Mayan community. In spite of the friars' campaign against traditional Mayan religion, the Spanish conquest and evangelization did not destroy traditional village life. "Although it is unlikely that any native community escaped the ravages of epidemic diseases brought across the Atlantic, native regions unevenly experienced direct conquest violence. For centuries after the arrival of Spaniards, the majority of natives subject to colonial rule continued to live in their own communities, speak their own languages, work their own fields, and be judged and ruled by their own elders. These elders wrote their own languages alphabetically . . . and engaged the colonial legal system in defense of community interests skillfully and often successfully" (Restall 2003: 73). The Spanish employed the principle of indirect rule. The farther a town was from Spanish authorities and towns of residencia, the fewer were the pressures for any change in the traditional culture.

Preservation of the Traditional Worldview

The continuity of the Mayan communities under their own authorities preserved the cultural logics of the traditional worldview.

The Cycle in Mayan Metaphysics

The Maya interpreted the Spanish intrusion, conquest, and colonization through the lens of their metaphysical principle of the cosmic cycle. "Most of the Mayan elite . . . tended to downplay the significance of the Conquest by emphasizing continuities of status, residency, and occupation from pre-Conquest times. Mayas placed the Spanish invasion, and the violence and epidemics it brought, within the larger context of history's cycles of calamity and recovery, relegating the Conquest to a mere blip in their long term local experience" (Restall 2003: 122). This experience included many wars between various Mayan groups. The Spanish were just another group with whom they had to contend, just as they had contended with the demands of the tributary Nahua and K'ichean empires in preconquest times.

Evidence that they continued to use the logic of the cycle is seen in Mayan books continuously compiled before and after the Spanish conquest. These books are known as Chilam Balam, meaning Spokesman, or Prophet, of the Jaguar Priest. Several texts of these books have been found and the place where each was found added to its title. Four have been translated: those of Maní (Craine and Reindorp 1979), of Tizimin (Edmonson 1982), of Chumayel (Edmonson 1986), and of Kaua (Bricker and Miram 2002). The first three deal primarily with Mayan history and prophecy; the Chilam Balam of Kaua deals primarily with astronomy, astrology, and medicine.

The metaphysical principle of the cycle provides the basic structure of the first three books. They are built around a series of cyclical prophecies and narratives. For each of the important cycles, a jaguar priest was appointed to preside over the prescribed rituals. The final part of the ritual was a "sermon" during which the jaguar priest predicted the events of the upcoming cycle (Edmonson 1986: 27–28). These sermons were taken down by scribes, who also added historical notes. "The Maya were clearly the people of the cycle in post-Classical and colonial times and had been for a very long time. . . . The cycle itself was called the *may*, and it was still going strong in the nineteenth century" (Edmonson 1986: 5).

The Covenant

The preservation of the traditional worldview included the prime importance of the Mayan covenant for interpreting everyday life: "each culture or cultural configuration contains a central set of ideas about the way things are and ought to be—in other words, a core of general explanations and norms around which the shared cognitive map and social order are organized. These ideas comprise the most stable part of the system both because they are central and because, being general rather than specific, they are open to varying interpretations in the ancillary concepts that flow from them and in the way they are expressed through social action. As core concepts, they provide not only the principles according to which change will take place, but also the measure of its extent; they indicate whether we are dealing with variations on a theme or an altogether new theme" (Farriss 1984: 8). This describes how the Mayan covenant functioned in defining and interpreting new situations. "The application of the cultural logic underlying the k'u'x model is not uniform; indeed the generative quality of cultural logics allows for infinite variation . . . these competing interpretations are mutually intelligible, for they are based on common logical principles. . . . In acting on cognitive models of *k'u'x* through concrete activity and in applying the k'u'x paradigm to observed behavior and relations, the standards are constantly modified in light of circumstantial contingencies. Still, continuity is maintained through the logical transposition of salient cultural schemas" (Fischer 2001: 161). Monaghan (2000: 24–49) has surveyed some of this variation.

Transmission of the Covenant

The obligation of transmitting the covenant primarily fell upon the older members of each generation.

> The traditions ought to be preserved, and for this reason, the efforts of the Tzotziles and Tzeltales strive to protect the given order or destiny of the world just as it has been handed down from generation to generation [the templates]. This is a task for the older people since they have been endowed with the ability and special knowledge for it. These include the shamans and those who know the stories from long ago. It is said about them: they have learned (*chanbil yu'unik*) or that their souls have fully arrived (*vulem xa xch'ulelik*). It is also said: they know how things really are, or they know how to conduct themselves in the proper manner (*snabeik sjamsmelol*, or *yich'ojbeik sjam-smelol*). . . . This last expression is that aspect of things which explains the why; the raison d'etre of things. (Arias 1991: 38)

The Covenant in the Late Twentieth Century

The depth and continuity of the covenant in the Mayan psyche during the colonial and national periods can be seen in Ignacio's diary, quoted in chapter 4. Upon assuming his final cargo role that would make him a principal, a respected elder of the community, he echoed the traditional perspective of the covenant by addressing his fellow cofrades in this manner:

> In the name of God, who is the heart of heaven [sky] and heart of earth, in the name of our fathers, who have given us a heritage, we ought to preserve and take care of our Mayan culture. Our fathers have bequeathed our culture in place of themselves—they have gone and turned into dust, but their spirits are always with us. Also, we are going to die, but it will be our sons and our grandsons who will serve the representative of the heart of heaven and heart of earth, who is San Juan Bautista, patron and guardian of our town, a saint of god of the clouds and of the rain, who also is *dueño* of the origins of rivers and hills, a saint of god who also is *dueño* of the storms. And the image of the saint is what we are going to serve for a year. (Bizarro 2001: 231)

In some Mayan groups, grandchildren are named for their grandparents because they are seen as taking the grandparents' place in continuing the covenant (Mondloch 1980). The souls (*ch'ulel*) of the grandparents or great-grandparents can be reincarnated in the grandchildren.

The Need for the Mayan Covenant

During the colonial period the Maya felt they needed the added protection of the Spanish gods to strengthen the power of the Mayan covenant. This perception arose out of the multiple experiences of natural disasters in the Mayan regions. "Between the arrival of the Spanish and independence in 1821, the area which comprises the modern nation of Guatemala experienced *at least* seventeen volcanic eruptions, thirty earthquakes, seventeen locust infestations, numerous epidemics, a half-dozen frosts and droughts, as well as floods. Environmental hazards prompted the Spanish to move their capital on three occasions" (Claxton 1986: 139, see also 156–63). Similar events were taking place in the Cuchumatán region, Chiapas, and Yucatán (Lovell 1985: 150–53, 158–59; Wasserstrom 1983a: 72; Farriss 1984: 61–62; MacLeod 1973: 99–100). Mayan communities felt helpless in the face of these overpowering threats to their survival. Their only recourse was to seek the protection of the gods by performing the ceremonies prescribed by the terms of the covenant. Given the high incidence of epidemics and natural disasters in all three regions, the tenacity of the Maya in maintaining their covenant was strengthened in spite of the friars.

Modes of Communication

In part 3 the Mayan and Spanish covenants were expressed as verbal or written forms that communicated the concepts of their respective worldviews. In part

4 the friars perceived conversion as a process of communication by preaching and teaching theological concepts expressed in the words of the fourteen articles. But all this has neglected another kind of communication, visual forms. In daily life there are many examples of this communication: interpreting a person's thoughts by reading his or her body language, facial expressions, or the look in the eyes, those "windows of the soul." In nature, weather conditions can be forecast by looking at cloud formations. Visual communication has been raised to a performing art, pantomime. In all these examples, the communication takes place through what is seen in the absence of words, either spoken or written. The Maya, both during the hiatus between the conquest and evangelization and during much of the confused verbal communication of evangelization itself, were still seeking to understand who the Spanish gods were and what they wanted in order for the Maya to adopt them into their covenant.

To find out about the gods, the Maya observed what the friars and Spanish laity did rather than what they said. Visual communication, like all communication, does not simply absorb the raw material of the visual field but also interprets it. In this case the interpretation was by the Mayan cultural logics described in chapter 5. The Maya minds were not empty, the blank tablets of passive children that many Spaniards perceived them to be. They had their own culture with its concepts and cultural logics that became the tools they used to digest the visual structure of evangelization and the actions of the Spanish laity. This process provided the answers to their questions.

Preliminary Visual Communication

Before the friars even began preaching and erecting churches, Spanish banners and pictures provided the first clues about Spanish gods.

The Battle Banners of the Conquistadors

Chapter 7 described the decisive battle outside Quetzaltenango in which the K'iche' were defeated. The K'iche' attributed their defeat to Spanish gods whom they described as a very fair maiden ("una niña muy blanca") protected by footless birds surrounding her ("muchos pájaros sin pies . . . rodeada a esta niña") and a very white dove above all the Spaniards ("una paloma muy blanca encima todos los españoles"). The account is taken from a Spanish translation of a K'iche' document that is now lost ("Titulo de la Casa Ixquin-Nehaib," Recinos 1957: 87). These were the first indications to the Maya as to the identity of the Spanish gods. But who were these gods?

We know from the Cortés model that the conquistadors marched into battle with banners inscribed with the cross (possibly the Santiago cross) and the Virgin Mary. In every town they entered, Cortés had the image of the Virgin placed on an altar along with a cross. Probably Alvarado, Montejo, and other

Cortés' captains continued this tradition in some fashion during their conquests. Bricker (1981: 39) translates "niña" as "a very fair maiden" and identifies her as the Virgin Mary. *Niña* in Spanish usually means a female child, whereas the English word *maiden* implies a female older than a child, one who has reached sexual maturity but has not yet married or given birth. However, Arias in a personal communication says that in San Pedro Chenalhó *niña* was formerly used in the English sense of maiden.[1] Some Spanish painters in this period showed Mary as a very young maiden. But there are other clues. The phrase "muy blanca" probably refers to white skin. The Maya always noticed the difference in skin tone between themselves and the Spaniards (Gossen 2002: 355). The *Título C'oyoi* (Carmack 1973: 301) explicitly notes this with regard to Alvarado's men. Therefore the phrase could be freely translated as "the young white goddess of the Spaniards" who would be the Virgin Mary.

The footless birds ("muchos pájaros sin pies . . . rodeada a esta niña") are heavenly cherubs whose traditional function in Judaism, Christianity, and Islam is to attend the celestial thrones of divine persons. Angelic cherubs are frequently shown in religious paintings of the Virgin, especially those portraying the Annunciation, the Immaculate Conception, the Assumption, and Mary's Coronation as Queen of Heaven. The cherubs surround the Virgin, who is either standing in glory or seated on a throne. In this scene the cherubs could easily be interpreted as protecting her. They are pictured as small winged children clothed in flowing white garments floating in clouds. Their wings probably gave rise to the Mayan description of them as birds. In a number of paintings, the flowing white garments and clouds cover all the lower extremities of the cherubs, therefore they appear footless.

In Christian iconography the Holy Spirit is often symbolized as a single white dove hovering over those on whom special graces are conferred. In Pentecostal scenes the dove hovers above the apostles. In many paintings of the Virgin, the Holy Spirit is symbolized as a single white dove hovering above her and the attending cherubs ("una paloma muy blanca encima todos los españoles"). The dove symbolizes the bestowal on the Virgin of her special prerogatives as understood by Catholic theology.[2]

There are a number of famous sixteenth- and seventeenth-century paintings of the Virgin illustrating this iconography. Notable paintings of the Annunciation include that by Titian (1559–64), several by El Greco (1570, 1575, 1590), and especially those of Bartolomé Murillo (in 1660–65). The Immaculate Conception was painted by El Greco in 1610, by Francisco de Zurbarán in 1660, and by Murillo in 1678. Peter Paul Rubens in 1626 and Murillo in 1670 depicted the Assumption.[3] This does not suggest that the conquistadors used copies of these paintings, most being done later than the initial conquest. The point is that the elements, composition, and themes of these paintings show artistic conventions during that period which could easily have produced renditions that matched the K'iche' description. This interpretation for all three symbols is confirmed by Vazquez's (1937: 25) briefer description. Therefore, some visual communication about the Spanish gods took place in the very first battles. But for the Maya many questions remained about the maiden, the footless birds, and the dove.

Mass Kits

Another indication as to the identity of the Spanish gods came in the initial days of evangelization before the construction of churches. For the mass, the friars used portable altars and mass kits containing items used in the ritual such as the chalice, a plate for the wafer, and vestments. They were similar to the kits used by military chaplains. Their use could stretch over a period of seven to eight years before enough resources were available for the construction of a church (Remesal 1966: 181). The kits usually included

> a picture of the glorious Apostle Santiago, the patron of Spain, as he appeared to King Alfonso at the battle of Clavijo—riding on a white horse, armed, engaged in combat with many Moors falling beneath the horses' hooves, etc. . . . When transported, the picture was doubled over and wrapped. When opened out for public display, it was creased and dull due to the poor quality of the paint. It was not discarded, however, but usually hung on a twisted tree branch or suspended with two wooden nails. For the Christian hearts of the Spaniards, its poor condition meant little because upon seeing the picture of their Santiago, they would kneel down and make a thousand manifestations of their devotion by bringing to the picture their rosaries, swords, and hats, and they would kiss the worn-out, unadorned corners of the picture. Because of this veneration, the Indians understood that the image was the god of the Spaniards, and since they saw it armed and on horseback with a bloody sword waving on high and men dead on the battlefield, they considered it to be a valiant god, and through serving this god, the Spaniards had the same qualities [see figure 6.2]. The Indians came to believe that this was the reason they were easily overcome and lost their strength in battle as soon as they met the Spaniards. Since this deception of the Indians was such an advantage for the Spaniards, they deliberately did not attempt to disabuse them of it, although they never openly claimed it was true. The rumor was thus spread among the enemies of the Spaniards that the armed Santiago on horseback was the god of the Christians, and for this reason, they conquered. (Remesal 1964: 422)

The Mayan reaction was based on visual information as interpreted in light of their cultural logics. In addition to the details of the image itself, an important clue for their interpretation was the behavior of the Spaniards acting out the popular devotion model of Christianity discussed in chapter 7. The pictures of Santiago were widespread, and they can be found in many churches and Mayan homes. Sometime around 1700 Ximénez (1965: 762) found one in a small chapel of an isolated Zinacanteco settlement. He noted that the chapel resembled a chicken coop.

The Images of the Saints

In addition to the mass kits, church architecture and furnishings as well as the ritual behavior of friars and laity provided visual clues that were more important for the Maya than the sermons of the friars.

The Churches and the Friars

Although the early churches were relatively small, they were the largest edifices in their towns and were often built on sites of pre-Columbian temples. The open interior resembled a cave, the dwelling place of the traditional gods. In place of the traditional gods were the images of the saints, especially the town patron in a place of preeminence over the main altar. Before these images the friars performed their rituals, especially the saying or singing of the mass. These visual images finally answered the Maya's questions about the identity of the Spanish gods. They were these images—Jesus, the Virgin Mary, the patron saint of the town, and the other saints.

Behavior of the Spanish Laity

This interpretation was confirmed by what the Maya observed about the manner in which the Spaniards paid reverence to the saint images. It was similar to the way they paid homage to the Santiago picture in the mass kit. The Maya saw the Spaniards praying to suffice their needs and frequently invoking Holy Mary, "Santa María" (Remesal 1964: 387, 422; Ximénez 1965: 713–14). They heard this name so often that they began calling anything connected with the Spanish religion "Santa María." The church was the house of Santa María; the mass, the ritual of Santa María; holy water, the water of Santa María; the priest's sermon, the word of Santa María. Even Santiago was occasionally called María. The Spaniards had great devotion to the Virgin Mary. They invoked her intercession continually and attended the Saturday mass in her honor more regularly than the obligatory Sunday mass (Remesal 1964: 103).

Profusion of Saint Images

Originally, the colonial churches had few saint statues due to the friars' early bias against them. When the friars realized that ornamentation and statues attracted the Maya to the churches, some began to encourage their use. This decision led to dissension among the Franciscans, but eventually the Mayan wish for images won out.

> In the beginning the ritual items used in the church services were very poor, the altar backings and images because of a lack of anyone to take care of them, very dirty; but with the passage of time and with the efforts of the friars, the Indians began to acquire a fondness for these things and have been very generous in offering them to God. This is something to be thankful for considering that Guatemala is less prosperous than other areas of the Indies. Every church has at least ten or twelve or more images, each one with its banner which the Indians carry in procession as the relatives and friends of the saint. At first these images were the private property of the one who donated them and were kept in the owner's house on a well-decorated altar. Later the priests did not like this arrangement and ordered the images to be kept in the churches, which caused a number of disputes. . . . The Indians have lavished on the churches many ritual items and each day they continue to give more, some individuals trying to outdo others and some towns trying to compete with other towns. (Remesal 1966: 181)

From the description of the ownership and care of pre-Columbian images (see chapter 5), it is clear the Maya were extending the same cultural logics to the saint images.

Gage's comments from the first part of the seventeenth century show that the profusion of images took place fairly early in the colonial period:

> All Indians are much affected unto these popish saints, but especially those who are given to witchcraft, and out of the smallness of their means they will be sure to buy some of these saints and bring them to the church, that there they may stand and be worshipped by them and others. The churches are full of them, and they are placed upon standers gilded or painted, to be carried in procession upon men's shoulders, upon their proper day. Upon such saints' days, the owner of the saint maketh a great feast in the town, and presenteth unto the priest sometimes two or three, sometimes four or five crowns for his Mass and sermon, besides a turkey and three or four fowls, with as much cacao as will serve to make him chocolate for all the whole octave or eight days following. So that in some

churches, where there are at least forty of these saints' statues and images, they bring unto the priest at least forty pounds a year. (1958: 235)

The Maya were fond of ceremonies and attended them with relish (Ximénez 1971a: 253). They employed trumpets, percussion instruments, tinkle bells, and dances. They were attracted to saints whose statues include animals, especially those on horseback such as Santiago (see introductory photograph to chapter 7) and Saint Martin and the stag of Saint Eustacius. In Christian iconography the four evangelists are associated with animal figures. Although these vary, Saint Matthew is typically associated with a winged man, often perceived as a bird; Saint Mark with a lion; Saint Luke with an ox, and Saint John with an eagle. In Santiago Atitlán there is an image of Saint John holding a book, presumably the gospels, with a small lamb on top that has been spotted with black dots by the Maya to represent a jaguar (see the introductory photograph to this chapter). Their preference for saints with animals may be related to seeing these saints as possessing stronger naguals as their animal spirits. It demonstrates the greater importance of what the Maya observed in the images than of any verbal communication about them.

In the early eighteenth century Ximénez observed that Mayan churches contained more ornamentation than the cathedral in Ciudad Real. Some Maya set up endowments, called *guachibales*, for the cult of a saint whose image they had either donated to the church or kept in a private shrine.

[They] are mainly found in parishes administered by the friars, and they consist of endowments of land, feathers, coloring dye, cattle, or money from the wills of rich Indians who have commissioned an image of a saint with the same name as their own or one to whom they had special devotion. These rich Indians leave their wealth entrusted to their heirs in the form of an endowed chaplaincy so that every year a mass may be celebrated, sometimes with a sermon and other solemnities. The heirs, acting as if they were mere administrators of the inheritance, fulfill this charge with such punctuality that never is there a case in which they must be reprimanded or compelled to do it. Before the fiesta date, they come to the priest to make arrangements and pay at times two pesos, and at other times twenty reales and even three pesos. (Ximénez 1971b: 158)

Fuentes y Guzmán (1969: 331–32) mentions a case where there were four or five guachibales in each descent group of a town.

These descriptions from the sixteenth and seventeenth centuries are repeated in archival materials from the eighteenth century:

There is no doubt that Guatemala's Indians were most serious in their religious beliefs, considered themselves devout Catholics, and took an active part in the official cult. Christian saints claimed their particular attention.... Innumerable examples show that Indian communities spared neither effort nor expense in filling the churches with altars, retables, and sculpted images depicting their particular devotions. Eleven carpenters of Tecpán, Guatemala, made nine separate retables for their church over a seven year period in the 1720s. In 1781, at least thirty-eight carved statues of saints adorned the modest church of Olintepeque. The altars and ornaments inside many churches represented enormous material investments, often exceeding the values of the structures that housed them. The gilding of a single side retable in the church of Salamá cost an estimated 850 *pesos*. The main retable of the church in Asunción Izalco cost 800 *pesos* to construct, and 2,500 to gild. In order to combat such "useless" expenditures, the *Audiencia* went so far as to prohibit Indian confraternities and towns from contracting artisans without special permission.

No one listened. During the period 1779–1803, the confraternities of the parish of Texacuangos alone spent 2,000 *pesos* on ornaments, altars and improvements to the temple. Poorer communities fabricated their own images, even if they met with clerical disapproval such as the sculptures in the church of San Antonio Palapó, judged so poorly done that they deserved burning. Similarly, Archbishop Ramón Francisco Casaus y Torres fulminated against "the many images" he found in the church of San Cristóbal Verapaz, "made by the Indian themselves, ignorant of the principles of sculpture, indecorous to the very saints they represent and incapable of inspiring the devotion ordered by the Council of Trent. ... When the Indian town of Santa Catarina Ixtahuacán split into opposed bands in a 1792 land dispute, the two sides fought each other over possession of the statue of Saint Catherine, "profaning the church with the blood we spilled" as a participant recalled. The leader of one of the bands based his claim to the town's governorship on the grounds that he had spent more than 4,000 *pesos* on an altarpiece to the Immaculate Conception decorated with silver and mirrors, as well as "a Saint Peter, Saint Paul, and a Saint John," all cloaked in silver. (Oss 1986: 150–51)

The preceding passages make clear that it was the Maya themselves who initiated the making of many of the images and the placing of them in their private residences and the churches. Originally, the friars had reservations about the images and their later openness to them appears to be as much passive acceptance of the initiative of the Maya as active promotion of the saint cult.

The Mayan Perception of the Images

Pre-Columbian Maya viewed the large interior spaces of caves as points of contact between surface and inner sky-earth. These were the places where the cosmic force in its various emanations poured forth its sustaining and protective power to surface sky-earth. From observing how the Spaniards used the churches, the Maya concluded the cavelike church interiors were the homes of the Spanish gods.

How did the Mayan perception of images of the saints lead to all their devotional activity? Chapter 5 discussed how the pre-Columbian Maya viewed their gods, their images, and the rituals they performed for them. These attitudes and practices were carried over to the Catholic saints once the Maya had identified them as the powerful Spanish gods who had defeated the Mayan protecting gods: "they yield unto the Popish religion, especially to the worshipping of saints' images, because they look upon them as much like unto their forefathers' idols" (Gage 1958: 234). This writer found that in Zinacantán, the soul (*ch'ulel*) of the saint is present in the image, or, since in Mayan thinking all things are sustained by the cosmic force, the better expression may be that the *ch'ulel* of the wooden image *is* the saint. Freidel (1993: 177) found much the same thing in Yucatán. A K'iche' Maya from Momostenango expressed it this way: "The images hear what one says and see what one does. This is the mystery [*secreto*] of the images. The Protestants say all of them in the church are but chunks of wood. Maybe it's true, but he who walked with Jesucristo in the first days was Santiago and this image has power because it has the spirit of Santiago" (Cook 2000: 95).

In summary, the Maya believed the ch'ulel of the saint was incarnated in the image and treated it with rituals in much the same manner as they had preconquest images; this treatment was modified only by some small external differences they observed in the devotions of the Spaniards. Making the sign of the cross on the forehead, breast, and shoulders before the image would be an example. Given this view of the saints and the Mayan devotion to them, the profusion of images in the churches becomes understandable.

There is confirmation of this worldview from Nahua materials. The Nahua concept of *ixiptla* denotes the way the cosmic force exists in the god images: "the envelope that received, the skin enclosing a divine force that erupted from crossed influences emanating from the cycles of time. The *ixiptla* was the container for a power; the localizable, epiphanic presence; the actualization of the power infused into an object, a 'being-here'; native thought did not take time to distinguish between divine essence and material support. It was neither an appearance nor a visual illusion harkening back to an elsewhere, or a beyond. In this sense the *ixiptla* and the image were poles apart; the *ixiptla* emphasized immanence of the forces surrounding us; whereas the Christian image, in a reverse, upward motion, is meant to raise us toward a personal god, the copy moving toward its prototype, guided by the resemblance uniting them" (Gruzinski 2001: 51).

Integration of the Saints and the Traditional Mayan Gods

The Mayan perception of the saint images as specific manifestations of the cosmic power leaves open the question of how the saints were related to the existing Mayan gods who remained on the scene. Within Mayan groups there are no theologians or officially appointed interpreters of the Mayan mind to determine norms of orthodoxy. The shamans do a certain amount of interpretation, but their thinking carries no official status and is usually communicated to a small group of their clients, who are free to accept or reject it. Consequently, there is no necessity that all Maya perceive the saints' relation to the traditional gods in any specific manner.

The Saints as an Additional Group of Gods

In Zinacantán most of the saints were incorporated as an added group of tutelary gods, or as additional emanations of the cosmic force to use a more accurate expression. "It is not merely a substitution of a Christian saint for an ancient deity nor the adoption of an additional god that is expressed in these identifications [of saints with specific functions]. In line with the general pantheistic tendency, both concepts exist side by side, as two manifestations of the same [cosmic] power. So far as the esoteric [Mayan] religion goes, the effect of Christian theology has simply been to give the ancient powers another dimension and greatly enrich the philosophical and ritualistic structures" (Bunzel 1952: 268). The saints reside in the churches and are perceived as similar to the ancestral gods living in the mountains surrounding the valleys where the settlements were located. Like the ancestral gods, the saints watch over the communities and their observance of the Mayan covenant. They protect the community from natural disasters and evil beings if the people are observant, and if they are not, punish their failures by withdrawing their protection.

That the saints remain a distinct category from the ancestral gods was confirmed by the discovery that the saints are perceived as ladinos. This is a common perception in all the Tzotzil-Tzeltal area of Chiapas (Arias 1990: 76, 132, 1991: 56–57) and is also found in Santiago Chimaltenango (Watanabe 1992: 76, differing with Wagley 1949: 62). Arias explains the perception as based on the ladino-Indian social relationship. Although the Maya resent ladinos, they consciously or unconsciously have an image of the economic and political superiority of the ladino and retain this in incorporating the saints as ladinos.

This attitude is in agreement with the original reason the Maya adopted the saints: their superiority at the time of the conquest. Arias notes that the various descriptions of the traditional earth gods as rich, fat ladinos is a variation of the same process.

The perception of the saints as ladinos was used for propaganda purposes in the Chamula uprising of 1868. "Cuscat's next move was to exhort the Indians to cease worshipping images fabricated by ladinos in honor of White gods and urge them to crucify a member of their own race whom they could worship" (Bricker 1981: 121 based on Pineda 1888: 77). Many historians and anthropologists have accepted this account and the crucifixion itself as fact. However, Rus (1983: 156–60) has made a strong argument that Pineda's account was part of a mendacious propaganda campaign by the conservatives of San Cristóbal to depict the Chamulas as religious fanatics deserving of ladino repression. Whether the account be fact or falsified propaganda, it drew on the regional belief that the saints were ladinos.

To perceive the saints as a separate category of gods does not mean they are isolated. Every week the saints, ancestral gods, and other beings of internal sky-earth concerned with the welfare of the Zinacantecos meet in the sacred mountain, Kalvario, and together they discuss the observance or nonobservance of the Mayan covenant and the consequent reward or punishment. On the second day of the major festivals the prayer of the ritual advisor over the food offered by the departing alférez is addressed to the sun, the ancestral gods, and the saints (see chapter 3).

Personas of the Saints

Not all the saints are incorporated into the oral tradition as distinctive persons. Some are seen simply as saints residing in the church with candles burning before them who share the group characteristic of powerful beings in offering assistance obtained by the faithful under the terms of the covenant. There is no myth attached to such an image and its name is often unknown or subject to debate.

Multiple images of the same saint, especially those of Christ and the Virgin, may be perceived as distinct individuals. Each image is considered a distinct person if a different ch'ulel is in each one. In Zinacantán the image of the infant Jesus lying in the Christmas manger is perceived as a child saint unrelated to any of the other Christ images or stories. There is also an image of a bloodied Christ, wearing a crown of thorns, and bound to a scourging pillar (see introductory photograph to chapter 6). This image is not identified with any of the other Christ images and has no descriptive myth attached. The people are somewhat fearful of it because of all the blood. The same is true of the Sacred Heart images.

Fusion of Mayan and Catholic Personas

Another possibility is fusion or conflation of existing Mayan deities with Catholic saints, particularly some of the Christ and Virgin Mary images. For example, a Christ image may be fused with the sun and the traditional corn gods as the giver of life (Gossen 1974: 41; Christenson 2001: 165–66). The basis for the fusion is the cyclic birth, death, and rebirth of all three which may be collapsed into a single complex cycle—the sun's daily and seasonal cycles and their effect on corn's daily cycle of consumption and seasonal cycle of growth.

In many Mayan churches one of the Christ figures is used in a dramatic Good Friday reenactment of the crucifixion. During the year a large cross and a life-size image of the crucified Christ are kept on or near a side altar. During Holy Week the cross is set up in the church, and on Good Friday the life-size image is raised and fixed to it to remain for three hours (see introductory photograph to chapter 8). The Catholic priest, if present, or the fiscal recites the standard Latin prayers of the Catholic Good Friday service while the Maya crowd the church with their offerings. But as Christenson (2001: 78, 79, 185) has shown in Santiago Atitlán, the Maya interpret the service as the death of Christ, his descent to the inner sky-earth, and his reemergence at the end of three hours to renew the community. The Maya celebrate the crucifixion and the resurrection on the same day. Easter Sunday is usually ignored in Mayan communities.

The various statues of the Virgin may also be perceived in diverse ways. The Maya were introduced to the Virgin as a protectress via the battle banners of the Spanish conquerors, the important role she played in Spanish devotions, and the use of her various titles as the patroness of towns. The Maya see her as either the wife or the mother of the Christ/Sun/Corn God who assists him as the patroness of female roles. The similarity between the monthly orbital cycle of the moon and the female ovarian cycle appears to have provided a basis for the fusion of the Spanish female goddess and the Mayan moon goddess.

In Mayan communities in the Tzotzil and Tzeltal areas Christ and Mary are perceived to be ladinos like the other saints. These identifications and their fusion with the sun and the moon are illustrated in murals painted on the walls and ceiling of the sacristy of La Merced Church in San Cristóbal by an Indian artist some time in the 1770s. Included in the murals are oval images of the sun and the moon as human faces (see figures 12.1 and 12.2). The sun has a large, thick mustache, which defines him as ladino. Indians have sparse body hair, and an Indian male could never grow such a mustache. It obviously represents Spanish descent. Likewise, the moon is pictured with very light skin and large rosy cheeks, again a ladina image. Both images have relatively large eyes to emphasize their function of watching daily community behavior. Recall the titles

Left: Figure 12.1. Portion of a mural from San Cristóbal depicting the sun god as a ladino.

Below: Figure 12.2. Portion of the same mural depicting the moon goddess as a ladina.

of address used several times by the mayordomos in their prayers at the flower changing ceremony described in chapter 3. There Christ is called "divine and glorious ladino" and the Virgin "Woman of the sky, ladina of the sky."

The Saints as Tribal

Chapter 5 discussed the gods of the pre-Columbian covenant as being tribal. The Maya have continued to view their saint-gods in the same manner.

> For the Tzotziles and Tzeltales, the harmony of man and the universe requires the permanent residence of each individual within the confines of his community. This creates a certain sentiment of belonging to one place and its shared land symbolized by the . . . ceremonial center. The patron saints live in the ceremonial center and watch over the whole community. Around the ceremonial center there are other sacred places that the community respects and fears and to which they owe obligations. In addition, there are small residential clusters . . . where the ancestors and powerful gods reside in sacred places. Again the inhabitants of these places have obligations to their divine protectors.
>
> . . . When a person abandons once and for all his community, all the divine beings of that place feel offended because the parting implies a renunciation of the obligations to them, and they feel rejected because that person can now offer what had been theirs to some other group of powerful beings in another place. (Arias 1991: 64–65)

The Zinacantecos identify themselves as "the sons of San Lorenzo," the patron of those villages whose residents wear the distinctive Zinacanteco clothing and look to Zinacantán center and its church as the home of their patron, Saint Lawrence, and to the town hall as the focus of authority for the group. The Zinacantecos speak Tzotzil, as do a number of other groups in Chiapas. But there is no sense of unity based on language among these groups. The Zinacantecos consider themselves superior to their Tzotzil neighbors, especially the Chamulas. A common Zinacanteco put-down is "stop acting like a Chamula," which means "quit acting stupid."

There is a concern that communities might steal each other's saints. If the Chamulas should ever succeed in stealing Saint Lawrence from Zinacantán and place him in the church in Chamula, he would no longer protect the Zinacantecos but would become one of the Chamulas' tribal gods and protect them instead (Early 1963–64: 82). In a striking example, the Mayan community of San Luis, Petén, fissioned and one group moved to Belize (then British Honduras) and founded a new community, San Antonio. At first this community suffered from poor crops and fever sickness. A town meeting was called to discuss their problems. The unanimous conclusion was that their old saints were no longer protecting them since their images were still in San Luis. "The council finally decided to raid San Luis and seize the saints so that they might be set up in the new church in San Antonio, where they would be able to see all the evils that were besetting the community and take steps to set them right" (Thompson 1930: 38–39). The armed raid, complete with dynamite to blow open the church door if necessary, was successfully carried out at night and the saints brought to San Antonio, where they remained, and the community began to prosper.

Summary

By means of visual clues, the Maya identified the saints as well as Christ and the Virgin Mary as the powerful Spanish gods that bestowed military victory in the conquest. As a result, they incorporated the saints into the Mayan covenant so that they would offer their protection and thereby strengthen it. The elaborate cult of the saints with its images and ceremonies is the way the Maya fulfill their covenant obligations to these saints. This explains the first part of the anomaly: the essential presence of the Catholic saints in Mayan religion.

The Necessity of the Mass, Baptism, and the Catholic Priest in the Mayan Worldview

The incorporation of the saints into the Maya pantheon as sacred protectors dictated a mutual relationship of assistance between the saints and the Maya in accordance with the Mayan covenant. In return for the saints' protection, the Maya were required to nurture and praise them as they did their traditional gods. Consequently, the Maya had to determine what ceremonies constituted the praise and nurture the saints wanted. With the friars' efforts to communicate the doctrina creating more confusion than enlightenment, the Maya could only watch how the Spaniards treated their saints.

The Ritual of the Saints

In the visual structure of evangelization the Maya saw that the mass was the ritual the priests continually celebrated on an altar beneath a statue or painting of the patron saint of the town. As described in chapter 9, this was a weekly

Figure 13.1. A priest celebrating mass in Santiago Atitlán during the festival of Santiago. Behind him is the image of Santiago brought to the church from his cofradía house for his festival.

event for the whole community in the towns of residencia and frequently visited visitas, and an occasional occurrence in the other visitas.

The Priests' Intention in Celebrating Mass

For orthodox Catholics the mass is a Christ ritual reenacting the sacrifice of the cross. Its relationship to the saints was reiterated at the Council of Trent in 1562: "And though the Church has been accustomed to celebrate Masses now and then in honor and in memory of the saints, yet she does not teach that the sacrifice is offered to them, but to God alone, who has crowned them [the saints]. Hence the priest is not accustomed to say: 'I offer sacrifice to you, Peter and Paul,' but giving thanks to God for their victories, he implores their patronage, so that 'they themselves may deign to intercede for us in heaven, whose memory we celebrate on earth'" (Denzinger 1955: 290, #941). The theological distinctions contained in this passage were from a universe unknown to the Maya as well as to a number of popular devotion (folk) Catholics.

The Mayan Understanding of the Mass

Watching the Spaniards with greater attention than they listened to the garbled rote instruction they received, the Maya observed that the mass was the ritual constantly performed in the presence of the saint images (see figure 13.1). "Ecclesiastical structures in Yucatán were designed so that Indians could *watch* the Mass while being physically segregated from its participants. The Mass would remain something of a mystery even to those Indians—schoolmasters and boys from the village school—who helped to serve it: all they would *see* at certain moments would be the back of the priest as he muttered over the chalice" (Clendinnen 1987: 184, emphasis added). Since many of the first churches were small, an altar was often placed on a raised outdoor platform next to the church where mass was celebrated as the Indians watched from the *atrio*, a large patio in front of the church. The importance of the visual experience is confirmed in Nahua documents. "It is significant that the sixteenth century Nahua Indians in New Spain did not speak of attending mass but of seeing mass" (Poole 1992: 127–28).

Visually, the mass used candles and sometimes incense. During it, wine and a food wafer were offered and consumed to the accompaniment of a fixed set of prayers that the priest read from a book or recited from memory. While the arrangement of these elements was different, there were a number of visual similarities with pre-Columbian ceremonies in which the Maya fed their gods with offerings of candles, liquor, incense, and blood accompanied by formulaic prayers (see chapter 5). The Spanish laity would kneel during the mass and show signs of great devotion. Therefore the Maya concluded that the mass was the ritual they were now required by their covenant to provide for the saints, their new set of gods:

> One should remember that the communal effort is oriented toward the maintenance of harmony in the visible world as well as the invisible. On any important occasion, bringing in a priest "to give a mass" in the church constitutes one of the community's obligations to the saints and other powerful invisible beings, and at the same time it is both an offering and a payment for the effort that they have expended in the invisible world. This obligation must be fulfilled, and if it is not, the powerful invisible beings will punish the community by sending sickness, drought, and other calamities that will break the ideal equilibrium in the social order and everyday relationships. (Arias 1991: 56)

Arias compares the mass with the traditional Mayan Year Ceremony mentioned in chapter 3 as an example of the Church-Mountain pattern. The Year Ceremony is conducted by shamans without a priest because it is primarily intended for the ancestral gods, although the saints are invoked as well. "The only difference [between the two rituals] is based on the fact that the mass is a celebration in honor of the powerful invisible ladino beings, the Catholic saints" (Arias 1991: 56).

This explains the second component of the anomaly. According to Mayan cultural logics, adopting the Catholic saints entailed performing the mass as the ritual for their praise and nurturance. The saints, in return, protect and provide for the community and its members, thereby maintaining its equilibrium and ensuring the people's survival to the end of their allotted time. The logic of the Mayan covenant was defining their religious practices.

Providing for the Ritual of the Saints

One of the purposes of the cargo/cofradía system was to provide the goods and services needed for the saints' masses. Although the system was founded by the friars as part of the evangelization effort, its members probably conceived of their roles in pre-Columbian terms. Like the other gods of the Mayan covenant, the saints were to carry the burden of their historical cycles of time. In turn, the cargo/cofradía members were to help carry the burden by offering their prayers and service and by paying for those of the priests along with needed ritual goods as exemplified by the Zinacanteco model described in chapter 3. Eber recounts a conversation with the wife of a cofrade in San Pedro Chenalhó about the relationship of these servants to the Mayan covenant and the important roles women played in assisting their husbands with the rituals: "I was moved by the devotion Angélika expressed in her ritual work and the dignity and good humor with which she carried it out. Later, when we talked about the fiesta, she explained how she saw her role. She told me that she had to go on with her work because St. Peter and her people depended on her to fulfill her duties at prescribed times, so that the world would continue and her people would prosper" (Eber 1995: 107).

The cargeros/cofrades retained some of the pre-Columbian ritual patterns in their care of the saints. As Barbara Tedlock observes, in Momostenango there is

a large complex of community wide rituals performed in accordance with the Prehispanic Quiché calendars, together with other rituals that follow the Gregorian calendar. These two types of ritual, however, do not constitute a simple dualistic opposition between Pre-conquest and Post-Conquest ritual, or between paganism and Christianity. Rather, there are always "catholic" elements in pagan ritual and "pagan" elements in Catholic ritual. For example, although the famous 8 Batz celebration takes place largely at outdoor shrines and hearths, it includes a visit to the church. Conversely, the image of San Antonio Pologuá is removed from the church each year on August 14–24 and taken to twenty-two different earth shrines where copal is burned in its honor. The various confraternities wash the clothing and change the flowers of their respective saints according to the Prehispanic 260-day Quiché calendar, while many priest-shamans preface their divinations with the Lord's Prayer. (1982: 37)

Baptism

In the early colonial period some friars insisted that the Maya be baptized immediately. The Maya interpreted baptism as an act of submission to the Spanish king and an acknowledgment of his religion (Remesal 1964: 422). The Maya submitted to it in hopes of receiving better treatment from the Spaniards. When dealing with Spanish authorities, the Maya were required to identify themselves by the name of the saint given them when they were baptized. Some were baptized two or three times because they could not remember their baptismal name.

Gradually the custom evolved so that when the Catholic priest visited Mayan villages to say mass, he would baptize the infants afterwards. The writer found in Chiapas and Guatemala a compulsive insistence among Mayan parents for the quick baptism of their newborn. A couple that was unwilling to wait for the next festival would go to the nearest town where there was a resident priest and have the infant baptized there. Thus, the Mayan insistence on baptism is another part of the anomaly. Why are the Maya so insistent on this Spanish-derived ritual?

Baptism evolved as a type of shamanic curing ceremony to protect against ever-present infant sickness. While the festival mass was performed as a ritual of supplication for the whole community, baptism was a ritual for an individual. Anointing the infant with oil, placing salt on the tongue, and pouring water on the head while reciting a fixed prayer formula during baptism are customs similar to shamanic curing patterns (see figures 13.2 and 13.3).

> [Baptism] is considered a symbol of the act of "implanting the soul in infants". . . . The soul is separable from the body and does not inform it immediately but gradually enters it in proportion to the child's physical growth and acquisition of knowledge and wisdom. For this reason the mother of a newborn infant takes precautions to avoid any danger that could cause the loss of the soul of her infant. . . . The soul of the child is not yet totally set in the body; it is near it but not yet firmly set. It has been found that baptism is capable of correcting this defect. Thanks to this ritual, the infant will receive powerful protection against sickness; upon his soul entering his body . . . the infant will be better endowed to resist dangerous attacks against his person. (Arias 1991: 54–55)

The act of uniting the child's body with its soul is the initiation of civilizing the child. "Education is a long process that begins with the birth of the child and lasts until the last moments of life. Education is the slow but constant, step by step acquisition of a soul (*ch'ulel*)" (Arias 1991: 28–29). By the Mayan logics, the doctrina about baptism was understood as referring to the goals of in-

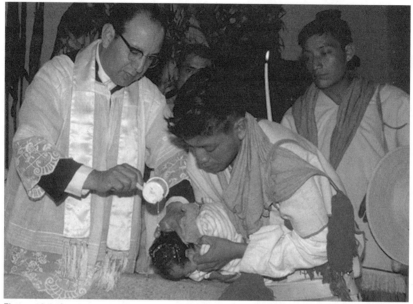

Figure 13.2. A priest pours water on an infant's head during a baptism in Zinacantán.

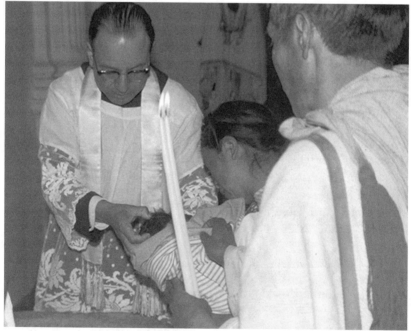

Figure 13.3. The priest then anoints the infant with oil during the same baptism.

creasing the likelihood of physical survival and rearing civilized humans who would take their place in the Mayan community. The fiscales may have been an important factor in this interpretation. They substituted for the priest for many years in visitas. In some dioceses they were allowed to perform baptisms in the absence of a priest.

The Mayan understanding is reflected in the petitions by the child's father to the prospective baptismal godfather. Accepting the godparent role means entering into fictive kinship with the parents of the infant. This relationship involves serious reciprocity obligations between parents and godparents that are an essential part of everyday Mayan social and economic life. In petitioning a prospective godparent, the father of the infant offers a bottle of cane liquor and uses such phrases as, "Won't you just be so kind as to let me borrow your feet, your hands, to sustain for me the soul of God's angel [the infant]?"; "if it got sick I would feel bad if it hadn't been baptized"; "I would like its soul to enter a bit"; "do the holy favor a little, sustain for me the soul of God's angel." After the ceremony, the father of the infant thanks the godparent: "See, *compadre* . . . with this ceremony, there has entered the spirit, there has entered the soul of the angel of God. O my *compadre*, many thanks, may God repay you" (Early 1965: 79–81).

Ritual Prayers

The Maya observed that all the rituals for the Spanish gods involved the recitation of prayers. In their praise and nurturance of these gods, could the Maya use their own prayers or would they have to learn new ones?

What the Friars Taught the Maya

The purpose of four hundred years of evangelization was to communicate and consequently convert the Maya to basic Christianity summarized in the doctrina that consisted of some introductory prayers, the fourteen articles of faith, and a summary of moral principles for life (see table 8.1). Given all the problems of evangelization, in many instances the doctrina was reduced to the mechanical memorization and recitation of the exact words of the preliminary prayers. The assumption seems to have been that recitation of these prayers signified an instructed and believing Christian.

Early Colonial Period

From the very beginning of evangelization, the manpower problems prevented friars from teaching the entire content of the doctrina. In 1550 Tomás López, a judge of the Royal Audiencia, noted in his report to the king that in Guatemala the priests were content to teach only the words of the Our Father and the

Hail Mary, which the Maya repeated like parrots without any understanding (O'Flaherty 1979: 170). The following year in response to a decree that the Indians should be taught Spanish, the Franciscan provincial replied that to do so was essentially impossible because they lacked the manpower to teach even the Our Father, Hail Mary, Credo, and Hail, Holy Queen (O'Flaherty 1979: 176).

The Eighteenth Century and Later

In 1770 Archbishop Cortés y Larraz summarized the situation in Guatemala:

> The schools where the doctrina is taught consists of an Indian, called the fiscal, chanting the prayers with boys and girls together. They attend these schools with reluctance and their parents view it with even greater reluctance. They use any pretext to take them away from the school—because their labor is needed to help pay the tribute, or that they are about to be married, frequently at age twelve for the girls and fourteen for the boys. Their reluctance to attend is overcome by the vigilance of the priest and the punishments given for those who fail to do so. As a result, some learn to chant the prayers but others are unable to do even this. No one acquires any understanding of them. Usually all quickly forget what they have learned because upon leaving school, they neither chant nor recite the prayers. (Cortés y Larraz 1958 I: 42–43)

During Lent in 1780 the residents of the town of Chamula were summoned for an interrogation about their knowledge of the doctrina. Fewer than two hundred adults appeared and gave answers: forty-one men and seventy-eight women replied with a number of errors, and the remaining seventy-seven had little knowledge at all (Laughlin 2003: 89). In Yucatán,

> as the numbers of clergy in the colony increased, the level of enthusiasm declined. Most were creoles and therefore bilingual from infancy, yet by their own admission the vast majority of curates continued to leave the catechism completely to the Maya *maestros cantores* [fiscales] and counted these successful if the catechumens learned to repeat from memory the "Four Prayers" (the Creed, Hail Mary, Our Father and Salve Regina), by the time they were ready for communion. The more conscientious priests reexamined the adult parishioners before admitting them to the sacraments for their annual Easter Duty and sent those with faulty memory back to remedial catechism class on Sunday afternoon. Even so, the bishops who bothered to examine candidates for confirmation during their diocesan tours found the majority grossly ignorant of even these rudiments. And the few clergymen who ventured to inquire whether the rote learning had inculcated any understanding of Christian

precepts came to the painful conclusion that the gospel seed had borne little fruit among the Maya. (Farriss 1984: 305)

Of the twenty-eight sections outlined in Molina's catechism as the desired content of evangelization (see table 8.1), memorization of the four introductory prayers and repetition of them by rote memory without any understanding appears to have been the typical outcome of evangelization.

The Mayan View of Prayer Formulas

If the Maya learned one thing from the doctrina, it was a confirmation of their preexisting belief in the importance of fixed prayer formulas, understood or not.

The Pre-Columbian View

Chapter 5 demonstrated that the use of fixed prayer formulas was a ritual necessity. Based on preconquest traditions recorded in the Popol Vuh, the Maya viewed a spoken word as having an intrinsic power to bring forth the being it signified. The gods gave the prayer formulas to the first shamans as part of the ceremonial templates and these had to be followed in all subsequent performances.

The Chilam Balam Books

The importance of ritual prayer formulas from the perspective of the Mayan covenant is documented in Chilam Balam books compiled both before and after the conquest. In the Chilam Balam of Chumayel, there is a great deal of preoccupation with rituals and their prayers (Edmonson 1986: 20). The Chilam Balam of Kaua was concerned with the practical arts and sciences required for protection against natural disasters and sickness. "It is clear to us that the scribes who compiled the *Kaua* used it as a kind of encyclopedia or reference book. Whenever they encountered an interesting European or Mayan text, they would either copy it directly or make a translation of it before incorporating it into the Book" (Bricker and Miram 2002: 12).

Of interest to the scribes and inserted into the Kaua book were twelve Catholic religious texts, all concerned with prayers. Six were prayer formulas: five in Latin from the doctrina (Sign of the Cross, Our Father, Hail Mary, Creed, and the Hail, Holy Queen)[1] and a devotional prayer in Yukatek of unknown origin (Bricker and Miram 2002: 210, 283, 284, 295)[2]. The other six entries were instructions about prayers. Two are concerned with the worldview behind the prayers, commentaries on Genesis copied from Spanish almanacs that reveal who are the "our Father in heaven" and "Mary full of grace" (Bricker and Miram 2002: 280, 283). Two other texts were instructions about wearing Marian medals or scapulars,[3] the recitation of some doctrina prayers while doing so, and the indulgences and benefits to be gained (Bricker and Miram 2002: 296, 297). Many kinds of protection are promised: not to die suddenly without having confessed; a remedy to ease painful childbirth; protection against attacks of fainting, windstorms, madness, or getting lost while traveling; forgiveness of sins; protection in times of wars and sea voyages; and protection against injustices and captivity. The last two texts appear to be instructions that accompanied prayer sheets (Bricker and Miram 2002: 299, 301). One was an account of the Passion of Jesus explicitly named a prayer. It describes the rewards for those who carry the account with them and recite seven Our Fathers and seven Hail Marys for the suffering Jesus. The rewards were indulgences and protection against enemies, storms, sudden death without confessing in situations such as drowning or fire, lawsuits, and false charges. At the hour of death the Virgin, Joseph, and the Virgin's parents were promised to appear, presumably to lead the departing soul to heaven.[4]

In summary, these twelve passages were prayer formulas or instructions about them that when recited, provided protective rewards from the Spanish gods against life's dangers. They fit perfectly with the continuing logic of the Mayan covenant and for this reason, they were of interest to the scribes who copied them into their Chilam Balam book.

Mayan Use of Doctrina Prayer Formulas

Given the power of the Spanish prayer formulas for the saints, the Maya incorporated them into their traditional rituals. In the 1950s in Chenalhó the sign of the cross, Our Father, and Hail Mary were recited as the prayers for the risings of the sun and moon and in times of danger (Guiteras-Holmes 1961: 235, 237). In Guatemala these prayers were recited by some Mayan diviners seeking to understand the future through probing the divine cycles (B. Tedlock 1982: 154; D. Tedlock 1996: 57). In Yucatán during the 1930s a Mayan group who had retreated from national and church jurisdiction during the Caste Wars used the word *doctrina* to signify six specific prayers: the Our Father, the Hail Mary, the Hail, Holy Queen, the Creed, the General Confession, and the Act of Contrition, all in Yukatek (Villa Rojas 1945: 118). These prayers were recited repetitively in almost all their religious ceremonies including one for the purification of the shamans (Villa Rojas 1945: 73, 105, 120).

The Essential Requirement of a Ritual Specialist

Given the necessity of using the power of fixed prayer formulas to fulfill the obligations of the Mayan covenant, learning and reciting their exact words became the essential requirement of every specialist conducting covenant rituals.

Cargo/Cofradía Members

During his lifetime Manuel Arias, a native of San Pedro Chenalhó and father of Jacinto Arias, was a specialist in all aspects of Mayan ritual: the *pasión* (mayordomo) for the festival of Carnaval, a shaman, and a fiscal. Reflecting on memorizing the long prayers required for his role during the Carnaval festival, he says, "The prayer should be repeated word for word. A word not belonging to the prayers cannot be introduced into it. That is no good. One may know half, or almost all; but if two or three words are different, it is no good. My brother was the one, the only one [who taught Manuel the prayers]. Others knew a little, but they do not pass their cargo as it should be: it rains a lot. The people can testify to it, that I prayed as I should pray, that it did not rain, the sun shone even brighter" (Guiteras-Holmes 1961: 193–94). One of the prayer petitions was that it would not rain on the main day of the festival so that the people could pay homage to the saint and enjoy themselves. Therefore a requirement for a cargador/cofrade was knowledge of the exact words of the required prayers. A cofrade in Momostenango echoed this necessity: "The image is very sensitive. One or two incorrect words and we are punished" (Cook 2000: 164).

Shamans

The shamans perform rituals calling on the divinized ancestors and other Mayan gods including the incorporated saints. Manuel was also a shaman, as was his mother. When asked how he learned the shamanic prayers, he said, "It felt good; I felt pleasure in the words of my mother. I would hear them and then I would think and think [about them], and in that way I would dream of them and so I learned them" (Guiteras-Holmes 1961: 176). This statement implies knowledge of the exact words. In Zinacantán the shamans are taught the ritual prayers by the ancestral gods in their dreams as well as by older shamans. But for the shaman to conduct a successful curing ritual, "The h'ilol [shaman] role demands control of a fair quantity of esoteric knowledge, including ritual manipulation and prayers in which the h'ilol is supposed to be word-perfect. . . . The prayers and basic ritual operations, in other words, are largely outside the areas of permissible deviation" (Fabrega and Silver 1973: 58).

Another type of shaman is the day-keeper, a diviner. In the mid-1970s, while Allen Christenson was undergoing training as a day-keeper in Momostenango, he had to learn prayer texts containing archaic terms and phrasings that he did not understand. His K'iche' teacher, a man well known in the area for his divinations, explained that he himself didn't know what the phrases meant.

He advised Christenson, "You just have to learn them because they are in the prayers" (Cook 2000: 243). Once again, the essential requirement of a ritual specialist is the ability to recite the exact words of the prayer formula whether he understands it or not. In Santiago Atitlán the shaman must know how to perform the rituals, but there are nuances in the wording of the prayers of some shamans. "A shaman received his prayers and procedures from that power that owned him. Although the prayers fit closely into a basic format of shamanic rituals, they were always unique unto the individual shaman. This was not a balance between personal expression and tradition, but between tradition and the shamanic nature spirit's personality" (Prechtel 1998: 13).

In Mayan communities another important way of addressing the gods is through sacred music and songs learned from the ancestors and performed by musicians especially called to this form of community service (Landa 1941: 294; O'Brien 1975; Prechtel 1999; D. Tedlock 2003). In San Pedro Chenalhó, Pedranos say that song and music are God's favorite sounds (Eber 1995: 94). The music and songs must employ exact repetition of a basic format. Tozzer (1941: 104) cites an incident in 1586 from the Lacandones. During a ceremony of human sacrifice, the drummer missed his beat and upset the traditional rhythm. The ceremony was stopped and it was decreed that the drummer was to be sacrificed for his misdeed in place of the intended victim. The drummer escaped.

Another way of addressing the gods is through dance performances. "In the festival of the towns' patron saints, they dance weighed down by adornments of rich and precious feathers, a variety of coins, mirrors, and beads of green stones. They are indefatigable as they continuously dance all day in the church-yard for one to eight days as required by the importance of the festival. . . . They dance singing the praises of the saint of the festival, but in the prohibited dances they used to sing the histories and deeds of their ancestors and false gods" (Fuentes y Guzmán 1969, I: 216–17). The Zinacanteco festivals described in chapter 3 involved a number of dances.

An Ethnographic Account

Guiteras-Holmes in her summary of Manuel Arias' worldview reiterates the necessity of a ritual specialist knowing the exact words for addressing the gods:

> Man approaches the gods after fasting; and the offering of the required ritual objects, disposed in the prescribed manner, is accompanied by the recitation of formulas of which no word may be changed or spoken out of proper order. Personal prayers for aid and blessing may be said before the sacred images in the church, or to the holy earth for the cleansing of sins. Cultural tradition provides the layman with the means to face nor-

mal situations, but it is up to the specialist to confront the uncommon and the powerful. The deities are seldom invoked by the non-specialist.

The difference between personal prayer and that performed by the specialist is not difficult to ascertain. One is apology or supplication spoken in the clumsy words of the anxious and the needy; the other is magic formula—even though it be a Catholic prayer—repeated word for word, accompanied by prescribed gestures and intonations, a command rather than a request, describing the part to be performed by man and the part to be expected of the deity. These formulas are based on a sense of reciprocity, or, to put it another way, on the idea of cause and effect. (1961: 295)

Again an essential characteristic of a ritual specialist is knowing the exact words of the prayer formulas used in ritual. This shows the continued influence of the preconquest logics described in chapter 5. The word *doctrina* originally signified the pedagogical content of the Hellenized formulation of Christianity, but due to all the problems involved in evangelization, it was finally reduced to signifying the use of the correct verbal formulas of several traditional Catholic prayers by Mayan shamans, cofrades, and Catholic priests.

The Necessity of the Catholic Priest in the Mayan Ritual Matrix

The elite were the ones who dealt with the Catholic priests. "The Maya leaders regarded themselves rather than the Catholic clergy as the guardians of the saints and all that belonged to them. The clergy could not be trusted with the responsibility. Curates came and went; they did not have the same stake in the community as the elite. And even if they had stayed permanently, they remained outsiders who never became integrated into Maya society, never shared the same values, and were therefore incapable of understanding the true significance of the saints in the world order" (Farriss 1984: 338).

Why then is the non-Mayan Catholic priest necessary for the rituals of baptism and masses for the saints, rather than a capable Mayan person who is a participant in the Mayan covenant and leader of the community? By observing the Spanish priests, could not shamans, or especially the fiscales, have learned to perform these rituals for their own people? LaFarge raised the same question: "At present the Indians believe that baptism is necessary and that the Fiesta would be incomplete without the priest's assistance. It would take but little for them to dispense with him in these matters also and for control of ritual meaningless to them to pass entirely into the hands of native church attendants, who are already closely interlocked with the non-Christian hierarchy" (LaFarge 1947: 81).

The priest's knowledge and ability to recite the exact words of the prayer formulas for the ladino saints provides the answer. The non-Mayan Catholic priest is the only one who knows how to read or recite from memory the mass and baptismal prayers in Latin. Based on the similarity of purpose and structure between the traditional Mayan and imported Catholic rituals, the Maya view the Catholic priest as having a similar shamanic power in relation to the ladino saints as their own shamans have to the traditional gods. Both are seen as learning their prayer formulas from the gods themselves. A Maya shaman compares his divining table to the altar in the church used by the priest (Christenson 2003b: 95). In Yucatán the same word is used for both the shaman's table and the altar in the church where the mass is celebrated (Green 2003: 105, 111). The purpose of the altar and shaman's table are the same: communication with the respective gods whereby both kinds of shamans intercede for the well-being of the client or community. During the baptismal ceremony the priest introduces the infant's soul into its body, much as a shaman has the power to recover lost soul parts in order to prevent sickness.

The celibacy of the Catholic priesthood is also a shamanic characteristic, although the former is permanent and the latter temporary. Sexual intercourse is viewed as inimical to ritual efficacy. As noted in chapter 5, Landa found that priestly celibacy was required for seventy-eight to one hundred days before the festival rituals and for the idol makers while they fashioned the images. The Maya practiced celibacy before planting their fields so that the earth would retain its strength (Ximénez 1929: 88). The *nabeysil*, the shaman par excellence of renewal in Santiago Atitlán, must remain celibate for a year. The Maya consider the permanent celibacy of the Catholic priesthood as unnatural. But in a seeming contradiction, if a priest is found to have a mistress, they become highly upset. The loss of celibacy means a loss of spiritual power that weakens or destroys the efficacy of the masses and baptisms the priest performs. The unique role of the non-Mayan priest during evangelization was perpetuated with the exclusion of the Maya from the Catholic priesthood.

This answers the final question about the anomaly, why the non-Mayan Catholic priest is necessary. When in later years some Mayan fiscales and others learned to read Spanish, the shamanic quality of the priest mitigated against their assuming the priest's role. It did not mean that the Maya gave up their desire to have one of their own as the ritual specialist for the saints' covenant rituals. This cultural logic remained latent and would reveal itself when circumstances allowed, as will be discussed in chapter 14.

Conclusion: Endurance of Cultural Logics

This chapter has described how the pre-Columbian Mayan cultural logics explain the necessity of the Spanish-derived mass, baptism, and the non-Mayan Catholic priest within the Mayan ritual matrix. The mass was seen as the ritual that fed and nurtured the saints as demanded by the Mayan covenant. This ritual required knowledge of the exact words of prayer formulae that only the priest knew as a result of his shamanic status. The same was true of baptism. The preconquest logics continued to define Mayan consciousness and decisions for almost five hundred years after the conquest. Their continued use explains all the elements of the anomaly described in the first chapter.

14

The Fiscal

The fiscal has been mentioned a number of times in the preceding chapters. He was in charge of the church in Zinacantán and a ritual specialist for the major-domos of the cargo system (see chapter 3). In the friars' plan of evangelization he was the funnel of communication between them and the Mayan communities. This chapter describes the role in greater detail and examines cases that provide striking examples of how the cultural logics that explain the anomaly also define how the Maya expanded the role of the person most closely associated with the priest.

The Title and the Role

The first meaning of the Spanish word *fiscal* is treasurer. The treasurer of the Real Audiencia was designated by this title. In Mayan churches the term had a wider meaning. In small communities it referred to the person who took care of the physical maintenance of the church and the priest, taught the doctrina, and assisted with ritual. In larger communities these duties were divided into specialized roles such as doctrina teachers, bell ringers, sacristans, mass servers, and so on. In some communities the term was used for the overall supervisor (Farriss 1984: 337), while in other communities the term applied only to one of the more specialized functions (Collins 1977: 242–43). In Yucatán the fiscal was the choirmaster (maestro cantor) and this was the term used in that region. In the ethnographic present the term has various usages in Mayan communities, the common denominator being a Mayan person who has an important task connected with the church.

Importance

In colonial times the fiscal was one of the most important persons in a Mayan community. Usually, the position was occupied by a person from the Mayan elite (Thompson 1999: 54, 278). The ex-Dominican Gage described the role as it existed in Guatemala around 1630:

> To the church there belong according to the size of the town, so many singers, and trumpeters, and waits [musicians], over whom the priest hath one officer, who is called *fiscal*. The *fiscal* has a white staff with a little silver cross on the top to represent the church and shew that he is the priest's clerk and officer. When any case is brought to be examined by the priest, this *fiscal* or clerk executes justice by the priest's order. He must be one that can read and write, and is commonly the master of music. He is bound upon the Lord's Day and other saints' days, to gather to the church before and after service all the young youths and maids, and to teach them the prayers, sacraments, commandments, and other points of catechism [doctrina] allowed by the Church of Rome. In the morning he and other musicians, at the sound of the bell, are bound to come to church to sing and officiate at Mass, which in many towns they perform with organs and other musical instruments . . . as well as Spaniards. So likewise at evening at five of the clock they are again to resort to the church, when the bell calleth, to sing prayers, which they call *completas*, or completory [compline], with *Salve Regina* [Hail, Holy Queen], a prayer to the Virgin Mary.
>
> This *fiscal* is a great man in the town, and bears more sway than the mayors, jurats and other officers of justice, and, when the priest so wishes,

attends him, goes about his errands, and appoints such as are to wait on him when he rides out of town. Both he and all that belong to [that is, work for] the church are exempted from the common weekly service of the Spaniards, and from giving attendance to travelers, and . . . other officers of justice. But they have to attend with their waits, trumpets, and music, upon any great man or priest that comes to their town, and to make arches with boughs and flowers in the streets for entertainment. (1958: 230–31)

In the Franciscan parishes of Yucatán,

the sergeant-major of parish administration was the *maestro cantor* [fiscal] of each church. From the beginning of evangelization the Franciscans had to rely on native assistants to help preach the gospel and supervise the material and spiritual affairs of the newly created parishes. . . . They were the parish secretaries, keeping notes for entry into the registries of births, marriages and deaths, and often recording the entries themselves. They supervised the catechism [doctrina] and selected and taught the youngsters who would receive special training in vocal and instrumental music, in liturgy, and in reading and writing; and they thus controlled who would become church functionaries, *escribanos* and their own successors. . . . They examined and coached the candidates for the sacraments of adult baptism (in the early period), confession and communion, confirmation, marriage and extreme unction. They made the matrimonial inquiries concerning prospective marriage partners to avoid bigamy and unions within the prohibited degrees of kinship. They were responsible for all the music, vestments, and sacred vessels, they organized the liturgy and led the daily recital of the rosary in the churches and a modified Sunday and holy-day liturgy if a priest was not present. They buried the dead and baptized the newborn when the curate was absent or could not be bothered. . . . The face that Christianity presented in day-to-day contact with the faithful was a Maya face. (Farriss 1984: 335)

Bishop Landa described the fiscals as the indispensable persons "on whom everything depends, because of the confidence placed in them, having been the friars' colleagues in preaching and instructing the Indians in the things of our Holy Faith" (Farriss 1984: 335). The fiscal became the narrow funnel of communication between the Catholic priest and the Mayan community. The number of sacraments mentioned in the preceding accounts indicates that they more aptly describe the situation in towns of residencia or oft-visited visitas.

In the seldom-visited visitas and the surrounding areas where the majority of the Mayan population lived, the role of the fiscal can be seen in two possible ways. In some instances, due to the infrequent presence of the priest, the role of the fiscal would have been enhanced so that he became the de facto priest. Farriss notes that he baptized the newborn in the absence of the priest. This would have allowed him wide latitude in his interpretations of the doctrina, some of which were probably not what the friars intended. The interpretation of baptism reported in chapter 13 (as an act of submission to the king and protection against illness for infants) may have been an example of this. On the other hand, the infrequent presence of the priest may have meant that there was little concern for the doctrina and that the fiscal's duties were mostly restricted to helping the seldom-appearing priest. This was the case in Santiago Chimaltenango, as described in chapter 10.

A Memorial to the Fiscal

The historical importance of the fiscal in the Mayan community is enshrined in a wooden altarpiece sculpted between 1976 and 1981 in Santiago Atitlán, Guatemala (Christenson 2001: xiii). Sometime in the colonial period, a large, elaborately carved altarpiece was placed behind the main altar. Over the years it had been badly damaged by the earthquakes that have tumbled the colonial church. In 1976 the Catholic priest commissioned two Atiteco woodcarvers to restore and embellish this altarpiece. It consists of four tiers, each occupied by saint statues set in alcoves. The tiers are set on a base of five carved panels showing scenes of important community rituals (Christenson 2001: 5). The first panel depicts origins and is divided into three scenes (see figure 14.1). The middle scene shows a seated Mayan shaman performing a divination ceremony to reveal the future of a newborn child held in the mother's arms. The right and left scenes of the panel continue the theme of origins by showing the beginnings of the word of God in Atitlán. The right side depicts Moses with the Ten Commandments. The left side depicts the traditional fiscal delivering the first Christian sermon in Atitlán (Christenson 2001: 144–54). There is no depiction of a Catholic priest in this panel in spite of Atitlán having been a Franciscan town of residencia for many years (see table 10.3).

The Fiscal and Mayan Cultural Logics

Mayan cultural logics defined the non-Mayan Catholic priest as a shaman-like person who knew the exact words of the rituals to honor the incorporated Spanish saints. The Maya could have removed this part of the anomaly by becoming Catholic priests themselves, but this alternative was closed to them during the colonial period. But the preference for their own people remained latent.

Figure 14.1. A panel from the carved altarpiece in Santiago Atitlán; the fiscal as teacher and preacher is to the left (photo courtesy of Allen Christenson).

Figure 14.2. A catechist, the contemporary successor to the fiscal's teaching function, instructs in the church of Santiago Atitlán. In the background are the images of its patron and other saints.

Conflict over the Fiscal's Role

This preference for Mayan ritual specialists surfaced temporarily in the early period of evangelization. It is implied in the prohibitions decreed by the Mexican synods of 1555 and 1565 that applied to all the suffragan dioceses of the Mayan area. They forbade Indians to recite the canonical hours of the Divine Office, to say mass, to hold funeral services, or to organize processions without the presence of the Spanish priest (Ricard 1966: 67). These explicit prohibitions imply that fiscales were celebrating rituals that were reserved for the Catholic priest. In spite of the prohibition, the preference remained and would surface again when open conflict between the Maya and Spaniards or nationalists upset the accepted ways of everyday life.

The Cancuc Rebellion, 1712

The Cancuc rebellion took place during Ximénez's lifetime, and he describes it in detail (Ximénez 1971a: 249–357). His account is interspersed with passages where he vents his burning fury at the corrupt bishop of Chiapas. Gosner's (1992) archival research uncovered testimonies from Mayan participants taken after the rebellion that expand and correct some of Ximénez's descriptions. The following is a summary account that gives the background for understanding the Mayan cultural logics revealed during this period of conflict.

Preliminaries to the Rebellion

Due to economic depression, and more immediately to the economic abuses of highland Mayan groups by the civil *alcalde mayor* (governor of the province) and the bishop, Chiapas in the first part of the eighteenth century was in turmoil. The alcalde was misusing the king's tribute while an avaricious bishop was constantly seeking money by making excessive visits to Mayan towns to generate fees and by demanding the removal of costly ornaments from parish churches for his personal gain. The Maya so despised the bishop that some plotted against his life.

Against this background, in a four-year period from 1708 to 1712, there were four apparitions of Catholic saints, three by the Virgin Mary and another by St. Sebastian. In Zinacantán and Santa Marta Chamula, the Virgin said that she had come to help the Mayan people. After each of these two incidents, a chapel was erected for the ceremonial cult of a Marian image. The Catholic priest was asked to approve the cult and say mass in the chapels. In both cases he refused and burned the chapels. In 1711 in San Pedro Chenalhó the image of San Sebastián was said to have visibly sweated several times and rays of light were seen coming from the image of San Juan. This was interpreted as a sign that God was offended by the sins of the community and that unless they repented, the community and the world would come to an end.

The Apparition and the Cult of the Virgin in Cancuc

In early June of 1712 the Virgin with or on a cross appeared to a young Mayan girl with the same message of assistance. The girl informed her family. Her father had been the fiscal of Cancuc for forty years. They built a small shrine at the site of the apparition. They were soon joined by four other men, one a former fiscal in Bachajón who had quarreled with the priest there and the other two, former civil officials in Cancuc. They approached the local priest for his approval of the chapel and cult, but were rejected. A week later and for the same purpose, they went to see the bishop who was visiting Chamula for the festival of San Juan, the town's patron. Again, they were unsuccessful. Because of these rejections the group of the Virgin became hostile to church authorities. The friar of Cancuc was warned to leave town. He did so, and in his absence the cult attracted a large following.

The friar informed the Spanish authorities in Ciudad Real. These authorities, always wary of independent Mayan gatherings, summoned the Cancuc authorities to Ciudad Real, ostensibly to discuss the matter. Instead, upon their arrival the Cancuc authorities were imprisoned. They escaped, returned to Cancuc, and gave their approval to the cult that had already expanded to the surrounding areas. With this approval the skeptical were won over and the cult following grew even greater. The chapel of the cult was enlarged and the interior divided into two sections by hanging straw mats. One section contained an altar with images of the Virgin, Saint Anthony, and some other saints taken from the church. There were two rows of benches in front of the altar where officials of the cult sat in hierarchical order. When a decree of the Virgin was to be proclaimed, the young girl would retire to a space behind the hanging mats, remain there a short time, and then return to proclaim whatever the Virgin had commanded. Daily prayer ceremonies took place in the chapel.

An invitation was issued to Tzeltal towns to come and see the Blessed Virgin and aid in her defense should the rumor prove true that the Jews of San Cristóbal were coming to kill her. The invitation added that since the Maya had been refusing to pay the alcalde mayor the tribute he unjustly demanded, not the king nor the president of the Audiencia nor the bishop would come to defend her, only the local community. A short time later a mandate of the Virgin was sent to the authorities of Tzeltal communities:

> Jesus, Mary and Joseph. Esteemed alcaldes of [such and such community]: I, the Virgin, have descended to this sinful world and call upon you in the name of Our Lady of the Rosary and command you to come

to Cancuc and to bring with you all the silver of your church, and the ornaments, canopies, chests, drums, and all the books and money of the cofradías because no longer is there a Spanish god nor a king. And come as soon as possible because if you do not, you will be punished because you have not listened to my summons. . . . The most Holy Virgin María of the Cross. (Ximénez 1971a: 264)

The resources from the churches were needed to finance an army, the soldiers of the Virgin. A rebellion was underway. The Spaniards were alarmed. They called on the civil authorities in San Cristóbal to do something. The bishop was scheduled to make one of his unwanted visits to the doctrinas of the area for his usual purpose of demanding fees and church ornaments. He was asked to cancel his visits but refused.

The Armed Rebellion

Some Tzeltal communities had refused the summons to Cancuc. They became the first targets of the Virgin's army. In a number of these towns the army killed the local fiscales who had been firm in their opposition to the cult. Then beginning in Chilón, they began a murderous revenge on Spaniards for their past condescending and unjust treatment. Friar Colindres of Chilón confronted the rebels and tried to negotiate a surrender of the town's weapons in exchange for sparing the lives of the Spaniards. He was unsuccessful and they were killed.

Friar Colindres however was spared. At the beginning of the rebellion the order to kill the Spaniards did not include the local priests. It appears that the Cancuc rebels hoped eventually to win over some of the priests who were needed to say mass for the Virgin. But later the Virgin commanded their deaths because of their continued opposition to the cult. Colindres and another Dominican friar were murdered on their way to Cancuc to preach against the cult. A Dominican from Bachajón was imprisoned in Cancuc and killed because it was feared that he would later reveal some adverse things he had found out about the cult during his imprisonment. A Dominican taken prisoner in Ocosingo and brought to Cancuc with hostage women and children was killed when he refused to celebrate mass in the chapel of the Virgin. In Simojovel, a town that had refused to answer the summons, the Franciscan friar and the fiscal were killed. In Tumbalá, a town that contributed a number of soldiers to the army of the Virgin, a secular priest was killed.

Founding a Mayan Church

Sebastián Gómez, who had been involved in promoting the apparitions in San Pedro Chenalhó, came to Cancuc and assumed the role of the Catholic priest in the cult group. He sent this message to the rebellious communities:

Esteemed Sebastián Gómez of Glory, as the delegate of Saint Peter, sends this message, which is not mine but an order from heaven . . . that the world cannot endure if there is no authority on earth. Our father, Saint Peter, became our bondsman before God, and for this reason the word of God came from heaven. It is not of the earth because in every community there is a priest who has power before God because of the mass. Since there will always be sinners in the world, the world would end if there were no masses. It is because of the masses celebrated by the priests that God's anger is turned aside. And so that your children may be well instructed, you must send them to church to learn the doctrina and be taught the Christian laws as ordered by heaven. (Ximénez 1971a: 276)

The priests' rejections of the cult created a problem: there was no one to celebrate masses for the Virgin. Sebastián Gómez solved the problem by claiming that he had been taken up into heaven where he had been named by Saint Peter as his vicar with the commission to ordain priests and bishops. To legitimate his claim, he preached, "Christ gave the authority to Saint Peter, Saint Peter to the pope, and the pope to the bishops, and therefore bishops have the authority to ordain the priests we know. These priests are men like ourselves; therefore Saint Peter can also give me the authority to ordain priests" (Ximénez 1971a: 275).

He then summoned the fiscales from the rebellious communities to find out who were qualified to be ordained, the qualification being that they could read. Eight were selected. The ordination ceremony took place in the chapel. The person to be ordained remained kneeling for twenty-four hours reciting the rosary. Sebastián took out a bundle, probably containing an image of Saint Peter, placed it on the head and chest of the future priest while reciting some prayers, and then blessed him with holy water. This probably took place during a mass. On September 23, Gómez ordained a second group of at least thirteen fiscales. The ordained fiscales returned to their communities to administer the cult of the saints. They said mass, preached, and administered those sacraments that were customary in the community. Ximénez describes the fiscales as tyrannical, demanding that community members show them the same respect given the friars and threatening that if they refused, they would be whipped.

Bishops were also needed for the Virgin's cult. The consecration ceremony for a bishop was preceded by a notification that the prospective person must accept the call to this high office or be drowned, that while fasting he had to kneel in the chapel for three days and nights, that on the final day he must hold a large lighted candle, and that if because of frailty he was unable to endure, he must die because that was the order of heaven.

The cult of the Virgin in the chapel continued. In place of María's father sat the newly consecrated bishops. Behind the two rows of benches previously described, there were two more rows occupied by the captains of the Virgin's army. There was constant music and singing for the Virgin and daily mass followed by recitation of the rosary. The chapel received the offerings of the faithful as well as the booty taken from Spaniards, wealthy Indians, and priests of the region. Internal divisions arose among the followers of the Virgin concerning the distribution of these resources.

The cult and its priesthood were short-lived. In a few months the Spaniards rallied, retaking the towns of the Virgin, and the rebellion collapsed. With it ended this attempt to establish the fiscales as a Mayan priesthood for the Catholic saints.

Cultural Logics at Work

Situations of sharp conflict tend to bring out underlying attitudes and logics that are not always evident in everyday life. The Cancuc rebellion did this for some of the Mayan cultural logics. The Virgin who had been incorporated into the Mayan covenant as an important saint was the sacred figure who legitimized this rebellion. Although the rebellion was against Spanish abuse, it was not a nativistic movement that called upon preconquest gods and rituals. Catholic saints, masses, and priests were involved in all phases, showing that they had been Mayanized.

The friars' rejection of the cult, as well as their murders, created a problem because of the cultural logic dictating the mass as the necessary ritual for the saintly Virgin. Therefore, the Maya decided to get their own priests. Cultural logic required finding Maya who knew how to read the proper words of the mass and other Catholic-derived rituals. The solution was the ordination of fiscales who could read the mass book and perform the ceremonies because of their association with the Catholic priests.

The Virgin's proclamation states the logic behind the insistence on masses: without them the present cycle of existence would come to an end. Since the priest knew the prayer formulas of the mass, he had the power to maintain the cycle. At every step of this rebellion the cultural logics of the cycle and covenant continued to play a role in the thinking of the Maya, confirming the earlier analyses of them.

The Chamula Rebellion, 1867–70

The same cultural logics were at work again in the rebellion that took place in Chamula led by the fiscal, Pedro Díaz Cuzcat (Rus 1983: 127–68; Bricker 1981: 119–25). In late 1867 a Chamula woman, Augustina Gómez Checheb, said she found some talking stones in the village of Tzajalhemel that had a message of assistance for the Maya. At some point saint images, including ones of the

Virgin, were added to the talking stones. The fiscal, Cuzcat, came to the village, said a shrine should be erected, and preached there for several months. In February 1868 the Catholic priest of Chamula came to the village and found burning candles and incense being offered to the stones and images. Attendance at the shrine swelled to the discomfort of the Chiapas civil authorities and merchants. In May ladino civil officials with twenty-five armed men invaded the shrine, seized the images and stones, and imprisoned Checheb. But because of internal fights among the ladinos themselves, the state governor ordered Checheb released and the images returned. In August the shrine was enlarged, bells and trumpets were obtained for the services, sacristans and acolytes appointed, and a mayordomo designated to organize the festivals of the saint. During this period Cuzcat had vestments made and acted as a Catholic priest, preaching and administering the sacraments.

Cuzcat functioned as a Catholic priest for less than six months. On December 2 a ladino force of fifty armed men invaded the village, arrested Checheb again, and seized the shrine adornments. Cuzcat escaped, but was soon taken prisoner. In June the Catholic priest of Chamula with several of his helpers visited the shrine village and demanded to take possession of the images and stones. Some Chamulas, while asking for the priest's blessing, handed them over to him. When another Chamula group found out what had happened, they pursued and overtook the priest and his companions, killing them while recovering the sacred objects. These murders triggered a series of raids and killings by both ladinos and Chamulas. Eventually, the ladinos regained control of the area and the rebellion died down. Once again in keeping with the cultural logics regarding ritual and the latent preference for a Mayan specialist, the fiscal took the place of the Catholic priest for the purpose of conducting the Catholic-derived rituals.

The Cruzob: Mayan Priests for Mayanized Catholic Rituals

In the two previous cases the Maya were unsuccessful in maintaining the fiscales as priests for the Mayanized Catholic rituals. With the defeat of the uprisings, the rebellious areas reverted back to the situation described in previous chapters. In the latter part of the nineteenth century in Yucatán, however, a Mayan group was successful in permanently installing fiscales as the priests of the Mayanized Catholic rituals.

Chapter 4 described how Yukatek Maya kidnapped Mexican Catholic priests and forced them to perform the required rituals for the saints during the early part of the Caste Wars. As the Caste Wars continued, some Mayan groups retreated into the unsettled forest areas of southeastern Yucatán to isolate themselves from the Mexicans. The Mexicans became embroiled in disputes among themselves in western Yucatán and ceased sustained efforts against the retreating Maya. A Mayan group took advantage of this respite to create a military theocracy, the Cruzob, presided over by a high priest who modeled himself on Catholic bishops (Villa Rojas 1945; Reed 1964: 159–280; Bricker 1981: 87–116). The cult of the theocracy centered on a talking cross kept in a large church constructed by the community. Since the Cruzob were now isolated from the Mexicans and unable to kidnap Catholic priests, they ordained their own people to administer the sacraments as part of the cult of the cross. The high priest transmitted the wishes of the cross to subordinate generals and priests, the latter ordained by the high priest. The majority of the newly ordained priests had been fiscales in their communities before the retreat. In the Cruzob villages they celebrated masses, performed baptisms and marriages, and conducted the devotional rituals of the rosary and novenas. They called themselves Catholic priests and in these villages functioned in the same manner as Mexican Catholic priests did in the rest of Yucatán.

This group remained isolated and independent for about fifty years. In 1901 a Mexican army invaded and defeated the Cruzob, bringing them back under Mexican political control. But the religious aspect of the theocracy continued. Villa Rojas (1945: 73) described the role of the priest and former fiscal for the Tusik area in 1932–36. The Cruzob priests continue to perform Catholic-derived rituals in the Cruzob communities in complete independence of the bishops and priests of the Mexican Catholic Church. The Cruzob consider the Catholic clergy to be fellow priests and allow them to celebrate mass in their inner sanctum if they so wish (Farriss 1984: 316).

Conclusion: Endurance of Cultural Logics

This chapter has demonstrated the extension of the pre-Columbian Mayan logics to the role of the fiscal. In circumstances of ethnic conflict, the Maya rejected the dominant culture, including the non-Mayan Catholic priests, and substituted the fiscales because they knew the prayer formulas of the required rituals. The preconquest logics continued to define Mayan consciousness and decisions for almost five hundred years after the conquest. Around roughly the middle of the twentieth century, the cultural logics of both the Maya and Catholicism were subjected to strong forces of change. Both have undergone some transformations since that time. But that is the subject of another volume.

The Mass of the Talking Saints

The preceding chapter examined how the cultural logics of the Mayan covenant explained the role of the fiscal as a substitute for the priest. This chapter examines how these same logics fused the saints with a characteristic of the traditional gods.

Mayan Tradition of Talking Gods

During the late Pre-Columbian Period in Yucatan, the interpreter of talking oracles was a recognized religious role: "The duty of the Chilans was to give the replies of the gods to the people, and so much respect was shown to them that they carried them on their shoulders" (Landa 1941:112). The Chilam Balam of Tizimin describes the manner in which the Jaguar Priest gave his prophecy. Roys (1933:182) thinks that in addition, this passage probably describes the experience of the *Chilans*: "He retired to the inner room of his house and lay motionless, apparently in a trance while a supernatural being, perched on the roof, vouchsafed a solemn communication in 'measured words.' Other priests were assembled outside the room, and they appear to have heard the words but could not understand them. They waited with their faces bowed down to the floor, until the chilan came out and delivered the prophecy to them"(Roys 1943:79).

Sharer (1994:542) raises the possibility of the use of psychotropic substances to alter the state of consciousness of the Chilans during this period. On Cozumel, there was a talking image that drew pilgrims from many parts of Yucatan and Tabasco.

> Anciently all this country and the Indians went ordinarily to the said island [Cozumel] to worship a certain idol which they had in certain ancient buildings and which they venerated greatly; . . . as if they went to gain pardons because they went from Tabasco and Xicalango and Champoton and Campeche and from other distant pueblos, they came to see and to worship the said idol . . . there was an old Indian who was called *Alquin* (*Ah Kin*) which means . . . cleric or priest. And the Indians went to see the idol speak with the said *Alquin* and told him why they came and that which they wished. And the said old Indian spoke with the idol and with the demon which they said was inside of it, he replied to all which was asked and they learned from him all that which they wished and the said old Indian, *Alquin*, returned the answer which the idol gave to them. (Landa 1941: 109 n. 500 and sources cited therein)

The sources say that the idol was kept in a square temple.

> It [the idol] was very singular and different from all the others; its material was baked clay; it was a large hollow figure joined to the wall with mortar. At its back was something like a sacristy in which the priests had a small hidden door opening into the back of the idol. Into this one of the priests entered, and from there he replied to the requests which were made. The unhappy dupes believed that the idol spoke to them and credited what was said to them; and so they venerated it more than the others with various offerings, sacrifices of blood, birds, dogs and sometimes even men. Since, as they believed, it always spoke to them, they came together from everywhere in such great numbers to consult it and to beg for help in their troubles. (Landa 1941: 109 n. 500 and sources cited therein)

The pattern described here consists of a talking sacred image who listens to requests for help and replies to a single person who, in turn, relays the answers to the petitioner.

Talking Saints of the Colonial and National Periods

The Pre-Columbian pattern continued into later historical periods. In the eighteenth century, as noted in chapter 14, statues of the Virgin Mary in Zinacantán and Santa Marta Chamula talked to single individuals who informed community authorities of the Virgin's message. A few years later the Virgin spoke again to a young girl and conveyed much the same message that became the source of legitimation for the Mayan revolt in Cancuc. A similar event preceded the revolt in Chamula in the following century.

The Christian cross, with or without the Christ image, was considered a Spanish saint by the Maya. As Nelson Reed explains in *The Caste War of Yucatan* (1964), in the nineteenth century crosses that talked were the ultimate authority during Yucatan's Caste War. Kept on an altar of an inner room in a thatched church, they were

> a sanctuary forbidden to all except a few assistants, guarded day and night. The congregation met in the main outer room. This arrangement added mystery and glamor to the hidden Crosses and was in keeping with the local tradition of using a substitute Santo for procession when the genuine article was too holy for public view. . . . A pit was dug behind the altar, and there crouched a hidden spokesman who used a wooden cask as an echo chamber to amplify, project and give resonance to his voice. Those who heard it said the words of God seemed to come from the middle of the air. (139)

The ritual for the talking cross was presided over by the theocratic high priest. He summoned his god, with a whistle, just as the shamans called the rain gods. Reed states that "According to all reports, each interview with the Cross would be announced during the afternoon by the ringing of bells and a performance by a military band. All normal work came to a halt. Catholic prayers and chants sustained the religious enthusiasm through the afternoon and evening, as the Cruzob gathered in and before the Temple. At midnight, with suspense at a high pitch, the whistle sounded, followed by a profound silence" (139).

The third official of the Speaking Cross was called the Organ of the Divine Word. "He was," Reed notes, "the man who did the actual speaking. The fact that his existence was admitted in a year when the cross was still speaking suggests that the Cruzob didn't believe that the voice came physically from the Cross, but rather that the words of God were given sound through the medium of a possessed man. . . . A variation of the sound chamber and the spoken word was the use of the whistle to stimulate the voice of God, which was then interpreted by the Tata Polin [the High Priest]" (215).

Talking Saints of Chiapas in the Twentieth Century

Ethnographic research has found talking saints in several communities of Chiapas.

San Pedro Chenalhó

According to Guiteras-Holmes (1961: 164) a talking saint was owned by a town official in 1944. Her consultant, Manuel, had a box similar to the ones in which the talking saints were kept. He relates how an owner of a talking saint came to his house. He proceeded to make Manuel's box talk even though it had no image. The voice prescribed medicines sold by the visitor and said the people were in danger of death if they did not use them. Manuel became disenchanted with the man and decided the whole thing was a hoax.

San Andrés Larraínzar

This community had a number of talking saints (Holland 1963: 199–206). Their owners, whether shamans or not, were the most esteemed of the all the traditional healers. During the ceremony, those present could barely hear the falsetto sound of the saint's voice and were unable to understand it. Consequently, the owner of the saint repeated and interpreted what had been said to those present: "Although these divinities are often confused with those of Catholic origin—St. Lorenzo, St. Antonio, St. Manuel and St. Miguel—they are in reality gods of the earth or angels of the mountains, caves and springs, and consequently the concepts attached to the talking saints are more Mayan than Catholic" (Holland 1963: 201). The soul of the image is a Mayan god of nature who bestows the necessities for survival within an allotted cycle.

A talking saint can initiate a pact with a prospective owner by appearing in a dream or by speaking directly from a small box in their house:

> the saint will explain that he is god-owner of a nearby cave, mountain or spring and he would like to make a covenant, proposing to be permanently at their command [to talk when summoned] as long as they live if they keep the required fasts and offer candles, incense and fireworks during the community celebration of the saint's feast day. If these are done in a satisfactory manner, the saint will return and order that a box be built and adorned either in the owner's house or one specially constructed for this purpose. (Holland 1963: 201)

This is a restatement of the reciprocity of the Mayan covenant.

Holland notes that the role of an owner of a talking saint in an outlying village is analogous to that of the Catholic priest in the ceremonial center of the municipio. Both conduct baptisms. The home of the talking saint is the focal point of the village's festival calendar. The festivals are sponsored by a cargo official, but on a smaller scale than those celebrated in the ceremonial center for the whole municipio as described in chapters 2 and 3.

Zinacantán

This municipio had a number of talking saints in villages away from the ceremonial center (Vogt 1969: 365; 1977: 199; Fabrega and Silver 1973: 43–46). In contrast to San Pedro and San Andrés, the owners of talking saints were regarded with considerable suspicion:

> the typical pattern of consultation is as follows: a patient goes to the house of a talking—saint owner . . . with standard payment of liquor, chickens, flowers and so on, and places them in front of the box in which the saint is kept. Often, the owner covers his head and the box with his chamarra [blanket] while he explains the patient's problems to the saint and waits for a response. Several informants who have witnessed consultations claim that a high-pitched, squeaky noise is emitted, construed to be the voice of the talking saint. Others claim that no sound is heard, that the owner acts as transmitter of the saint's message. . . . The reputation of the talking—saint owner is extremely dubious in Zinacantan today [1960s and 1970s]. In several cases the diagnosis of a talking saint has resulted in the murder of a suspected witch, thus drawing the censure of Zinacanteco and ladino authorities. In other cases, the cure prescribed involved continual payments to the owner, with patients paying out of fear for their lives. When the cures are unsuccessful the owners are accused of theft and become the objects of hostility and suspicion. Enough cases have been brought to court so that both Zinacanteco and ladino authorities have adopted a negative attitude. (Vogt 1977: 199)

Talking Saints in Guatemala

In most of the previous cases, the saint talked with a single person who in turn transmitted the saint's message to others. The person doing the talking was concealed in some manner so that the client did not see him while talking with the saint. In the post-Columbian cases, the one who owned a talking image (figure 15.1)[1] was a private individual, perhaps a shaman, but not in any

Figure 15.1. An angel's head (17" × 7", bright red color) used by a shaman as a talking saint. It is usually kept in a box with an open front.

way connected with the civil or religious officials of the community and their duties for its care.

In Guatemala, in the Mam-speaking municipio of San Juan Ostuncalco, department of Quezaltenango, talking saints play an integral role in the official community ritual.[2] By the terms of the Mayan covenant, the welfare of the whole community depends in a special manner on the reciprocity between its civil and religious officials and the talking saints, San Pedro Pascual and San Pedro Nolasco. In the colonial period, Ostuncalco was a Mercedarian town of residencia for the surrounding area. San Pedro Nolasco (St. Peter Nolasco) was the founder of the Mercedarian Order and San Pedro Pascual one of its early members. There are statues of them in the town church and cofradías are assigned to take care of them and celebrate their festivals. They may be consulted by individuals as in the Chiapas communities. But their more important role is communal because of a ritual that only shamans can perform.

Divination

Many shamanic ceremonies are preceded by a divination. Its most frequent use is to diagnose individuals who are suffering a physical discomfort of some type. The divination tries to determine the source of the discomfort and what is required to remove it. Other uses include determining a course of action in a problematic situation or determining the best day for the performance of a ceremony. Among his ceremonial tools, each shaman has a small gourd con-

Figure 15.2. A shaman's divination beans, usually kept in a small gourd with a corn cob stopper.

taining red beans (figure 15.2). Some use small crystals instead of beans, while others combine the two. Horace Peck describes the divination in the following passage.

> The shaman sits on his chair beside the low divination table. He takes up the gourd containing the red beans and asks its pardon, kissing it and calling on the mountains. He scatters a chance handful on the table. After blowing on his hands, he scoops up some and as he calls the name of each pair, he places them on the table with prayer to the gods to answer the question of restoration of the sick one to health. If the handful results in pairs, the shaman declares that the sick one will get well. If the result is odd, he says that the patient will die. After various throws, the shaman may state that there are two answers: one, that the patient will recover, and the other, that he will die. This result indicates that a series of ritualistic ceremonies are to be held at the river three times to cool the fever. (1970:19–20)[3]

The Ritual Patterns

The shaman then performs the prescribed ceremonies composed of one or several of the following ritual patterns whose purpose, place, and time will be described in the next section.[4]

Food Offerings

Before the altar of a sacred place or in a family home, the shaman enters and blesses himself. He has a bundle wrapped with a striped cloth containing candles and packets of incense. While praying, he raises and offers the bundle to the divinities that dwell in this place. In some ceremonies he touches the heads of those present with the bundle. Unwrapping it, he places on the altar a row of five lighted candles and some lighted kindling for the packets of incense. The shaman prays that the gods of the sacred place will accept these offerings as their food and, in the spirit of the covenant, grant the petition that is the objective of the ceremony. (Later in the text and in the tables, this ceremony will be called pattern 1.)

Blood Offerings

This pattern is similar to the previous one but in addition to the candles and incense, the shaman slits the throat of a rooster or turkey and pours its blood over the burning candles and incense and over the staffs of office in the ceremony for the civil officials of the community (figure 15.3). (In the text and tables this ceremony will be called pattern 2.)

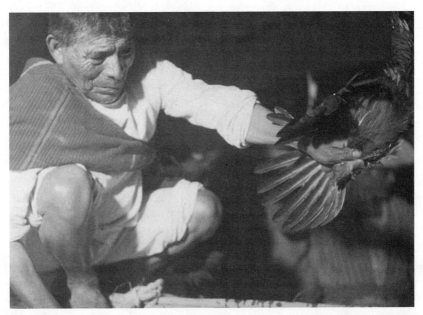

Figure 15.3. A shaman squats on top of a bundle of staffs to be distributed to the civil officials of the coming year. He has slit the throat of a rooster letting its blood splatter on the staffs. Only a small portion of the top of the bundle of staffs appears at the bottom of the picture.

The Shaman's Mass

In the Mam language this ceremony is called *santamis*, a loan word from the Spanish *santa misa* meaning holy mass. This is the most important shamanic ceremony in San Juan because during it, two saint-gods arrive at the summons of the shaman and vocally address both the shaman and those in attendance(Peck 1970: 24–25; 43–44; 64–66). The use of a Spanish loan word for this important shamanic ceremony may be based on the fact that the assistance of two Catholic saints is called on, in the same way that the Catholic priest's mass calls on assistance from all of the saints.

When a shaman is initiated, he receives the instruments used in divination and in the shaman's mass: a small gourd containing the red divination beans, a piece of cloth (a banner) attached to a wooden stick handle (figure 15.4), and a section of metal chain links (figure 15.5). During the ritual, the shaman snaps the handle of the cloth to make a flapping sound that announces the presence of San Pedro Pascual. Then the chain is shaken to make a rattling noise announcing the arrival or departure of San Pedro Nolasco.

The shamanic mass is usually preceded by offerings involving patterns 1 or 2 described above. All present cover their heads with blankets or shawls and all candles are extinguished. The mass takes place in darkness, usually at night. Children up to nearly age fifteen are not allowed to attend.

> In the dark he [the shaman] whistles. He flaps the banner, the angel's wings, nine times. He again whistles and again flaps the banner six times. He impersonates San Pedro Pascual, declaring in a high falsetto voice, "You who are not my children, I have been called by one of incense, one of candles. I have come. My feet are clean, my hands are clean. There is life, there is health for you (plural). You (plural) have given me this little gift here (incense, candles) with all your heart, with all your strength. I have taken it. Don't think there has sounded a skunk bell, a white bell. I am called to another place. See to yourselves. (Peck 1970: 25)

The saint emphasizes that he is not a human being but a divinity by declaring that those present "are not my children." Among the Maya, candles and incense are perceived as the food of the gods. Here, in the spirit of the Mayan covenant, San Pedro Pascual accepts the food offerings and upholds his part of the covenant by bestowing health. The divinity departs while the shaman reassures the assembled group that the saint has heard their prayers and accepted their offerings.

Next, the sounds of chains rattling against the door and a series of nine sighs are heard. These announce the arrival of the elderly San Pedro Nolasco. He enters and in deep falsetto voice speaks to the assembled group and tells them

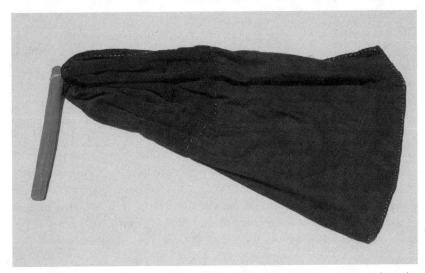

Figure 15.4. A cloth banner and its handle is snapped by the shaman to produce the sound of wings.

Figure 15.5. Chain links are shaken by the shaman to announce the arrival and departure of a talking saint.

who has called him— "a user of incense, a user of candles"—and why he has come: "Thanks to him that I have been called, cried for. . . . Now then, there is life. There is health. You will continue to be happy." The chain rattles again and Nolasco's sighs sound as he retires to respond to calls "from all over the earth" (Peck 1970: 44).

With these messages from the two saints, the ceremony is over. The blankets and shawls are removed from the heads of those present and the candles are relighted. The shaman may reassure the group that their petitions have been heard. After a mass to petition rain, the shaman addresses the group with these words: "Good night, you have heard what was left said by our fathers San Pedro Pascual and San Pedro Nolasco. For this, don't be sad. Perhaps will come our father rain, standing over our crops, over everything. Also not only I may be petitioning but also perhaps at the same time a group of our companions have worshipped [performed the same ritual]. . . . Indeed, perhaps, all will unite together and all will join together at this midnight" (Peck 1970: 67). Then in front of the altar table the shaman kisses the dirt floor without actually touching it. Others follow and bidding each other good night, return to their homes.

Community Shamanic Rituals

Table 15.1 lists the yearly calendar of shamanic rituals performed on behalf of the community's civil and religious officials.

Civil Officials

These authorities reside in the ceremonial center and are concerned with the usual functions of public order, taxation, public works, administration of justice, and so forth. The municipio has outlying villages (*aldeas*), and the town itself is usually subdivided into smaller units (*cantones*). Each aldea and canton is under the jurisdiction of a regidor appointed by the municipio authorities. These civil authorities usually have staffs, some with silver tips, that they carry as symbols of their office.

During their term in office they are bearers of the yearly cycle. To successfully perform their duties for the community's welfare, they must have the assistance of the gods of the Mayan covenant. This means that by the covenant's terms of reciprocity rituals must be performed in order to feed the gods. These rituals are performed in each jurisdictional unit at the beginning, middle, and end of the year (table 15.1) by a shaman selected by the regidor (Peck 1970: 69–72). At the beginning of the year, the shaman and the regidor go early in the morning to the altar at the river where the shaman prays while making the offerings described above as pattern 2. They then proceed to the altar on a sacred mountain where the same pattern is repeated. In the evening, the sha-

Table 15.1. Shamanic Rituals for the Whole Community by Times, Places, and Ritual Patterns

Petitions for Community, Officials, and Crops	Times of the Year	Ritual Places	For Each Yearly Segment Ritual Patterns		
			Beginning	Middle	End
Civil officials	Beginning, middle, near year's end	River	2	1	1
		Mountain	1	1	1
		House	1	a	3
Cofradía members					
Each cofradía	Saint's feast, six months later, near next year's feast	River	2	2	2
		Mountain	-	2	2
		Crossroad	-	-	2
		House	3	3	a
All 28 cofradías as a group	Every 20 days	Mountain	1	x	x
		House	3	x	x
Festival dancers	Year prior, six months later	River	1	1 2	1
	Arrival of costumes, end of festival	House	3	a 3	a
Crop cycle:					
To bring rain	Ascension Thursday	Mountain	2	x	1
Harvest thanks	October	House	3	x	3

Source: Peck 1970: 53–79.

aGiven the overall pattern for this ritual, there is a possibility that pattern three, the talking saints ritual, also takes place. A dash indicates that no ritual is performed at this place and time but see end note five. An x indicates that the category is not applicable.

man comes to the house of the regidor where pattern 3, the shaman's mass of the talking saints, is performed.

At mid-year the altars at the river and mountains are again visited to make the same petition and to express thanksgiving if all has gone well during the first six months. Peck's brief description implies that ritual pattern 1 is enacted. He does not mention an evening, ritual pattern 3 ceremony at the house of the regidor, but there is a possibility that it takes place.[5] Toward the end of the year, a ceremony using ritual patterns 2 and 3 is performed at the same three places in thanksgiving for the assistance of the gods during their past year. This ceremony for the civil officials resembles the Year Bearers' ceremony performed in many Mayan communities.

Cofradía Members

Each of the twenty-eight cofradías in the San Juan municipio has one or more shamans in their membership. They perform shamanic rituals so that the cofrades will successfully perform their rituals and other duties for the saints (Peck 1970: 53–59). There are two types of shamanic ceremonies for this purpose.

Each cofradía seeks assistance by having a shaman perform ceremonies three times a year that are similar to those described above for the civil officials. The cycle begins with the feast day of the patron saint and ends shortly before same feast a year later. The shaman is selected by the cofradía leader. He, along with the second cofradía official, accompanies the shaman who conducts the ceremonies at the sacred places indicated in table 15.1.

The other ceremony is celebrated every 20 days and is a joint effort of all the cofradías. A single group consisting of one shaman and the first and second officials from each cofradía goes to a sacred mountain top. There, ritual patterns 1 and 3 are performed for the success of the cofrades' efforts in dealing with their saints.

Festival Dancers

The feast day of the Virgen de Candelaria is a major festival in San Juan that includes the Dance of the Conquest (Peck 1970: 72–79; Bode 1961: 203). The dancers are considered ritual performers. Consequently, there must be additional rituals for assistance similar to those for the civil officials and the cofrades (table 15.1). An extra round is added with the arrival of the rented costumes that must be sacralized before the feast day itself.

Nature and the Agricultural Cycle

Traditional Mayan communities are dependent on corn for their survival. The seasonal rains are an absolute necessity for the success of the corn crop. Consequently, the Mayan covenant dictates ceremonies to feed the rain gods so that they will be generous in supplying an abundant and timely supply. These rituals are performed on Ascension Thursday, a movable feast occurring forty days after Easter (Peck 1970: 60–69). This usually occurs in the first part of May, at the normal onset of the rainy season in the highlands of Guatemala. Four shamans, each leading a group of cofrades and musicians, proceed to four sacred mountains to perform pattern 2, the animal blood sacrifice (table 15.1). In the evening, at the houses of each of the four shamans, the shamanic mass with the talking saints, pattern 3, takes place to obtain the life-sustaining rain. The harvest season begins with the cessation of the rains in October. In November the same ceremony is repeated in thanksgiving for the new crop.

Shamanic Rituals for Individuals

Like the shamans in Chiapas, the shamans of San Juan Ostuncalco also perform rituals requested by individuals to alleviate their personal problems. Table 15.2 lists typical needs as well as the places and ritual patterns used for some of these ceremonies. For individual needs, the ritual of the shaman's mass with

Table 15.2. Shamanic Rituals for Individuals by Place and Ritual Pattern

Individual Needs	Place	Pattern
Healing	House	Divination
	River/Mountain	2 repeated
	House	3
Blessing on newlyweds	Church	1
	River	2
	House	3
For a child	Church	1
	River or Mountain	1
During pregnancy	Church	1
	River	2
At birth	River	1
	Church	Catholic baptism
Domestic problems	House	Divination
	River	2 repeated
Witchcraft	River	1
	Mountain	1

Source: Peck 1970: 19–52.

the talking saints is only used to petition for a successful marriage and to heal sickness. In addition to the rituals, the shamans also prescribe various herbal and pharmaceutical remedies.

Conclusion

In San Juan Ostuncalco, two Catholic saints talk during a ritual in which their assistance is petitioned for community and individual needs. Following Holland's suggestion, it appears that these two saints have been fused with the traditional gods of the mountains who control rain, fertility, and health. The souls of the images of San Pedro Pascual and San Pedro Nolasco in the church are the traditional mountain gods. Recall Ignacio's words to his fellow cofrades in chapter 12, "we are going to die, but it will be our sons and our grandsons who will serve the representative of the heart of heaven and heart of earth, who is San Juan Bautista, patron and guardian of our town, a saint of god of the clouds and of the rain, who also is *dueño* of the origins of rivers and hills, a saint of god who also is *dueño* of the storms. And the image of the saint is what we are going to serve for a year" (Bizarro Upjohn 2001: 231).

The shamanic mass with the two talking saints is celebrated on all occasions that call for the help of the gods to assist the civil and religious leaders in carrying out their duties for the welfare of the community. It shows how completely the Catholic saints were incorporated into cultural logics of the Mayan covenant. In this type of fusion the shamans have broken the necessary connection between the saints and the Catholic mass, including its celebrant. While the community has retained the Catholic elements, the shamans have developed a parallel system with their own mass which they perform as celebrants. This writer suspects that the San Juan case is not unique. As described in note 1, the photographs in this chapter are from nearby Mayan communities and suggest a similar pattern. To the writer's knowledge, this tight integration of the talking saints into the authority structure of the community has not been previously reported. In the other cases described, the rituals of the talking saints were conducted by private individuals or by shamans outside the authority structure of the community and sometimes in spite of their negative attitude.

PART 6

Conclusion

Questions Raised by the Research

The previous chapters have explored the anomaly of the presence of Catholic elements as intrinsic parts of the Mayan worldview and ritual matrix. The results help explain some questions that have been raised about the Maya-Catholic relationship as well as posing topics for further research.

Syncretism

From the viewpoint of comparative religion, can the Mayan religion with its Catholic elements be described as syncretistic, as a hybrid religion? *Syncretism* has been used in so many differing senses that the question is ambiguous (Colpe 1987). This study has found that the Maya by means of their own traditional cultural logics defined the saint images as Spanish gods to be recognized as emanations in the pantheistic universe. If one's definition of syncretism allows for this process, then the Mayan religion is syncretistic. If syncretism means the emergence of a third, distinct religious system out of two previous ones as implied by Wagley (1949; see chapter 1), then there is no syncretism but rather the continuation of the traditional Mayan system with some elements added and defined within the logic of that system.

The Maya and Monotheism

Given the concerns of classical theism, a frequent question concerns the multitude of gods assigned to the Maya by Mayan scholars (Montejo 1991). Chapter 5 identified the Mayan cosmos as pantheistic. In such a system, the monotheistic-polytheistic distinction breaks down. Pantheism can be both, depending on whether it is considered from the viewpoint of the ultimate cosmic force or its various pluralistic emanations.

An inquiry about monotheism and other characteristics of Mayan religion is somewhat esoteric for some Maya. Like adherents of many religions, they spend little time thinking about such matters and when asked about exact details, show little interest in the subject. The writer recalls talking with a Zinacanteco and trying to understand some of the gods and the relationships among them. The man somewhat impatiently remarked that the people do not think or talk much about such things. I then asked what were the things that occupied people's everyday thoughts and activities. At first he said working and eating and as long as people can eat, they were content. I asked, "Is that all?" He then expanded his answer: growing corn, transporting crops of all sorts, getting drunk with friends and visitors, smoking, and sleeping with their wives. To such Maya, the question of monotheism is irrelevant to their everyday life. But this does not mean that they take the Mayan covenant lightly. It means that they take it seriously without reflecting much on it. "To say the tales reveal the Zinacantec musing over his legendary journey, reminding himself of the supernatural dangers that persist even today, does not mean that he is staggering under the burden of the past, cowering from fear of the present. In fact, the past is borne very lightly, almost cavalierly. During most of his waking hours the ordinary man, caught up in the innumerable petty affairs of daily life, gives little thought to the supernatural world" (Laughlin 1977: 3). But among the Maya, as in any community, there are some philosophers who ponder and continually ask searching questions about the human condition. Most are corn farmers; some are shamans, although philosophizing is not a characteristic of all shamans.

Catholicism as it is practiced is both monotheistic and polytheistic. At the theological level, monotheism is carefully preserved by the doctrine of the Trinity and the theological distinctions regarding the Virgin Mary and the saints. But in the "little tradition" of Catholicism, the folk Catholicism of popular devotions described in chapter 7, these distinctions remain in the realm of the theologians and all the sacred beings are treated as divinities.

> Some of the early Spanish missionaries, influenced by the reformist Erasmian Humanism of the early sixteenth century, attempted to purge their religion of medieval accretions, which might more properly be called incorporations, and to present to the Amerindian neophytes a pristine form of Christianity. . . . The version that was transplanted to America fell short of this ideal. For the mass of the Spanish laity and the majority of the clergy as well, the uncompromising monotheism of the Old and New Testaments had become tempered in their Mediterranean version of popular Catholicism by the incorporation of a rich variety of sacred beings. Angels, saints, the Prince of Darkness and his minions, and a host of lesser spirits accompanied and aided or sometimes sought to foil the will of the supreme godhead. For most of the Spanish culture-bearers, the Christian cosmos was as densely populated as that of the Maya. (Farriss 1984: 295)

Conversion to Catholic Christianity

Chapters 8 to 11 described the goals, strategies, and problems of the Catholic Church in its attempts to evangelize and convert the Maya over more than four hundred years. In spite of all the problems, chapters 2 to 4 showed that these efforts had an impact on the Maya. So the question becomes, Did the Spanish convert the Maya to the sixteenth-century Spanish Catholic reform version of Christianity?

Criteria for Conversion

To decide whether conversion took place requires some criterion to assess it; otherwise any change induced by the friars could be interpreted as conversion. Given its evolutionary history as an outgrowth of Judaism, Christianity came to define itself as a set of theological concepts from which ascetical and moral conduct should flow. Faith in the truth of these concepts was the criterion of orthodoxy and therefore of conversion. The core concepts were embodied in the fourteen articles of faith.

The Fourteen Articles

Chapter 8 noted that the heart of belief was contained in the fourteen articles of faith. To review them,

> the following are the seven articles that pertain to Our Lord God as God. I believe (1) in one God almighty, (2) who is Father, (3) who is Son, (4) who is Holy Spirit, (5) in only one God who created and made heaven and earth and all things, visible and invisible, (6) who is the Savior, (7) who bestows the glory of eternal life. The following are the other seven articles that pertain to Our Savior Jesus Christ as man: I believe (1) that Our Lord Jesus Christ, for love of us, took on human flesh in the womb of Holy Mary who remained a Virgin by the power of the Holy Spirit, (2) that Our Lord Jesus Christ was born of the Virgin Holy Mary without her losing her virginity, (3) that Our Lord Jesus Christ suffered and died on the cross for us and was buried, (4) that after he died on the cross, his soul descended to Limbo to rescue the souls of the Holy Fathers awaiting there, (5) that Our Lord Jesus Christ arose from dead on the third day by his own power, (6) that forty days after he arose, he ascended into heaven and was seated at the right hand of God the Father Almighty, (7) that Our Lord Jesus Christ will come again at the end of the world to judge the living and the dead, the good and the bad, and on the good he will bestow the eternal glory of heaven because they observed his command-ments, and on the bad, he will inflict eternal punishment in hell because

they did not keep his commandments. And also I believe in the Holy Church, namely the union and fellowship of all the faithful of Lord Jesus Christ who are called Christians, who by their faith and the sacraments are linked together in unity. And also I believe that sins are forgiven by the sacraments, and I believe also that at the end of the world the dead shall rise, and I believe in eternal life. (Molina 1941: 36–37)

These articles represent the historical evolution of Christian expression away from its Jewish roots and its reinterpretation in a Hellenized form. Belief in the theological constructs of the Trinity and the Incarnation were emphasized. Although they functioned within the framework of the covenant, they became the touchstones of orthodoxy. The fourteen articles were a pedagogical expression of the theological model summarized and reaffirmed in the decrees of the Council of Trent that took place at same time as the early phase of evangelization, 1545–63.

The Saints

The Catholic theology of the saints gradually developed at the same time as Hellenized Christianity (Brown 1981). Catholic orthodoxy concerning the saints was stated in several decrees of the Council of Trent influenced by some positions of the reformers. For methodological purposes, the following decree can serve as a criterion of orthodoxy for the saint cult:

The holy Synod commands all bishops and others who hold the office of teaching . . . [to] diligently instruct the faithful on the intercession and invocation of the saints, the veneration of relics, and the legitimate use of images, teaching them that the saints, who reign together with Christ, offer up their prayers to God for men; and that it is good and useful to invoke them suppliantly and, in order to obtain favors from God through His Son Jesus Christ our Lord, who alone is our Redeemer and Savior, to have recourse to their prayers, assistance and support; . . . that the images of Christ, of the Virgin Mother of God, and of the other saints, are to be placed and retained especially in the churches, and that due honor and veneration be extended to them, not that any divinity or virtue is believed to be in them, for which they are to be venerated, or that anything is to be petitioned from them, or that trust is to be placed in images, as at one time was done by gentiles, who placed their hope in idols (cf. Ps. 134:15 f.), but because the honor which is shown them is referred to the prototypes which they represent, so that by means of the images, which we kiss and before which we bare the head and prostrate ourselves, we adore Christ and venerate the saints, whose witness they bear. This is what was sanctioned by the decrees of the councils, especially that of the second council of NICEA [AD 325], against the opponents of the images. (Denzinger 1955: 298–99, #984–86)

Did Conversion Take Place?

Figure 16.1 shows the factors that caused the progressive diminution in the numbers of Maya to whom orthodox Catholic Christianity could be communicated in any meaningful way. The diminishing size of the print represents the diminishing number of Maya involved in each factor as a result of the numbers eliminated by the previous problem. Using the fourteen articles of faith and the orthodox view of the saints as criteria of conversion, and given the problems of evangelization described in chapters 10 and 11, one can only conclude that there were few genuine conversions among the Maya. Chapters 12 and 13 showed that the Mayan perception of the Catholic elements was based on the Mayan covenant, which cannot be harmonized with Catholic orthodoxy. For many Maya, the only orthodox adoption was the memorization of some traditional Catholic prayers, typically without understanding their meaning.

Others who have examined the question of conversion have come to the same conclusion. Archbishop Cortés y Larraz, fresh from Spain and in despair after his initial tour of the Guatemalan diocese in 1769–70, concluded that "these miserable people have no religion . . . the Christian religion was introduced without any consideration of the laws of the gospel; baptism was administered prior to any instruction, the opposite of what was laid down by Jesus Christ. As a result, men [priests] may work as hard as they wish, but they

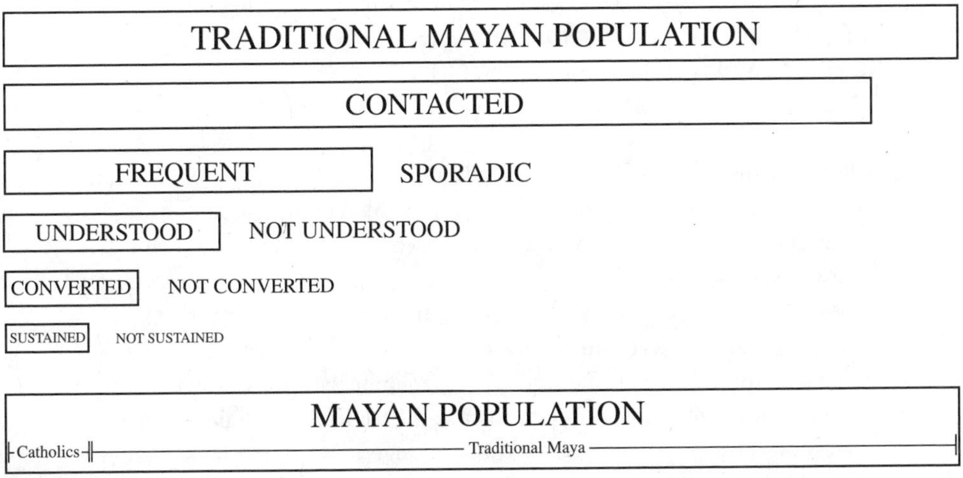

Figure 16.1. The problems of evangelization as they progressively limited the number of possible converts.

will gain nothing. Christianity has been founded contrary to what the gospel has ordered. No fruit whatsoever can be hoped for until the church, guided by the Holy Spirit, can find the means to place religion on its true foundation" (Cortés y Larraz 1958 II: 185).

LaFarge came to the same conclusion: "The task confronting a priest who wished to revive [introduce?] true Christianity among the people is made almost overwhelming by the fact that they are not merely non-Christians, but non-Christians who believe themselves to be the only maintainers of pure Christianity" (LaFarge 1947: 81).

Farriss agrees: "Whether the Indians 'really' became Christians is one of the more intriguing questions in Latin American history, . . . it is a perplexing one starting with the distinct lack of agreement among Christian theologians over the exact definition of 'Christian.' When asked, I take it to mean whether the Indians genuinely came to believe in 'One God, Father Almighty, Maker of Heaven and earth . . .' and so on down the articles of faith in the Nicene Creed. . . . Judging from the words and actions of the colonial Maya . . . the missionaries do not seem to have succeeded in converting more than a handful of their catechumens" (Farriss 1984: 301).[1]

The results of evangelization from the viewpoints of the Maya and the Spaniards is an example of what Lockhart has called "double mistaken identity": "Each side of the cultural exchange presumes that a given form or concept is functioning in the way familiar within its own tradition and is unaware of or unimpressed by the other side's interpretation" (Lockhart 1992: 445; 1999: 99). Because the Maya submitted to baptism, attended mass and doctrina sessions, and performed devotions to the saints, many of the Spanish friars thought the Maya had been converted. Within Spanish culture, these actions may have been indicators of orthodoxy. The friars were locked into this interpretation by the ethnocentrism of their worldview.[2]

The Exceptions

A few Maya were converted, specifically those who became partly Hispanicized and as part of the process, learned and assented to the Christianity taught by the friars. Some fiscales and the schoolteachers probably became converts. Their close association with the priest and the time spent with him permitted some of them to absorb what he was attempting to communicate. This is especially true of the youths trained in the monastery schools(Farriss 1984: 97). But for some of these students, their position as members of the Mayan elite probably brought family pressure not to forsake the traditional religion. Some real conversions probably also resulted from prolonged association with Spaniards among Maya who lived in the vicinity of the capitals of Santiago de Guatemala (Lutz 1994: 21), Mérida, and San Cristóbal and other important towns. These

Maya worked for years as servants and artisans in Spanish houses and work-shops, and some became Hispanicized (Ximénez 1965: 713).

Additional conversions probably took place in some towns where priests had been in residence for a number of years and began to have significant in-fluence. Evidence of this is found in a number of indigenous wills. The making of testaments was introduced by the friars as part of the evangelization effort (Cline 1998: 14). A section stipulated that masses be said for the departed soul. As part of his *Confesario*, which was as influential as his *Doctrina*, Molina drew up a model will with instructions for the town notary who was to interview the testator and transcribe the person's wishes. The first part of Molina's model contains the religious formulas that became boilerplates repeated in modified form in many indigenous wills.

> First, I commend and place my soul in the hands of our lord God, who made it, and I ask him for mercy. I beg him to keep my soul, and I desire that he pardon all my sins, and I wish that he carry me to his home in heaven, after my soul has left my body. And my said body, I leave and commend to the earth, from which it came, because it is earth and mud. . . . And this is my will, for the aid of my soul, in order that it not stay much time in Purgatory, a vigil and mass are to said for me when my body is entombed. (Cline 1998: 28)

Restall (1995) has collected sixty-eight testaments covering a twenty-seven-month period in 1765–68 from the town of Ixil in Yucatán. Sixty-three of these wills stipulate that a stipend be paid for a mass for the testator's soul. The formula used in these wills, or one similar to it, reads, "I supplicate our blessed lord the Padre Guardian that he say one mass for my soul and that he send up for me a prayer in the mass to provide protection of our lord in God through the suffering in Purgatory, and not to be burdened before our lord in God. Likewise the fee will be given, as we are believing Christians: six tomins and two tomins for Jerusalem" (Restall 1995: 72, 187–88). At times the formula is shortened and the part about Purgatory merely implied. Although constructed from boilerplate formulas, these wills indicate conversion. The mention of the priest implies that he was resident in Ixil, "in many ways a typical postconquest Maya community: it was close enough to Mérida—some thirty miles north-east of the colonial and present-day state capital—not to feel the pull of the independent Maya to the south and east of the colony, but not so close as to be pulled into the acculturative vortex that Mérida became in the late colonial decades. At the same time, Ixil was modest in size, large enough to have its own cabildo but not so large as to have attracted Spanish settlers. In the 1760s its population was probably a little over one and a half thousand; by 1794 it was well over two thousand" (Restall 1995: 15).

But these and similar cases represent a small minority in comparison to the many more typical Mayan corn farmers who clung to the Mayan covenant. Looking at the broad picture, evangelization was a failure. It is highly improbable that the friars communicated orthodox Catholic Christianity to the Mayan masses. A historical picture drawn from the centers of residencia or often-frequented visitas cannot be projected over the whole Mayan area. The historical materials are mostly silent about the majority of the Maya living in or surrounding the less-frequented towns of visita because there was no one present to write about them.

Further Research

As stated in the preface, the problem this book has attempted to analyze requires looking back over many centuries and covering many topics, each of which is a specialty in itself. As a result, much of this material has been treated in a very general manner, which in turn may help focus some questions for future research. Topics this writer considers especially important for further investigation follow.

The saints were swept up into the Mayan oral tradition. A sizable amount of this oral tradition is now available in the works of Shaw (1971), Laughlin (1976, 1977, 1979), D. Tedlock (1997), Sexton and Bizarro (1992, 1999), Gossen (2002), and others. This material needs analysis with regard to many topics, including how the saints, the mass, and the Catholic priests are treated in Mayan stories. Archival research is needed to examine the extent and influence of the monastery schools in the colonial period. Ethnographic research is needed about the Mayan usage of shamanic logics. This research has traced the common trends found in Guatemala, Chiapas, and Yucatán. But there are variations in the specifics of these trends that need investigation. Village-level variations within these regions, for example, need to be researched if we are to understand in greater depth how the Maya applied their cultural logics.

Conversion to Christianity or retention of the traditional Mayan religion are only the two endpoints of possible reactions to the stimulus of evangelization. Over the four-hundred-year period, the Maya experienced a continuum of reactions. Working with the richer Nahua materials from an area of greater friar penetration, León-Portilla (1974) and Klor de Alva (1982) have discussed a variety of responses to evangelization. Probably, the Maya experienced a number of the same reactions, given that their underlying cultural logics were similar to those of the Nahua. Klor de Alva (1982: 351–52) has compiled a list of fifteen possible ideal type responses grouped into three general categories—accommodation, conflict, or apostasy—which, for the purpose of this book, have been edited and regrouped in a slightly different way:

A. Christianity believed and understood: conversion
 1. With acculturation to creole customs
 2. With retention of those Mayan cultural patterns not excluded by Christianity or considered offensive by the clergy
B. Christianity misunderstood
 1. Christian elements accepted on the premises of the native religion
  a. With active participation only in apparent Christian rites
  b. With active participation in both rites
 2. Belief in both Christianity and the native religion, with active participation in both rites (By Christian orthodoxy, this position is a logical contradiction that would constitute a misunderstanding.)
 3. Christianity neither assimilated nor understood and the native religion lost or disfigured; participation in either or both rites often characterized by anomie and confusion (In social science language, this is the marginal man; see Stonequist 1961.)
C. Resistance to Christianity
 1. Passive
  a. Indifference to both Christian and native religious beliefs
  b. Belief in native religion and active participation in indigenous rites, perhaps with forced or casual participation in Christian rites
 2. Active belief in the native religion and active participation in indigenous rites
D. Apostasy: Following conversion, rejection of Christianity and adoption of one of the preceding positions

These and many of the other topics discussed in this book need clarification. Much research remains to be done.

Conclusion

This study has surveyed the protracted encounter between Mayan and Western cultures, the latter of the Spanish and later Latin American varieties. It has shown the importance of worldviews and cultural logics for understanding their interactions and the problems encountered. The quick journey through the four and a half centuries of history may help religious systems and their worldviews reflect on the historical evolutions that all of them undergo as they incarnate themselves in changing historical circumstances. The Mayan metaphysics of the cyclical nature of all of reality speaks to all ages.

Appendix

Evangelization as a Case of Applied Anthropology

Chapters 8 to 11 described the attempt to convert the Maya to Catholic Christianity. This was probably one of the largest programs of attempted religious change about which social scientists have information.

Applied Anthropology

The loosely defined field of applied anthropology uses anthropological knowledge to help a cultural group (the change agent) construct and implement programs of social change in an area with a different culture (target population). The colonial empire of Great Britain in the nineteenth and twentieth centuries stimulated development of the field. The decade of the 1960s, with its efforts at economic development of the third- and fourth-world countries gave it added impetus. Government and economic bureaucracies are only two examples of groups involved in such programs. Educational, medical, religious, and other bureaucracies also undertake many such efforts.

Intercultural contact is always problematic. The principal problem for the change agent is ethnocentrism; that is, considering the goals and methods of one's own culture to be the only correct or the best way to structure social action. For many people, ethnocentrism operates on a subconscious level, as one takes for granted without reflection the customary ways of one's own culture. Ethnocentrism in a cross-cultural situation leads to the use of inappropriate models because the requisite assumptions of the introduced model do not exist in the target culture. Every person is ethnocentric to some extent. Change agents need to realize their ethnocentrism and take it into account in structuring a change program. Doing so requires a reflective knowledge of both their own culture and the target culture. This task is not easy because ethnocentrism blinds change agents to the difficulty of attaining a deep understanding of both cultures. In addition, there is the ethical question of whether the proposed change should even be attempted.

The problem for the target culture is the acceptance of social change and the price to be paid for this acceptance. Change is threatening when it involves redefining one's traditional worldviews and social roles with the psychological security they provide. Frequently, the traditional ways of a culture are seen as moral imperatives, and any change in them is considered immoral.

The Strategy of Evangelization as a Case of Applied Anthropology

The evangelization effort was an attempted program of culture change without the aid of cultural knowledge. The change agent was the Catholic Church as a ministry within the royal bureaucracy. Its fieldworkers were the friars. The target population were the Maya in Guatemala, Yucatán, and Chiapas. A brief review of this case provides some classical examples of the problems of intercultural contact.

The friars manifested ethnocentrism in almost every aspect of their program. They knew nothing about the Mayan culture and the majority saw no purpose in learning about it. They made no attempt to prove the truth of the Spanish worldview and the Maya never asked for reasons (Borges 1960: 308, 313). The friars preached the doctrina, presenting orthodox Christian theological constructs, and assumed it would be accepted by all people of goodwill. The only problems they saw were literal translation of the catechetical materials and suppression of idolatry. For the moment, the reader is asked to hypothetically grant the validity of the friars' goals in order to assess the appropriateness of the strategy they used to implement these goals. Any hope of conversion in the already well-established Mayan culture required the friars to become members of Mayan communities and spend considerable time conversing with community members. This was the original model of Christianity demonstrated by Saint Paul and the early Christian communities.

In contrast, the friars had a subculture of a semimonastic order that militated against both their becoming members of Mayan communities and their spending the time required to accomplish their task. Their withdrawal into monasteries isolated them from the Mayan community and prevented them from becoming part of it. The strategy of establishing towns of residencia and visita was based on the requirement of monasticism. In addition, friars were periodically transferred from one doctrina to another precisely to prevent their becoming attached to any particular community.

When the friars did leave the monasteries, they spent most of their time celebrating mass and preaching, or more often having the fiscal do the actual instruction. In this they were following the model they had developed in Europe for their activities outside the monastery. There they specialized in a single function, preaching, that supplemented the wider range of ministerial activities performed by the resident parish priest for a congregation with a similar cultural background. But in the Mayan doctrinas there were no parish priests and the congregation came from a completely different cultural background. The friars were encased in a structural model that was inappropriate to accomplish the task they had set for themselves.

In addition, most of the friars did not appreciate the problem of attempting to translate between two languages based on very different worldviews. They assumed that literal translation would be sufficient to transmit the concepts of Christianity. But literal translation is impossible between two languages with so many conceptual differences.

These are easy criticisms to make in the twenty-first century about a sixteenth-century project; yet, even at the time Marroquín and Molina recognized most of them. In that historical period of small kingdoms and tribal groups, little was understood about the structure of cultures within a global context. The ethnocentrism of the Europeans of that period was similar to that of the Chinese in their first contacts with the West.

Evangelization and Worldviews

The appropriateness of inducing change in worldviews introduces questions of individual and group values, their expression through religion, and their philosophical-theological foundations. Analysis at this level becomes more problematic because of a lack of consensus about such matters. As often happens in cases of applied anthropology, a discussion of the appropriateness of the model to the situation requires specialized knowledge of disciplines that are far beyond the scope of anthropology. From the writer's perspective and without an attempt to give any answers, here are some contemporary philosophical-theological questions suggested by the study of the evangelization effort among the Maya.

Within Catholicism, the Model of Hellenized Christianity

Hellenized Christianity was based on a fundamentalist reading of the Bible rationalized by the application of categories drawn from Greek philosophy. This model still pervades much of Catholic thinking. The question is, Is this one of many possible models of the God-human relationship, or is the use of the word *model* to describe what is considered the absolute and only truth a blasphemy? Catholicism is currently wrestling with this question. It raises the question of the evolution of dogma (or the evolution of religious expression to use the semantic this writer prefers). In the encounter with Mayan religion, was the "all or nothing" stance necessary? If Catholicism is to function in an intercultural world, can only one theological model be the basis of orthodoxy? Does conceding that theological systems are models imply complete relativity of theological expression and morals?

Within Christianity, the Question of Unity

Can Christianity recover its original unity broken apart by theological models closely tied to political struggles? In many instances particular forms of Christianity became tribal religions. In Christian ecumenism the problems are much the same as those within Catholicism, only on a broader scale.

Within Christianity, Recognition of Native American Spirituality

Within the Mayan worldview, spirituality is based on a pantheistic theology characteristic of many Native American religions. Orthodox Christianity needs to examine the pantheistic foundation of these religions and find points of congruence. This writer would suggest that the mystical traditions within Christianity as well as the works of Christian Platonists can be of great value in such an effort.

Within Mayan Religion, the Question of Reform

The Spaniards encountered a Mayan religious system in as much need of reform as their own. Archaeological and historical research has revealed a unity between kingdoms and religion much like the Spanish unity. The Mayan system was a tribal religion that had become a religion of war leading to frequent combat between the numerous Mayan groups. In some cases the wars were stimulated by the need to take prisoners to fulfill the perceived requirement of the Mayan covenant for human sacrifice. In the context of the contemporary world, there is a need to develop a group of professional Mayan theologians to examine contemporary Mayan religion, to understand it at a philosophical level, and to develop commentaries to help the Mayan people better understand their own traditions.

Within the World Community, the Encounter of the World Religions and the Necessity of Religion

The sixteenth-century encounter between Catholicism and the Mayan religion raises a question presently confronted by all religions in their global encounters with one another and with secular humanism that substitutes for religion in many people's lives. Religious ethnocentrism and tribalism can only crumble in the long run in a world made smaller by the revolutions in transportation and communication. Studies such as this raise the following question: Are the often antagonistic relations between religions, sometimes leading to the complete rejection of all religions, based on the tribal characteristics of their models, on the rigidity of their formulations presented as all-encompassing truth? Are theological models ends in themselves or means to living a moral life, however such may be defined? Is there only one model that can properly accomplish this?

Somehow, somewhere, humankind must find meaning in order to survive; without it, there is only psychological if not physical suicide. This writer sees religion as an integral part of this search, but at the same time, all religions are in constant need of reform. The Mayan cycle of birth, death, and rebirth continues, or as the same cycle is described in biblical terms of election, sin, and redemption. Part of the rebirth is accepting the theological tenet that God is ultimately a mystery. Partial insight into the mystery comes from the manifestations, or emanations, of this mystery in our world. These partial insights are codified in various theological models and myths that attempt to throw some light on the God-human relationship. Their symbolic structures are to be taken seriously but not literally. A thin line separates theism from agnosticism because of the mystery of God. Perhaps the description in the previous chapters of four hundred years of cultural encounter between Maya and Spaniards along with their national descendants may assist in the study of questions about religion and culture raised in this appendix.

Notes

Chapter 2. The Saints, Their Homes, and Their Servants

1. For discussions of the forms of organizations that provide for the community cult, see Cancian 1967; Farriss 1984: 265–67, 329–30; Chance and Taylor 1985: 1–26.

2. For more detailed descriptions of this structure, refer to Cancian (1965) or Vogt (1969).

Chapter 3. Mayan Festivals for the Saints

1. Because Mayan invocations and prayers have frequent repetition of phrases and an optional order, this version has been edited for purposes of clarity and conciseness from that given in Early 1965: 225. If a particular text is used again in other segments of the rituals, this will be noted but the text not repeated.

Part 3. Cultural Logics

1. The search for cultural logics embedded in worldviews is similar to the approach Colby and Colby (1981: 248–66) used in their study of a Mayan diviner and Fischer (2001: 15–22) used in his study of Mayan identity.

Chapter 5. Traditional Mayan Worldview

1. Some of the ethnographic materials are based on the writings or testimonies of Mayan people about their traditional practices. Jacinto Arias is frequently quoted. He is from a family well versed in the traditions of San Pedro Chenalhó, Chiapas. Arias has moved through many worlds since his childhood, a story that should be a book at some future date. But after his experiences in these worlds, he returned to his roots in San Pedro and served as one of its traditional civil-religious officials. The work quoted and cited here was one of the first by a Mayan anthropologist to explain Mayan practices. It was originally his master's thesis from the Anthropology Department of the Catholic University of America.

Ethnographic data have also been drawn from Santiago Atitlán in Guatemala. This town has long been known for its preservation of traditional Mayan culture. This was confirmed during my residence there. It has been the site of some excellent ethnographic work, yielding considerable knowledge about Mayan traditions. The work of Allen Christenson about the altarpiece of the church is particularly valuable for our purposes. Methodologically, his work is similar to a theological TAT card (Thematic Apperception Test) as he interviewed the two woodcarvers who were restoring this visual book of Mayan theology. He states, "The altarpiece represents an attempt on the part of the Chávez brothers to assert the legitimacy of traditional Atiteco Maya faith as an independent complement to Roman Catholicism. As such it presents an invaluable visible display of important Tz'utujil rituals and beliefs that are otherwise poorly accessible to Western researchers" (Christenson 2001: 11). Author Early knew the father of the Chávez brothers and their talented older brother, Miguel. In the 1960s as part of the Micatokla project (Early 1973), Tom Stafford (Padre Tomás) spotted Miguel's artistic talent. Tom had initiated credit, weaving, and agricultural cooperatives and wished to add one for woodcarving. He arranged for Miguel to learn woodcarving in Huehuetenango. Miguel returned, but his genius as a painter was more intense than his interest in woodcarving. He worked for the famous Atiteco artist Juan Sisay, married Sisay's daughter, and left his woodcarving tools with his father, who became a master carver. The father encouraged the talent of his two younger sons, Diego and Nicolás. The restoration of the altarpiece was the result, and the rest of the story is told by Christenson (2001).

Another important source of traditional practices from Santiago Atitlán is the work of Martín Prechtel. Prechtel was raised on an Indian reservation in the southwestern United States. He wandered into Santiago while on a trip "to find himself." He settled in, immersed himself in Atiteco culture, and because of his talents, became one of the most important officials in the Atiteco ritual system. His work has been somewhat ignored because he is not an anthropologist, at times critical of anthropologists, and because of his later embodiment as a New Age guru. This writer believes Prechtel's books have some valuable ethnographic material.

The work of Robert Carmack in Momostenango is another important in-depth ethnography. For the purposes here, the ethnography of Momostenango religion by Garrett Cook (2000) has been most helpful, and many of its findings reinforce the presentation in this and other chapters.

For Yucatán, Bishop Landa compiled an account of traditional Maya culture in the sixteenth century. Nancy Farriss' award-winning work focuses on the colonial period, but as background, synthesizes the literature about important aspects of the pre-Columbian period.

2. The information that Kaqchikel shamans gave to Edward Fischer is explicit about the metaphysical unity in Mayan thought:

> traditionalist day-keepers appear to use the term *ahua* ("lord" or "god"), *ruk'u'x ulew*, *ruk'u'x kaj* (the *k'u'x* [heart/soul/essence] of earth, the *k'u'x* of sky," and the Spanish *dios* ("god") interchangeably in their prayers and ceremonies. . . . The monotheistic-polytheistic distinction breaks down in its application to traditional Maya beliefs. As day-keepers repeatedly informed me, there is but one "god" in Maya religion, best conceived of as a cosmic vitalistic force rather than the corporeal entity "god" denotes in Western tradition. This force has various aspects and is manifest in various manners that may appear as distinct "gods". . . . Despite having different names, different symbolic associations, and different contexts of activity, these gods are described by most *aj q'ijab'* as aspects of a single unified force that animates the cosmos. Viewing unity in diversity is characteristic of Maya cultural logics in a number of domains, and such unity is conceptually associated with balance and harmony within and between both the physical and metaphysical worlds. (Fischer 2001: 180)

Earlier Fischer had noted, "The *k'u'x* of the sky and earth is the essence of the cosmic force that animates nature" (154). He places it at the heart of Mayan identity, "the concept of *k'u'x* provides a stable cultural logic with a transcendental point of reference, realized through practical activity, that centers identity" (165).

Allen Christenson's conclusions about the use of *k'u'x* in Santiago Atitlán, although not explicitly addressing the monotheism-polytheism question, are much the same as Fischer's. He usually glosses *k'u'x* as "heart," and describes it as "spirit essence," "life-sustaining presence," and "some aspect of divine nature essential to existence." He describes the beings it animates as "receptacles for divine power" (Christenson 2001: 4, 12, 101, 143–44).

David Freidel with a more archaeological than ethnographic emphasis, has expressed much the same thing. He takes shamanism as his point of departure and notes that "the most important premise [of shamanism] is that the spiritual force that every human being has personally experienced is ambient, of the world, of the cosmos and everything in it" (Freidel, Schele, and Parker 1993: 12). For them the Yukatek word *itz*—which they gloss as "the cosmic sap"—expresses this idea (210). Further, "*Itz* and *ch'ul* are fundamentally related substances—magical and holy stuff" (211). Literally, *itz* refers to excretions of humans or plants, and to dripping wax from burning candles. Possibly *itz* is a visual metaphor for emanation. Just as objects visually expand by outward excretions (emanations) that remain relatively small compared with the excreting object, the cosmic force emanates out as the animating force of other beings. Consequently, these other beings can be viewed as both the same as and different from the cosmic force itself. Freidel expresses the same idea when he glosses *ch'ulel* as the "soul stuff of the universe" (217) and later refers to "Ch'u and ch'ulel, Maya words for 'god,' 'divinity' and 'inner soul'" (436).

In a study of the Lacandon worldview, Bruce identifies a single god, K'akoch, as the source of all the other gods. In spite of this, K'akoch is not the most important god of the Lacandon pantheon (Bruce, Robles, and Ramos 1971: 11, 74).

Regarding the importance of the cyclical nature of the cosmic force, León-Portilla's work is the classic. He takes *kinh* (*kin* in Yukatek, *kih* in K'iche') as the key Mayan word for expressing this cycle. "*Kinh*, sun-day-time, was not an abstract entity but a reality enmeshed in the world of myths, a divine being, origin of the cycles which govern all existing things. Many are the faces of *kinh*, but its essence is always divine. . . . *Kinh* appears, as the heart of all change, filled with lucky and unlucky destinies within the cyclic reality of the universe and most probably inherent to the essence of divinity itself" (León-Portilla 1973: 33). "*Kinh* is a cosmic atmosphere with visages of gods who become manifest cycle after cycle. . . . Since the cycles were gods, knowledge of time was the root of theological thought" (110).

3. Arias (1991: 25) emphasizes plant life.

4. This is well described in Carlsen and Prechtel (1991: 28).

5. There has been some discussion about whether the origin myth of the Popol Vuh was influenced by the biblical Genesis narrative. Carmack (1981: 318–19) cites a number of points where he sees adaptation, but he qualifies his views with "appears to be," "seems," and similar phrases. None of the similarities Carmack cites contradict the pre-

Columbian nature of the cultural logics cited in this chapter. D. Tedlock (1986: 81) and Christenson (2003a: 35) discuss the issue and find little or no influence from the biblical account.

6. In terms of physical pattern, the Mayan custom is to build their houses and lay out their cornfields in imitation of the quincuncial model of surface sky-earth (Vogt 1976: 58). The cultural patterns are those required for a harmonious community, in which everyone respects one another and contributes to community service. Both of these require the help and protection of the gods, who are sought through ritual activity.

7. For the various agents of punishment, consult Arias 1991: 42; Laughlin 1977: 2; and Blaffer 1972: 139–42.

8. Jane Collier (1973) reported that the principal areas of interpersonal disputes were witchcraft accusations; fighting; marital disputes; courtship disputes, especially when the termination of an engagement raised problems of returning gifts; inheritance disputes, especially about land; and disputes with neighbors about payment of debts.

9. The Popol Vuh origin account, taken literally, implies that the inability to perform ritual was the reason for terminating the three previous epochs. Consequently, the covenant duty of the Maya is to perform rituals following the templates of actions and words. Other sources indicate that more than mechanical performance of ritual is involved. Although some origin accounts fail to give a reason for the destruction of an epoch, others indicate the kinds of moral failures that bring the epoch-ending floods: because "the people became wicked," in an account from Yucatán (Thompson 1970: 340); because "they were taught to sin," in an account from San Pedro Chenalhó (Thompson 1970: 347); because the people ate their own children, in stories from Zinacantán (Laughlin 1977: 330) and Chamula (Gossen 2002: 235); and because of the rudeness of the people and their verbal disrespect for the gods, in another story from Zinacantán (Laughlin 1977: 258).

Another indication of the need for more than mechanical ritual performance is the oft-repeated phrase in Mayan communities: "ritual should be a showing of one's heart." The metaphor of the heart has an important role in Mayan speech. A Spanish friar at the end of the sixteenth century compiled a Tzotzil dictionary of more than ten thousand words. Among them were eighty heart metaphors. "He found in Tzotzil 'infinite expressions derived from this word, heart.' He learned that the heart was the seat not only of the soul and of emotion, but also of thought, of judgment. Everything we call 'human' was there in the heart" (Laughlin 2002). In Zinacantán it is dangerous to perform ritual with a bad heart.

Jane Collier (1973: 92) has described the Zinacanteco sense of committing a wrong that goes beyond ritual performance. "Zinacantecos use the single word *mulil* . . . to cover the concepts expressed in the English words 'guilt,' 'crime,' 'sin,' and 'blame' . . . , but a mulil is best understood as any act that displeases the gods and can provoke supernatural retaliation. The act may be as minor as an angry word spoken to a kinsman or as serious as murder."

10. See Polanyi 1977; and Foster 1988: 212–46.

11. Landa (1941: 131) also says the Maya believed in an afterlife of heaven or hell.

Tozzer (1941, n. 615) thinks this statement is probably a projection from Christian teaching on Landa's part. He quotes Redfield and Villa (1962) as confirming his position.

12. There is a theological position that sees the external versus internal god distinction as a false dichotomy. *Encyclopaedia Britannica* labels this view *panentheism*. A number of religious systems, including Christianity, see divinity as both transcendent and immanent. In Christianity the indwelling of the Holy Spirit is a long-accepted doctrine that recently has been emphasized by Pentecostal groups. The external-immanent distinction for these systems is a matter of emphasis rather than a metaphysical dichotomy. The mystical traditions within many religious systems focus on the immanent aspect of the god-human relationship. For example, consider this meditation for obtaining love written by the Spanish Catholic mystic St. Ignatius Loyola (1943: 75–76): "consider how God dwells in creatures, in the elements giving them being, in the plants giving them growth, in animals giving them feeling, and causing me to understand; making likewise of me a temple, since I am created to the likeness and image of His Divine Majesty; . . . consider how God works and labours for me in all created things on the face of the earth, as in the heavens, elements, plants, fruit, cattle, etc., giving them being, preserving them, giving them growth and feeling, etc." Similar passages can be found in the mystical literature of many religious systems. Many Mayan shamans would immediately understand it.

Because mysticism is not frequently emphasized in institutional religions, many of their adherents are not aware of it. Such emphasis has and could give rise to challenges to institutional authorities because it lessens the importance of their role as mediators. Given the basic theological tenet that God is ultimately a mystery, the transcendent-immanent distinction represents two different theological models showing aspects of infinite being that no model can fully comprehend. These considerations may be helpful in thinking about the Mayan worldview and putting it into some kind of philosophical-theological context.

Chapter 6. The Worldview of the Spanish Crown at the Beginning of the Sixteenth Century

1. All translations of the *Requerimiento* into English are mine from the original Spanish text in Las Casas 1986 (lib. 3, cap. 57, 210–12). Phrases were borrowed from the translations of Hanke (1973: I, 94) and Seed (1995: 69).

2. The early sixteenth century, called the Age of Discovery, was a time when the European world began its oceanic exploration of the globe and conquest of the newly discovered lands. Columbus found the Americas in 1492 and the Portuguese were continuing their explorations of the west and east African coasts, which eventually enabled Vasco da Gama to reach India, the gateway to the Asiatic world. Spain and Portugal were in competition to explore and exploit territories new to Europeans. To prevent disputes arising from the rivalry, in 1493 both countries agreed on a pact drawn up by the pope in exercise of his jurisdiction over the medieval European world. It was agreed that a line drawn pole to pole and passing 100 leagues west of the Cape Verde Islands should be a boundary. All the lands found west of it would belong to Spain and all to the east to Portugal, provided these lands did not already belong to other Christian countries. This

demarcation interfered with Portugal's exploration of the west African coast, and in 1494 the pope moved the line to 370 degrees west of the Cape Verde Islands (between 48 and 49 degrees west of Greenwich). Both countries accepted this demarcation by the Treaty of Tordesillas.

While conquering these lands, the monarchs also strengthened their control over the Catholic Church. "The most striking feature of the Roman Catholic Church in the New World was its *de jure* relationship to the Crown. This relationship, known as the *Real Patronato*, produced an overlap between the action of the king and the work of the Church in America, but since the work of the king was broader in its social implications, then the relationship of the Church to the king is viewed as one of subordination" (O'Flaherty 1979: 105). Pope Alexander VI, by a papal bull in 1493, assigned to the Catholic kings the exclusive right and responsibility for evangelization of the indigenous populations. In 1501 the tithes to be collected for the church were made the king's responsibility. In 1508 Pope Julius II granted the king universal patronage, the right to appoint all bishops.

By these papal concessions, the church and its personnel became another ministry within the royal bureaucracy. During the colonial period bishops and priests in their reports and written requests to the king made frequent use of the phrase "descargar la real conciencia" (fulfill the duties of the royal conscience) to remind the king of his responsibilities with regard to evangelization. Priests and royal officials also made frequent use of the phrase "en servicio de Dios y de Vuestra Majestad" (in service of God and Your Majesty), an acknowledgment of the divine right of kingship. "Religious and clerics assumed . . . obligations not only in the name of their calling but also as subjects of the king" and the "further obligation . . . to the king as beneficiaries of his largess was a right and duty at the same time" (O'Flaherty 1979: 111).

Chapter 7. Spanish Victories and Their Impact on the Mayan Worldview

1. Díaz's account is a combination of chronicle, memoir, and a *probanza de merito,* or report to the king by a conquistador describing the lands he has conquered in the name of the king and consequently seeking his reward (Restall 2003: 13). Díaz had been disappointed by his lack of recognition in both Mexico and Guatemala, so in his later years he wrote the memoir, which probably exaggerates his role as conquistador. The accounts referenced are not concerned with his role.

2. The first of these appearances is said to have taken place at the battle of Cintla in Tabasco. The account is contained in a book about the life of Cortés by his personal chaplain and biographer, Francisco López de Gomara (1964: 45–47). Díaz, however, rejected López de Gomara's claim on the basis of what he saw at the battle and the fact that López de Gomara was never in the New World. Valle (1946: 20–22) reprints the pertinent documents. For the background of the dispute, see Simpson (1964: xv–xxvi).

Chapter 8. The Goals of Evangelization

1. Not of concern here, but in the next stage of evolution, the Jesuits did away with the monastic routine completely so that they could devote themselves fully to ministry. And in a further evolutionary step, some contemporary congregations (the newer groups are not called orders) still take vows and live communally, but during the day they are

employed in secular occupations and wear no distinctive clothing. Time is allotted for spiritual exercises before leaving for work and after returning to the communal house in the evening.

2. Kung 2001 is a shortened version of the 936-page 1999 work. The shorter version will also be quoted because the writing is more concise.

3. Some notes about terminology: As used in this book, the term *doctrina* usually means some or all of the content of these manuals to distinguish it from the broader content of Catholic theology and popular devotions. In English the manuals are called *catechisms of Catholic doctrine* or simply *catechisms*, a term derived from the instructions given to catechumens before baptism in early Christianity. Another meaning of *doctrina* is a defined area (town of *residencia* with its *visitas*) served by a group of friars where they taught the *doctrina* in the first sense. The friar who taught was a *doctrinero*. Because the friars defined themselves as mobile preachers and teachers but did not live in many of the areas where they went for their ministry, they were not labeled pastors or curates living and working in parishes. These latter terms describe the ministry of secular (sometimes called diocesan) priests. Because the friars followed a structured, semimonastic lifestyle, they are also referred to as *regulars*.

Chapter 10. Problems Facing the Friars

1. These are a set of unpublished notes titled "Carpetas de Parish Geography." They were intended for the continuing research of Adrian van Oss, which was cut short by his untimely death. Each carpeta is a colonial district, and within each is a listing of all the colonial towns with their location coordinates and a series of historical notes and citations culled from various published and archival sources. The one carpeta that has been published, "Suchtepéquez," is typical of the whole collection (Oss 1984). The individual carpetas are Suchtepéquez, Escuintla, Sacatepéquez, Verapaz, Chiquimula, Totonicapán, Quetzaltenango, Sololá, and a single carpeta that includes Sonsonate, Santa Ana, San Salvador, San Vicente, and San Miguel. Oss' widow has a complete set. An incomplete set is available at the Archivo Histórico de CIRMA, in Antigua, Guatemala, and at Plumsock Mesoamerican Studies in South Woodstock, Vermont. The missing carpetas are: Sacatepéquez, Chiquimula, Quetzaltenango, and the sections on San Salvador and San Miguel.

Chapter 11. The Secular Clergy

1. The decrees of the Council of Trent were formulated in the context of the theological disputes at the time of the Protestant Reformation. It took place at the same time as the first evangelization efforts among the Maya.

2. Where this writer has inserted "the fiscales," Rus' text has "devout members of Catholic Action." But Catholic Action did not exist in Zinacantán at that time. It was the fiscales with whom this priest had dealt for many years.

Chapter 12. The Necessity of the Saints in the Mayan Worldview

1. The difficulty is that the K'iche' word translated as *niña* is not known. Many older K'iche' documents were written in archaic K'iche'. As Chonay (1953: 166) pointed out

in 1834 and as is even more true for later translations, it is sometimes impossible for even contemporary K'iche' speakers to understand sections of these documents (James Mondloch, personal communication).

2. Bricker (1981: 40–41) identifies the dove as the dove of peace and the footless birds as the Holy Spirit. It is doubtful that any conquistador group would carry a peace symbol. The Holy Spirit in Christian iconography is symbolized by a single dove, not a flock of them.

3. These paintings can be viewed on the web at <www.abcgallery.com>.

Chapter 13. The Necessity of the Mass, Baptism, and the Catholic Priest in the Mayan Worldview

1. The titles of the various texts in the Chilam Balam of Kaua were added by the translators. In this writer's opinion, some of them are not apt. The translators title this prayer "A Breviary Anthem." It is used frequently in the priests' breviary, but a more likely source is the doctrina teaching, where it was included as one of the necessary Christian prayers.

2. The section titled "Communion Prayer" on page 210 contains a short prayer sometimes used when making the sign of the cross. It has no necessary connection with Communion.

3. These texts were probably translated into Yukatek from instructions about the use of a Marian medal or a scapular. Instead of the literal translation "whoever brings this medal," a more apt and free translation would be "whoever wears this medal." Wearing such medals was a commonplace Catholic devotional practice. Marroquín distributed medals during his visitation of Soloma in 1557 (Ruz et al. 2002 I: 155). The medals frequently come with a small leaflet attached or a small picture of Mary with an explanation on the back about the prayers to be recited and the indulgence to be gained.

4. The text appears to have been influenced by the popular devotion movement exemplified in the faith of many conquistadors.

Chapter 15. The Mass of the Talking Saints

1. All the photographs in this chapter, except figure 15.3, depict the ritual items of a former shaman from the K'iche' town of Nahualá in the Department of Sololá. The shaman renounced his practice of shamanism and gave the articles to the town priest as a sign of his renunciation. The priest in turn gave them to the writer around 1966. The figure 15.3 photograph was taken in Colotenango, a Mam speaking community not far from San Juan Ostuncalco in the early 1960s.

2. All the information about the talking saints in San Juan Ostuncalco comes from a doctoral dissertation in religion by Horace Dudley Peck. He was a Presbyterian missionary in San Juan for about forty years, from the early 1920s until his retirement in 1963. He spoke Mam and published a Mam hymnal and a translation of the New Testament. He was involved in community activities, founding a medical clinic, an agricultural program, and a rural school. In the later years of his retirement, he attended the Hartford Seminary Foundation to obtain the doctorate and in 1970 at the age of 77 completed his dissertation, *Practices and Training of Guatemalan Mam Shamans*.

While Peck attended some shamanic ceremonies, the dissertation primarily draws on recorded interviews in Mam with ten shamans. The second volume of the dissertation, Appendix C, prints these interviews with interlinear English translations. This was done by computer at the University of Chicago by A. James Trabulse and Norman A. McQuown using *Un Sistema Modular de Programas Para El Procesamiento y La Recuperación de Información Lingüística.* Throughout the body of the dissertation, Peck provides references to these interviews. The complete dissertation can be obtained from University Microfilms 71–11,449.

3. For a more detailed account of the divination procedure, see B. Tedlock 1982: 153–71. Her materials are from Momostenango, a K'iche' town not far from San Juan Ostuncalco.

4. As the writer can testify from his own experience in Zinacantán (Early 1965), describing rituals that are very similar can become especially tedious in print. Peck had this difficulty in writing his dissertation where the descriptions are highly repetitious. This writer summarized his Zinacanteco data by constructing Weberian ideal types of the main ritual patterns. A list of the various rituals was compiled and, as observed in chapters 2 and 3, a simple code was used to designate what ritual patterns were enacted during the festivals. The writer has done the same with Peck's dissertation. Table 15.1 lists the time, place, and shamanic patterns of the various rituals. The patterns themselves are described in this chapter.

5. In an effort to avoid the excessive repetition often involved in describing ritual patterns, some of Peck's descriptions are very brief. This may indicate that some of the more extended patterns, such as 2 and 3, were actually used in more rituals than he indicates but were omitted because he thought it unnecessary to duplicate their description. Given the overall pattern of rituals that take place several times a year, this writer suspects there was some such omission.

Chapter 16. Questions Raised by the Research

1. The conclusion that the Maya were not converted to orthodox Christianity, Catholic or otherwise, may be upsetting to some readers who are fundamentalist Christians. They, like the friars, may see the eternal damnation of the non-Christian Maya as the consequence. This writer would suggest however that the various forms of Christianity should be considered primarily as the way in which individuals and their communities conduct their lives and that the purpose of theological models is to help them in doing this.

The Christ figure presents many faces. If the meek, kind, and gentle Jesus is emphasized—the Jesus of the Sermon on the Mount, the Jesus enjoying little children, and the Jesus forgiving sinners and bringing them redemption—then a number of Maya exhibit these qualities in their daily lives as any Mayan anthropologist can testify. If the prophetic Jesus is emphasized—the Jesus who denounced the degenerate priesthood exemplified by the hypocrisy and narrow-mindedness of the Sadducees and Pharisees, the Jesus who denounced greedy business activity as he drove the moneychangers out of the temple, the Jesus who denounced degenerate civil authority exemplified by Pilate and Rome, the Jesus who, because he took these prophetic stances, suffered terribly and finally was killed—then there are few Maya who are such Christlike figures in their communities, just as there are only a few in any human community. Viewed in this light, the question can again be raised: Are the traditional Maya Christians? A more complete answer would be, Yes and No.

2. The problem of mistaken identity continues among the Catholic clergy. In conjunction with the five-hundred-year anniversary in 1992 of Columbus' discovery of Latin America, and to celebrate the perceived success of the subsequent envangelization of its indigenous populations, the Catholic University of Argentina republished copies of the early doctrinas. The prologue, written by Bishop Antonio Quarracino in his capacity as the president of the Conference of Latin American Bishops (CELAM), exuberantly praises the success of the evangelization effort among indigenous populations (Duran 1984: 11–14). The research here shows that this repetition of the Ricardian thesis of a spiritual conquest is a wishful, ethnocentric projection by church authorities who have not fully understood the structure and evolution of cultural worldviews, both others' and their own.

References

Adams, Richard

1970　*Crucifixion by Power: Essays on Guatemalan Social Structure, 1944–1966*. Austin: University of Texas Press.

Anonymous

1941　El orden que las religiosos tienen en enseñar a los indios la doctrina, y otras cosas de policia Cristiana. In *Códice franciscano, informe de la provincia del Santo Evangelio al Visitador Lic. Juan de Ovando*, 55–74. Mexico: Editorial Salvador Chávez Hayhoe.

Arias, Jacinto

1990　*San Pedro Chenalhó: algo de su historia, cuentos y costumbres*. Tuxtla Gutiérrez, Chiapas: Gobierno del Estado de Chiapas.

1991　*El mundo numinoso de los mayas: estructura y cambios contemporáneos*. Tuxtla Gutiérrez, Chiapas: Gobierno del Estado de Chiapas.

Ashley, Benedict

1990　*The Dominicans*. Collegeville: Liturgical Press.

Aubry, Andrés

1988　*Los padres dominicos remodelan a Chiapas a su imagen y semejanza: secuencia histórica de la orden en los documentos del Archivo Histórico Diocesano de S Cristóbal de Las Casas*. Mexico: San Cristóbal de las Casas.

Bassie-Sweet, Karen

1991　*From the Mouth of the Dark Cave: Commemorative Sculpture of then Late Classic Maya*. Norman: University of Oklahoma Press.

1996　*At the Edge of the World: Caves and the Late Classic Maya World View*. Norman: University of Oklahoma Press.

Bataillon, Marcel

1966　*Erasmo y España, estudios sobre la historia espiritual del siglo XVI*. Translated by Antonio Alatorre. Mexico: Fondo de Cultura Económica.

Bizarro Ujpán, Ignacio

1981　*Son of Tecún Umán: A Maya Indian Tells His Life Story*. Translated by James D. Sexton. Tucson: University of Arizona Press.

1985　*Campesino: The Diary of a Guatemalan Indian*. Translated by James D. Sexton. Tucson: University of Arizona Press.

1992　*Ignacio: The Diary of a Mayan Indian of Guatemala*. Translated by James D. Sexton. Philadelphia: University of Pennsylvania Press.

2001　*Joseno: Another Mayan Voice Speaks from Guatemala*. Translated by James D. Sexton. Albuquerque: University of New Mexico Press.

Blaffer, Sarah C.

1972　*The Black-man of Zinacantan*. Austin: University of Texas Press.

Bode, Barbara
1961 The Dance of the Conquest of Guatemala. In *The Native Theatre in Middle America*, edited by Margaret Harrison and Robert Wauchope, 203–93. New Orleans: Tulane University, Middle American Research Institute, publication 27.

Borges Moran, Pedro
1960 *Métodos misionales en la colonización de América, siglo XVI*. Madrid: Departamento de Misionología Española.
1977 *El envio de misioneros a América durante La época española*. Salamanca: Universidad Pontificia.
1992 *Religiosos en Hispanoamérica*. Madrid: Editorial MAPFRE.

Bricker, Victoria R.
1981 *The Indian Christ, the Indian King: The Historical Substrate of Maya Myth and Ritual*. Austin: University of Texas Press.

Bricker, Victoria R., and Helga-Maria Miram
2002 *An Encounter of Two Worlds: The Book of Chilam Balam of Kaua*. Translated and annotated by Victoria R. Bricker and Helga-Maria Miram. Publication No. 68. New Orleans: Middle American Research Institute Tulane University.

Brown, Peter
1981 *The Cult of the Saints: Its Rise and Function in Latin Christianity*. Chicago: University of Chicago Press.

Bruce S., Roberto D., Carlos Robles U., and Enriqueta Ramos Chao
1971 *Los Lacandones 2. Cosmovision Maya*. Mexico: Instituto Nacional de Antropología e Historia.

Bunzel, Ruth
1952 *Chichicastenango*. Seattle: University of Washington Press.

Burkhart, Louise M.
1989 *The Slippery Earth: Nahua-Christian Moral Dialogue in Sixteenth-Century Mexico*. Tucson: University of Arizona Press.

Cancian, Frank
1965 *Economics and Prestige in a Maya Community*. Stanford: Stanford University Press.
1967 Political and Religious Organizations. In *Social Anthropology*, ed. Manning Nash, vol. 6 of *Handbook of Middle American Indians*. Austin: University of Texas Press.

Carlsen, Robert S.
1997 *The War for the Heart and Soul of a Highland Maya Town*. Austin: University of Texas Press.

Carlsen, Robert S., and Martin Prechtel
1991 The Flowering of the Dead: An Interpretation of Highland Maya Culture. *Man* 26: 23–42.

Carmack, Robert
1973 *Quichean Civilization: The Ethnohistoric, Ethnographic, and Archaeological Sources*. Berkeley: University of California Press.

1981   *The Quiché Mayas of Utatlán: The Evolution of a Highland Guatemala Kingdom.* Norman: University of Oklahoma Press.

1995   *Rebels of Highland Guatemala: The Quiché Mayas of Momostenango.* Norman: University of Oklahoma Press.

Castro, Américo

1971   *The Spaniards: An Introduction to Their History.* Translated by Willard F. King. Albuquerque: University of New Mexico Press.

Chamberlain, Robert S.

1966   *The Conquest and Colonization of Yucatan, 1517–1550.* New York: Octagon Books.

Chance, John K., and William B. Taylor

1985   Cofradías and Cargos: An Historical Perspective on the Mesoamerican Civil-Religious Hierarchy. *American Ethnologist* 12: 1–26.

Chonay, José D.

1953   Letter from Father Dionisio Chonay, Translator. In *The Lords of Totonicapán.* Spanish translation by José Dionisio Chonay, English translation by Delia Goetz. Norman: University of Oklahoma Press.

Chonay, José D., and Delia Goetz, translators

1953   Title of the Lords of Totonicapán. In *The Annals of the Cakchiquels,* translated by Adrian Recinos and Delia Goetz. Norman: University of Oklahoma Press.

Christenson, Allen

2001   *Art and Society in a Highland Maya Community: The Altarpiece of Santiago Atitlán.* Austin: University of Texas Press.

2003a   *Popol Vuh: The Sacred Book of the Maya.* New York: O Books.

2003b   Manipulating the Cosmos: Shamanic Tables among the Highland Maya. In *Mesas and Cosmology in Middle America,* edited by Douglas Sharon, 93–103. San Diego: San Diego Museum of Art.

Christian, William A.

1981   *Local Religion in Sixteenth-Century Spain.* Princeton: Princeton University Press.

Claxton, Robert H.

1986   Weather-Based Hazards in Colonial Guatemala. *Studies in the Social Sciences* 25: 139–63.

Clendinnen, Inga

1987   *Ambivalent Conquests: Maya and Spaniard in Yucatan 1517–1570.* Cambridge: Cambridge University Press.

Cline, Sarah

1998   Fray Alonso de Molina's Model Testament and Antecedents to Indigenous Wills in Spanish America. In *Dead Giveaways,* edited by Susan Kellogg and Matthew Restall, 13–33. Salt Lake City: University of Utah Press.

Colby, Benjamin N., and Lore M. Colby

1981   *The Life and Discourse of an Ixil Diviner.* Cambridge, Mass.: Harvard University Press.

Collier, Jane
1973 *Law and Social Change in Zinacantan*. Stanford: Stanford University Press.
Collins, Anne C.
1977 The Maestros Cantores in Yucatan. In *Anthropology and History in Yucatan*, edited by Grant D. Jones, 233–49. Austin: University of Texas Press.
Colpe, Carsten
1987 Syncretism. *Encyclopedia of Religion* 13: 218–26.
Cook, Garrett W.
2000 *Renewing the Maya World: Expressive Culture in a Highland Town*. Austin: University of Texas Press.
Córdoba, Pedro de
1970 *Christian Doctrine*. Translated by Sterling A. Stoudemire. Coral Gables: University of Miami Press.
Cortés, Hernán
1986 *Letters from Mexico*. Translated and edited by Anthony Pagden. New Haven: Yale University Press.
Cortés y Larraz, Pedro
1958 *Descripción geográfico-moral de la diócesis de Goathemala*. Vols. 1 and 2. Biblioteca "Goathemala" No. 20. Guatemala: Sociedad de Geografía e Historia de Guatemala.
Craine, Eugene R., and Reginald C. Reindorp
1979 *The Codex Pérez and the Book of Chilam Balam of Maní*. Norman: University of Oklahoma Press.
Denzinger, Henry
1955 *The Sources of Catholic Dogma*. Translated by Roy J. Deferrari. Fitzwilliam, N.H.: Loreto Publications.
Díaz del Castillo, Bernal
1928 *The Discovery and Conquest of Mexico 1517–1521*. Translated by A. P Maudsley. New York: Harper and Brothers.
1968 *Historia verdadera de la conquista de la Nueva España*. Vol. 2, 6th ed. Introduction and notes by Joaquín Ramírez Cabañas. Mexico: Editorial Porrúa.
Duran, Juan Guillermo
1984 Fr. Alonso de Molina: Introducción. In *Monumenta catechetica hispanoamericano*. Vol. 1, *Siglo XVI*, edited by Juan Guillermo Duran, 357–86. Buenos Aires: Facultad Teología de la Pontificia Universidad Católica Argentina.
Early, John D.
1963–64 Unpublished field notes in possession of author.
1965 The Sons of San Lorenzo in Zinacantán. PhD diss., Harvard University.
1970a A Demographic Profile of a Maya Community: The Atitecos of Santiago Atitlán. *Milbank Quarterly* 48: 167–78.
1970b The Structure and Change of Mortality in a Maya Community. *Milbank Quarterly* 48: 179–201.
1973 Education via Radio among Guatemalan Highland Maya. *Human Organization* 32: 221–29.

1974   Revision of Ladino and Maya Census Population of Guatemala. *Demography* 11: 105–17.

1982   *The Demographic Structure and Evolution of a Peasant System: The Guatemalan Population.* Boca Raton: University Presses of Florida.

1983   Some Ethnographic Implications of an Ethnohistorical Perspective of the Civil-Religious Hierarchy among the Highland Maya. *Ethnohistory* 30: 185–202.

2000   *La estructura y evolución demográfica de un sistema campesino: la población de Guatemala.* Prologue by Ricardo Falla. South Woodstock, Vt.: Plumsock Mesoamerican Studies/CIRMA. (Spanish translation of Early 1982.)

Early, John D., and Thomas Headland

1998   *The Population Dynamics of a Philippines Rain Forest People: the San Ildefonso Agta.* Gainesville: University Press of Florida.

Early, John D., and John F. Peters

1990   *The Population Dynamics of the Mucajai Yanomama.* San Diego: Academic Press.

2000 *The Xilixana Yanomami of the Amazon: History, Structure, and Population Dynamics.* Gainesville: University Press of Florida.

Eber, Christine

2000   *Women and Alcohol in a Highland Mayan Town: Water of Hope, Water of Sorrow.* Rev. ed. Austin: University of Texas Press.

Edmonson, Munro S.

1993   The Mayan Faith. In *South and Mesoamerican Spirituality: From the Cult of the Feathered Serpent to the Theology of Liberation,* edited by Gary H. Gossen, 65–85. New York: Crossroad Publishing.

Edmonson, Munro S., translator and annotator

1982   *The Ancient Future of the Itza: The Book of Chilam Balam of Tizimin.* Austin: University of Texas Press.

1986   *Heaven Born Merida and Its Destiny: The Book of Chilam Balam of Chumayel.* Austin: University of Texas Press.

Eliade, Mircea

1958   *Patterns in Comparative Religion.* New York: Sheed and Ward.

1959   *Cosmos and History: The Myth of the Eternal Return.* New York: Harper and Brothers.

Erasmus, Desiderius

1963   *The Enchiridion.* Translated and edited by Raymond Himelic. Bloomington: Indiana University Press.

1998   Modus Orandi Deum, translated by John N. Grant. In *Collected Works of Erasmus,* vol. 70, *Spiritualia and Pastoralia,* edited by John W. O'Malley. Toronto: University of Toronto Press.

Fabrega, Horacio, Jr., and Daniel B. Silver

1973   *Illness and Shamanistic Curing in Zinacantan.* Stanford: Stanford University Press.

Farriss, Nancy M.

1984   *Maya Society under Colonial Rule.* Princeton: Princeton University Press.

Fernández Tejedo, Isabel

1990   *La comunidad indígena maya de Yucatán, siglos XVI y XVII.* Mexico, DF: Instituto Nacional de Antropología e Historia.

Fischer, Edward F.

2001   *Cultural Logics and Global Economics: Maya Identity in Thought and Practice.* Austin: University of Texas Press.

Foster, George M.

1960   *Culture and Conquest.* Chicago: Quadrangle Books.

1988   *Tzintzuntzan: Mexican Peasants in a Changing World.* Prospect Heights, Ill.: Waveland Press.

Freidel, David, Linda Schele, and Joy Parker

1993   *Maya Cosmos: Three Thousand Years on the Shaman's Path.* New York: William Morrow.

Fuentes y Guzmán, Francisco Antonio de

1969   *Obras históricas de don Francisco Antonio de Fuentes y Guzmán.* Vol. 1, edited by Carmelo Sáenz de Santa María. Biblioteca de Autores Españoles No. 230. Madrid: Ediciones Atlas.

Gage, Thomas

1958   *Thomas Gage's Travel in the New World.* Edited by J. Eric S. Thompson. Norman: University of Oklahoma Press.

González Cicero, Stella María

1978   *Perspectiva religiosa en Yucatán,1517–1571: Yucatán, los franciscanos y el primer obispo fray Francisco de Toral.* México: Colegio de México.

Gosner, Kevin

1992   *Soldiers of the Virgin: The Moral Economy of a Colonial Maya Rebellion.* Tucson: University of Arizona Press.

Gossen, Gary H.

1974   *Chamulas in the World of the Sun: Time and Space in a Maya Oral Tradition.* Cambridge: Harvard University Press.

1986   Mesoamerican Ideas as Foundation for Regional Synthesis. In *Symbol and Meaning beyond the Closed Community: Essays in Mesoamerican Ideas*, edited by Gary H. Gossen, 1–8. Albany: Institute for Mesoamerican Studies, State University of New York.

Gossen, Gary H., editor and translator

2002   *Four Creations: A Epic Story of the Chiapas Mayas.* Norman: University of Oklahoma Press.

Green, Judith

2003   Altars for Ancestors: Maya Altars for the Days of the Dead in Yucatan. In *Mesas and Cosmology in Middle America*, edited by Douglas Sharon, 105–18. San Diego: San Diego Museum of Art.

Gruzinski, Serge

2001   *Images at War: Mexico from Columbus to Blade Runner (1492–2019).* Translated by Heather MacLean. Durham: Duke University Press.

Guiteras Holmes, Calixta
1961   *Perils of the Soul: The World View of a Tzotzil Indian.* New York: Free Press of Glencoe.

Hanke, Lewis
1973   *History of Latin American Civilization.* 2 vols. Boston: Little, Brown and Co.

Hill, Robert M.
1992   *Colonial Cakchiquels: Highland Maya Adaptations to Spanish Rule, 1600–1700.* New York: Harcourt Brace Jovanovich.

Hill, Robert M. and John Monaghan
1987   *Continuities in Highland Maya Social Organization: Ethnohistory in Sácapulas, Guatemala.* Philadelphia: University of Pennsylvania Press.

Holland, William R.
1963   *Medicina Maya en Los Altos de Chiapas.* Mexico: INI.

Holleran, Mary P.
1949   *Church and State in Guatemala.* New York: Columbia University Press.

Jones, Grant D.
1989   *Maya Resistance to Spanish Rule: Time and History on a Colonial Frontier.* Albuquerque: University of New Mexico Press.

1998   *The Conquest of the Last Mayan Kingdom.* Stanford: Stanford University Press.

Kamen, Henry
1991   *Spain 1469–1714: A Society of Conflict.* 2nd ed. New York: Addison Wesley Longman.

Kelly, John Eoghan
1932   *Pedro de Alvarado Conquistador.* Princeton: Princeton University Press.

Klor de Alva, J. Jorge
1982   Spiritual Conflict and Accommodation in New Spain: Toward a Typology of Aztec Responses to Christianity. In *The Inca and Aztec States 1400–1800*, edited by George A. Collier, Renato I. Rosaldo, and John D. Wirth, 345–66. New York: Academic Press.

Knowles, David
1966   *From Pachomius to Ignatius: A Study of the Constitutional History of the Religious Orders.* Oxford: Clarendon Press.

Kramer, Wendy
1994   *Encomienda Poltics in Early Colonial Guatemala, 1524–1544: Dividing the Spoils.* Boulder: Westview Press.

Kung, Hans
1999   *Christianity: Essence, History, Future.* New York: Continuum.

2001   *The Catholic Church: a Short History.* Translated by John Bowden. New York: Modern Library.

LaFarge, Oliver
1947   *Santa Eulalia: The Religion of a Cuchumatan Indian Town.* Chicago: University of Chicago Press.

Landa, Diego de
1941   *Landa's Relación de las Cosas de Yucatan: A Translation.* Translated and edited by

Alfred M. Tozzer. Cambridge, Mass.: Peabody Museum of American Archeology and Ethnology, Harvard University.

Las Casas, Bartolomé de

1958   *Apologética historia de las Indias.* Biblioteca de Autores Españoles No. 13. Madrid: Ediciones Atlas.

1986   *Historia de las Indias.* 3 vols. Caracas: Biblioteca Ayacucho.

Laughlin, Robert M.

1976   *Of Wonders Wild and New: Dreams from Zinacantán.* Washington: Smithsonian Institution Press.

1977   *Of Cabbages and Kings.* Washington: Smithsonian Institution Press.

1979   *Of Shoes and Ships and Sealing Wax: Sundries from Zinacantán.* Washington: Smithsonian Institution Press.

2002   *Mayan Hearts.* San Cristóbal de las Casas: Author.

2003   *Beware the Great Horned Serpent!: Chiapas under the Threat of Napoleon.* Albany: Institute for Mesoamerican Studies, University of New York at Albany. Distributed by University of Texas Press.

León-Portilla, Miguel

1962   *The Broken Spears: The Aztec Account of the Conquest of Mexico.* Translated by Lysander Kemp. Boston: Beacon Press.

1973   *Time and Reality in the Thought of the Maya.* Boston: Beacon Press.

1974   Testimonios Nahuas sobre la conquista espiritual. *Estudios de Cultura Nahuatl* 11: 11–36.

1993   Those Made Worthy by Divine Sacrifice: The Faith of Ancient Mexico. In *South and Mesoamerican Spirituality: From the Cult of the Feathered Serpent to the Theology of Liberation,* edited by Gary H. Gossen, 41–64. New York: Crossroad Publishing.

Lockhart, James

1992   *The Nahuas after the Conquest: A Social and Cultural History of the Indians of Central Mexico, Sixteenth through Eighteenth Centuries.* Stanford: Stanford University Press.

1999   *Of Things of the Indies: Essays Old and New in Early Latin American History.* Stanford: Stanford University Press.

López de Gomera, Francisco

1964   *Cortes: The Life of the Conqueror by His Secretary.* Translated and edited by Lesley Byrd Simpson. Berkeley: University of California Press.

Lovell, W. George

1985   *Conquest and Survival in Guatemala: A Historical Geography of the Cuchumatan Highlands, 1500–1821.* Kingston and Montreal: McGill-Queen's University Press.

Lovell W. George, and Christopher H. Lutz

1994   Conquest and Population. *Latin American Research Review* 29 (2): 133–40.

1995   *Demography and Empire: A Guide to the Population History of Spanish Central America, 1500–1821.* Boulder: Westview Press.

Lovell, W. George, and William R. Swezey

1990   Indian Migration and Community Formation: An Analysis of Congregación in

Colonial Guatemala. In *Migration in Colonial Spanish America*, edited by David J. Robinson, 18–40. Cambridge: Cambridge University Press.

Loyola, St. Ignatius

1943 *The Spiritual Exercises of St. Ignatius Loyola*. Westminster, Md.: Newman Bookshop.

Lutz, Christopher H.

1982 Population History of the Parish of San Miguel Dueñas, Guatemala 1730–1770. In *The Historical Demography of Highland Guatemala*, edited by Robert M. Carmack, John Early, and Christopher H. Lutz, 21–35. Institute of Mesoamerican Studies Publication No. 6. Albany: State University of New York.

1994 *Santiago de Guatemala, 1541–1773: City, Caste and the Colonial Experience*. Norman: University of Oklahoma Press.

Marroquín, Francisco

1905 Doctrina cristiana en lengua guatemalteca. Santiago de Chile: Imprenta Elzeviriana.

Marzal, Manuel M.

1993 Transplanted Spanish Catholicism. In *South and Mesoamerican Spirituality: From the Cult of the Feathered Serpent to the Theology of Liberation*, edited by Gary H. Gossen, 140–69. New York: Crossroad Publishing.

Maurer Avalos, Eugenio

1993 The Tzeltal Maya–Christian Synthesis. In *South and Mesoamerican Spirituality: From the Cult of the Feathered Serpent to the Theology of Liberation*, edited by Gary H. Gossen, 228–50. New York: Crossroad Publishing.

McAndrew, John

1965 *The Open-Air Churches of Sixteenth Century Mexico*. Cambridge: Harvard University Press.

Medina, José Toribio

1905 Biographical notes about Bishop Francisco Marroquín in *Doctrina cristiana en lengua guatemalteca*. No page numbers. Santiago de Chile: Imprenta Elzeviriana.

Mendelson, E. Michael

1957 Religion and World View in a Guatemalan Village. Microfilm collection of manuscripts on Middle American cultural anthropology, No. 52. University of Chicago Library, Chicago.

1965 *Los escándalos de Maximón*. Publication No. 19. Guatemala: Seminario de Integración Social Guatemalteca.

Molina, Alonso de

1941 Doctrina cristiana. In *Códice franciscano, informe de la Provincia del Santo Evangelio al Visitador Lic. Juan de Ovando*, 30–54. Mexico: Editorial Salvador Chávez Hayhoe.

1984 Doctrina cristiana breve traducida in lengua mexicana. In *Monumenta catechetica hispanoamericano*. Vol. 1, *Siglo XVI*, ed. Juan Guillermo Duran, 387–403. Buenos Aires: Facultad Teología de la Pontificia Universidad Católica Argentina.

Monaghan, John D.

2000 Theology and History in the Study of Mesoamerican Religions. In *Ethnology*. Supplement to the *Handbook of Middle American Indians*, vol. 6, edited by John D. Monaghan with the assistance of Barbara W. Edmonson. Austin: University of Texas Press.

Mondloch, James L.

1980 K'E?S: Quiche Naming. *Journal of Mayan Linguistics* 2:219–25.

Montalvo, Gregorio de

1938 [1582] Carta del Obispo Fray Gregorio de Montalvo a Su Majestad con un memorial sobre el estado de la iglesia de Yucatán. In *Documentos para la Historia de Yucatán*. Vol. 2, *La iglesia en Yucatán, 1560–1610*. Mérida: Compañía Tipográfica Yucateca, S.A.

Montejo, Victor

1991 In the Name of the Pot, the Sun, the Broken Spear, the Rock, the Stick, the Idol, Ad Infinitum and Ad Nauseam: An Expose of Anglo Anthropologists' Obsessions with and Invention of Mayan Gods. Paper presented at the American Anthropological Association Meeting.

Moorman, John

1968 *A History of the Franciscan Order*. Oxford: Oxford University Press.

Moreno, Robert

1984 Introduction to *Confesionario mayor en la lengua mexicana y castellana (1569)*, by Fray Alonso de Molina, 9–34. Mexico: Universidad Nacional Autónoma de México.

O'Brien, Linda Lee

1975 Songs of the Face of the Earth: Ancestor Songs of the Tzutuhil-Maya of Santiago Atitlán, Guatemala. PhD diss., University of California, Los Angeles. UMI 76–838.

O'Flaherty, Edward Martin

1979 Institutionalization of the Catholic Church in the Americas: The Case of Colonial Guatemala, 1524–1563. PhD diss., University of Pennsylvania.

1984 *Iglesia y sociedad en Guatemala: análisis de un proceso cultural*. Translated by Elias Zamora. Seville: Universidad de Sevilla. (Translation of O'Flaherty 1979.)

Oss, Adrian C. van

n.d. *Carpetas de Parish Geography*. Unpublished notes in possession of the author's widow.

1984 Pueblos y parroquias en Suchtepéquez colonial. *Mesoamerica* 1984: 161–78.

1986 *Catholic Colonialism: A Parish History of Guatemala 1524–1821*. Cambridge: Cambridge University Press.

2003 *Church and Society in Spanish America*. Amsterdam: Aksant.

Patch, Robert W.

2002 *Maya Revolt and Revolution in the Eighteenth Century*. Armonk, N.Y.: M.E. Sharpe.

Peck, Horace Dudley
1970   *Practices and Training of the Guatemalan Mam Shamans.* Ph.D. dissertation, The Hartford Seminary Foundation.

Phelan, John Leddy
1970   *The Millennial Kingdom of the Franciscans in the New World.* Berkeley: University of California Press.

Pieper, Jim
2002   *Guatemala's Folk Saints: Maximon/San Simon, Rey Pascual, Judas, Lucifer, and Others.* Albuquerque: University of New Mexico Press.

Pineda, Vicente
1888   *Historia de las sublevaciones indígenas habidas en el estado de Chiapas.* San Cristóbal: Tipografía del Gobierno.

Polanyi, Karl
1977   *The Livelihood of Man.* New York: Academic Press.

Poole, Stafford
1992   Iberian Catholicism Comes to the Americas. In *Christianity Comes to the Americas 1492–1776,* edited by Charles H. Lippy, Robert Choquette, and Stafford Poole, 1–129. New York: Paragon House.

Porrúa, Miguel Angel
1992   *Autos seguidos por algunos de las naturales del pueblo de Chamula en contra de su cura don Joseph Ordóñez y Aguilas por varios excesos que le suponían 1779.* Mexico: Gobierno del Estado de Chiapas, Universidad Autónoma de Chiapas, Facultad de Derecho, UNAM.

Prechtel, Martín
1998   *Secrets of the Talking Jaguar: Memoirs from the Living Heart of a Mayan Village.* New York: Penguin Putnam.
1999   *Long Life, Honey in the Heart: A Story of Initiation and Eloquence from the Shores of a Mayan Lake.* New York: Penguin Putnam.

Recinos, Adrian
1957   *Crónicas indígenas de Guatemala.* Guatemala City: Editorial Universitaria.

Recinos, Adrian, and Delia Goetz
1953   *Annals of the Cakchiquels.* Norman: University of Oklahoma Press.

Redfield, Robert, and Alfonso Villa Rojas
1962   *Chan Kom, a Maya Village.* Chicago: University of Chicago Press.

Reed, Nelson
1964   *The Caste War of Yucatan.* Stanford: Stanford University Press.

Remesal, Fray Antonio de
1964   *Historia general de las occidentales y particular de la gobernación de Chiapa y Guatemala.* Vol. 1. Biblioteca de Autores Españoles No. 175. Madrid: Ediciones Atlas.
1966   *Historia general de las occidentales y particular de la gobernación de Chiapa y Guatemala.* Vol. 2. Biblioteca de Autores Españoles No. 189. Madrid: Ediciones Atlas.

Restall, Matthew

1995　*Life and Death in a Maya Community: The Ixil Testaments of the 1760s.* Lancaster, Calif.: Labyrinthos.

1997　*The Maya World: Yucatec Culture and Society, 1550–1850.* Stanford: Stanford University Press.

1998　*Maya Conquistador.* Boston: Beacon Press.

2003　*Seven Myths of the Spanish Conquest.* Oxford: Oxford University Press.

Ricard, Robert

1933　*La "conquête spirituelle" du Mexique.* Paris: Institut D'Ethnologie.

1966　*The Spiritual Conquest of Mexico: An Essay on the Apostolate and Evangelizing Methods of the Mendicant Orders in New Spain, 1523–1572.* Translated by Lesley Byrd Simpson. Berkeley: University of California Press.

Roys, Ralph L.

1943　*Indian Background of Colonial Yucatan.* Washington: Carnegie Institution of Washington, publication 548.

Roys, Ralph L., France V. Scholes, and Eleanor B. Adams

1940　*Report and Census of the Indians of Cozumel, 1570.* Washington, D.C.: Carnegie Institution of Washington.

Rubial García, Antonio

1978　Evangelismo y evangelización: los primitivos franciscanos en la Nueva España y el ideal del cristianismo primitivo. *Anuario de Historia* 10 (1978–79): 95–124.

Rus, Jan

1983　Whose Caste War? Indians, Ladinos, and the "Caste War" of 1869. In *Spaniards and Indians in Southeastern Mesoamerica: Essays in the History of Ethnic Relations,* edited by Murdo J. MacLeod and Robert Wasserstrom, 127–68. Lincoln: University of Nebraska Press.

2002　Afterword to *Four Creations: A Epic Story of the Chiapas Mayas,* edited and translated by Gary H. Gossen. Norman: University of Oklahoma Press.

Ruz, Mario Humberto, Claudia M. Báez Juárez, et al., coords.

2002　*Memoria eclesial guatemalteca, visitas pastorales.* 2 vols. Mexico: Universidad Nacional Autónoma de México.

Sáenz de Santa María, Carmelo

1964　*El Licenciado Don Francisco Marroquín*: primer obispo de Guatemala (1499–1563). Madrid: Ediciones Cultura Hispánica.

Sahagún, Bernardino

1954　Prologue to Book 4 of the Historia General de las Cosas de Nueva España. In *Bibliografía mexicana del siglo XVI,* edited by Joaquín García Icazbalceta, 382–83. Mexico: Fondo de Cultura Económica.

1990　Coloquios y doctrina cristiana. In *La conversión de los indios de la Nueva España,* edited by Christian Duverger, 57–100. Quito: Ediciones ABYA-YALA.

Sanders, William T.

1992　The Population of the Central Mexican Symbiotic Region, the Basin of Mexico, and the Teotihuacán Valley in the Sixteenth Century. In *The Native Population of the Americas in 1492.* 2nd ed., edited by William M. Denevan, 85–150. Madison: University of Wisconsin Press.

Seed, Patricia
1995   *Ceremonies of Possession in Europe's Conquest of the New World 1492–1640.* Cambridge: Cambridge University Press.

Sexton, James D., and Ignacio Bizarro Ujpán
1992   *Mayan Folktales: Folklore from Lake Atitlán, Guatemala.* Albuquerque: University of New Mexico Press.

1999   *Heart of Heaven, Heart of Earth, and Other Mayan Folktales.* Washington, D.C.: Smithsonian Institution Press.

Sharer, Robert J.
1994   *The Ancient Maya.* 5th ed. Stanford: Stanford University Press.

Shaw, Mary
1971   *According to Our Ancestors: Folk Texts from Guatemala and Honduras.* Norman: Summer Institute of Linguistics of the University of Oklahoma.

Simmons, Marc
1991   Santiago, Reality and Myth. In *Santiago: Saint of Two Worlds*, edited by Joan Myers, 1–29. Albuquerque: University of New Mexico Press.

Simpson, Lesley Byrd
1964   Introduction to *Cortes: The Life of the Conqueror by His Secretary*, translated and edited by Lesley Byrd Simpson. Berkeley: University of California Press.

Smith, Anthony D.
2003   *Chosen Peoples.* Oxford: Oxford University Press.

Stonequist, Everett V.
1961   *The Marginal Man.* New York: Russell and Russell.

Tarn, Nathaniel, with Martín Prechtel
1997   *Scandals in the House of Bird: Shamans and Priests on Lake Atitlán.* New York: Marsilio.

Tax, Sol
1953   *Penny Capitalism: A Guatemalan Indian Economy.* Institution of Social Anthropology Publication 16. Washington, D.C.: Smithsonian Institution.

Tedlock, Barbara
1982   *Time and the Highland Maya.* Albuquerque: University of New Mexico Press.

Tedlock, Dennis
1986   Creation in the Popol Vuh: A Hermeneutical Approach. In *Symbol and Meaning beyond the Closed Community: Essays in Mesoamerican Ideas*, edited by Gary Gossen, 77–82. Albany: Institute for Mesoamerican Studies, State University of New York.

1997   *Breath on the Mirror: Mythic Voices and Visions of Living Maya.* Albuquerque: University of New Mexico Press.

2003   *Rabinal Achi: A Mayan Drama of War and Sacrifice.* Oxford: Oxford University Press.

Tedlock, Dennis, translator
1996   *Popol Vuh: The Mayan Book of the Dawn of Life.* New York: Simon and Schuster.

Thompson, J. Eric S.

1930   Ethnology of the Mayas of Southern and Central British Honduras. Field Museum of Natural History Publication 274. Chicago: Field Museum of Natural History.

1970   Maya History and Religion. Norman: University of Oklahoma Press.

Thompson, Philip C.

1999   Tekanto: A Maya Town in Colonial Yucatan. New Orleans: Middle American Research Institute, Tulane University.

Tovilla, Martín Alfonso

1960   Relaciones histórico-descriptivas de la Verapaz, el Manché y Lacandón en Guatemala. Guatemala: Editorial Universitaria.

Tozzer, Alfred M.

1941   Notes in Landa's relación de las cosas de Yucatán. Cambridge, Mass.: Peabody Museum of Archaeology and Ethnology, Harvard University.

United Nations

1950   Demographic Year Book, 1949–50. New York: Department of Economic and Social Affairs, Statistical Office, United Nations.

Valle, Rafael Heliodoro

1946   Santiago en América. Mexico: Editorial Santiago.

Vazquez, Fray Francisco

1937   Crónica de la Provincia del Santísimo Nombre de Jesús de Guatemala. Vol. 1. Biblioteca "Goathemala" No. 14. Guatemala: Sociedad de Geografía e Historia de Guatemala.

1938   Crónica de la Provincia del Santísimo Nombre de Jesús de Guatemala. Vol. 2. Biblioteca "Goathemala" No. 15. Guatemala: Sociedad de Geografía e Historia de Guatemala.

1940   Crónica de la Provincia del Santísimo Nombre de Jesús de Guatemala. Vol. 3. Biblioteca "Goathemala" No. 16. Guatemala: Sociedad de Geografía e Historia de Guatemala.

1944   Crónica de la Provincia del Santísimo Nombre de Jesús de Guatemala. Vol. 4. Biblioteca "Goathemala" No. 17. Guatemala: Sociedad de Geografía e Historia de Guatemala.

Villa Rojas, Alfonso

1945   The Maya of East Central Quintana Roo. Washington, D.C.: Carnegie Institution of Washington.

Vogt, Evon Z.

1969   Zinacantan: A Maya Community in the Highlands of Chiapas. Cambridge, Mass.: Harvard University Press.

1976   Tortillas for the Gods. Cambridge, Mass.: Harvard University Press.

1994   Fieldwork among the Maya: Reflections on the Harvard Chiapas Project. Cambridge, Mass.: Harvard University Press.

Wagley, Charles

1949   Social and Religious Life of a Guatemala Village. Washington: Memoir Series of the American Anthropological Association, No. 71.

Wasserstrom, Robert

1983a *Class and Society in Central Chiapas.* Berkeley: University of California Press.

1983b Spaniards and Indians in Colonial Chiapas. In *Spaniards and Indians in South-eastern Mesoamerica,* edited by Murdo J. MacLeod and Robert Wasserstrom, 92–126. Lincoln: University of Nebraska Press.

Watanabe, John M.

1992 *Maya Saints and Souls in a Changing World.* Austin: University of Texas Press.

Ximénez, Fray Francisco

1929 *Historia de la Provincia de San Vicente de Chiapa y Guatemala, Orden de Predicadores.* Vol. 1, Book 1. Biblioteca "Goathemala" No. 1. Guatemala: Sociedad de Geografía y Historia de Guatemala.

1965 *Historia de la Provincia de San Vicente de Chiapa y Guatemala.* 4 vols. with continuous numeration of pages. Guatemala: Ministerio de Educación.

1971a *Historia de la Provincia de San Vicente de Chiapa y Guatemala, Orden de Predicadores.* Part 4, Book 6. Biblioteca "Goathemala" No. 24. Guatemala: Sociedad de Geografía y Historia de Guatemala.

1971b *Historia de la Provincia de San Vicente de Chiapa y Guatemala, Orden de Predicadores.* Part 4, Book 7. Biblioteca "Goathemala" No. 25. Guatemala: Sociedad de Geografía y Historia de Guatemala.

1973 *Historia de la Provincia de San Vicente de Chiapa y Guatemala, Orden de Predicadores.* Book 5. Biblioteca "Goathemala," No. 29. Guatemala: Sociedad de Geografía y Historia de Guatemala.

Zamora Acosta, Elias

1983 Conquista y crisis demográfica: La población indígena del occidente de Guatemala en siglo XVI. *Mesoamerica* 6: 291–328.

Index of Persons and Places

Saints and other divinized persons are not listed here but in the index of subjects as analytical categories. Mayan towns have compound names. The first is usually the name of the town's patron saint; the second is the Mayan name. When searching for a particular town, look under the name of the patron saint and the Mayan name in the alphabetical listing below.

system, 17–19; case of creole priest's mentality, 183; chapels in hamlets of Apas and Salinas, 141; covenant as moral, 274nn8, 9; Dominican residence, 132, 154; festival calendar, 19–22; fiscal, 226; Mayan perception of saint images, 204–6; number of images in churches, 14–16; patron saint, 16; population size, 187; ritual patterns of festivals, 22, 32–41, 187; self identity, 209; shamans, 221; talking saints, 242; view of, 14; year ceremony, 71

Zulben, Verapaz, 158

Zumárraga, Bishop, 128, 132

Zurbarán, Francisco de, 198

Index of Subjects

This index includes gods, saints, and other divinized persons as subjects of analysis.

Franciscans, 118–19, 124; areas of evangelization, 132, 136, 151–58, 176, 187; on church
ornamentation and images, 201; dependence on fiscales, 228; early bishops, 167;
excessive transfers of, 168; monastic routine,
120; numbers from Spain, 133–35; percentage creole, 182; and secularization 180. *See
also* Evangelization; Friars
French Enlightenment, 185
Friars: goal of conversion, 117; historical background of, 118–24; teach doctrina, 124–30;
types of 133–34. *See also* Doctrina; Dominicans; Evangelization; Franciscans

Genesis, 219, 273n5
Godparent, 126, 217. *See also* Baptism

Harmony, 70, 77, 119, 209, 213, 272n2. *See also*
Balance; Equilibrium
Heaven: Christian usage of, 14, 63–64, 70, 82,
90, 127–29, 140, 178, 198, 212, 219–20, 257,
260–61; Mayan or Christian usage of, 20, 36,
191, 234, 251
Hell, 120, 130, 140, 257
Hellenization of Christianity, 95, 121–23, 129,
147, 223, 258, 267
Hinduism, 83

Idols. *See* Statues, of Mayan gods
Incarnation, 122, 129, 258
Infrastructure of church, 131, 150, 186
Inquisition, 45, 56, 89, 122, 155, 173
Islam, 45, 87–88, 90, 103, 120, 122, 198

Jesus: in Chilam Balam books, 226; discipleship versus revealed truth in, 122; Erasmian
view, 124; festival prayers to, 26, 31, 34–35;
in fourteen articles, 125, 129–30, 257–58;
images of, 14–15, 206; invocation of, during
conquest, 103; Mayan perception of, 200;
in Mayan rebellions, 232; mission mandate
of, 95; perception by folk religion, 100, 259;
relation to Jewish and Christian covenants,
91. *See also* Christ
Jews, 90, 92, 97, 121–24, 232
Judaism, 87–88, 95, 120, 122, 198, 257

Kaqchikel, 81, 105–7, 111, 125–26, 132, 272n2
K'iche', 71, 77, 105–11, 197, 199, 221, 277n1
(chap. 12)

Kinh, 62, 76, 272–73n2. *See also* Worldviews,
Maya
Kits for mass, 137, 199–200
K'u'x, 195, 272–73n2. *See also* Worldviews,
Maya

Labor service, 46–47, 57, 95, 99, 112, 116, 125,
136, 158, 160, 163, 218
Lacandón, 159, 222, 272–73n2
Ladino, 27, 43–46, 164–65, 182, 188, 205–7, 213,
224, 236, 242
Laity, 10, 197, 200, 213, 256
Languages, 8; problems of learning and trans-
lating of Mayan, 26, 169, 172, 182–83, 188,
193; for teaching doctrina, 125, 169
Latin, 41, 126, 130, 169, 178, 207, 219, 224
Liberalism, 185
Life cycle, 62, 68–69, 76, 79, 181
Lightning, 64–65, 75, 109–10
Liturgy, 53, 119, 138, 142–43, 146, 168, 228
Locust invasions, 101, 148, 196

Magic, 75, 100–101, 106, 123–24, 223, 272–73n2
Maryknoll, 14, 166
Maximon, 46
Mayan civil officials, 248; assisted by shamanic rituals, 248–51; as elite in schools,
144, 146; enforcers of mass and doctrina
attendance, 143; participation in cargo
rituals, 30, 33, 39–40; relationship to cargo
structure, 17–18, 146; role in Cancuc rebel-
lion, 231–35
Mayan elite, 78, 136, 139–40, 142, 144, 173, 223
Mayan gods, 207–8. *See also* Saints
Mestizo, 45
Memorization, 125, 172–73, 177, 217, 219, 259
Mercedarians, 120–21; areas of evangeliza-
tion, 150, 154–55; 166, 187; misconduct of,
167; numbers from Spain, 133–35. *See also*
Evangelization; Friars
Metaphysics, 61, 85, 174, 194. *See also* Cycles;
Worldviews, Maya
Mexica, 81–82, 107, 111–13
Middle Ages, 81, 95, 116, 119, 121, 256, 275n2
Mongols, 119
Monotheism, 130, 255–56
Moon, 28, 62, 76, 207–8, 220
Mountains, 92, 111, 158–60, 188; as homes of
the gods, 14, 35, 40, 65, 166, 205, 241, 244,
249–50. *See also* Caves

John D. Early, professor emeritus of anthropology at Florida Atlantic University in Boca Raton, is the author of *The Demographic Structure of a Peasant System: The Guatemalan Population* (UPF, 1982); the coauthor of *Population Dynamics of the Philippine Rainforest People: The Agta of the San Ildefonso Peninsula* (UPF, 1998), which received a Choice Outstanding Academic Book Award; and coauthor of *Population Dynamics of the Mucajai Yanomami* (UPF, 2000).